THROUGH
HIS EYES

God's Perspective on Women in the Bible

JERRAM BARRS

CROSSWAY BOOKS

WHEATON, ILLINOIS

Through His Eyes

Published by Crossway Books
a publishing ministry of Good News Publishers
1300 Crescent Street
Wheaton, Illinois 60187

Cover design: Amy Bristow

Cover photo: The Bridgeman Library

First printing, 2009

Printed in the United States of America

All emphases in Scripture quotations have been added by the author.

ISBN PDF: 978-1-4335-0567-6

ISBN Mobipocket: 978-1-4335-0568-3

Library of Congress Cataloging-in-Publication Data

Barrs, Jerram.
Through His eyes : God's perspective on women in the Bible / Jerram Barrs.
p. cm.
Includes bibliographical references and index.
ISBN 978-1-4335-0224-8 (tpb)
1. Women—Biblical teaching. 2. Women in the Bible. I. Title.
BS680.W7B36 2009
220.9'2082—dc22 2008037139

LB 18 17 16 15 14 13 12 11 10 09
15 14 13 12 11 10 9 8 7 6 5 4 3 2 1

THROUGH HIS EYES

Other Crossway Books by Jerram Barrs
The Heart of Evangelism
Learning Evangelism from Jesus

To Vicki,

*a woman of noble character who has been my partner
in marriage for forty-one years. You have been an excellent wife,
far more precious than jewels to me, my lover, my best friend,
an outstanding mother and grandmother, daughter, sister
and comforter to many. "Many women have done excellently,
but you surpass them all." Thank you, Lord.*

CONTENTS

INTRODUCTION

I have been deeply troubled in our churches by the way much teaching on women begins with the restrictive passages in 1 Corinthians 11 and 14 and 1 Timothy 2 and often ends there. It is not that those passages are insignificant, but I have been eager to ask a more foundational question: How does the Lord see women? I felt the best way to answer this question was to look at particular women whose stories are told in the Scriptures and to reflect on what God has to say. What does God think about women, and how does he treat them? My passionate desire and prayer is that the book will be an encouragement to women and a challenge to men to treat women with the same honor that the Lord himself shows. I originally gave these studies to about two hundred women in the setting of a women's ministry at a local church. They were greatly encouraged by the studies, and it was these women who urged me to write this book.

One particular example that stands out in my memory was that the study of the rape of Tamar by her half-brother Amnon encouraged women to be able to talk for the first time in their lives about sexual abuse they had endured, a couple of them fifty or sixty years before. Many other personal responses were greatly encouraging on a whole range of issues—singleness, motherhood, marriage, work, career, etc. Overall I think many of the women felt it was the first time in their lives that they had heard from Scripture about women being treated with such dignity and graciousness by the Lord. Since then I taught a class covering this material at Covenant Theological Seminary in St. Louis, and it was well received by both female and male students. This past year I preached on the rape of Tamar at the Seminary as part of a conference on sexual abuse. Again the reception and consequences were very moving to me. I have preached sermons from some of these chapters in many different kinds of churches (Presbyterian, Baptist, Pentecostal, black, white, Korean, Chinese) and on every occasion have been overwhelmed by the response. One time in a setting that was very hierarchical the women stood up and cheered for several minutes in response to what I said about Jesus' treatment of women and what it ought to mean for men (this astonished the men, as you might imagine).

This book begins at the beginning with the story of Eve and, in three chapters, considers her at creation, at the Fall, and as the bearer of the promise of redemption. Throughout the book I will put the woman's name first (Eve and Adam or Sarah and Abraham) simply because this is a book about women through God's eyes. We turn next to look at the lives of several very different women: Sarah, the mother of all God's people, both Jews and Gentiles; Tamar, a woman of faith who disguised herself as a prostitute to ensure that God's calling of her was fulfilled; Rahab, the prostitute in Jericho who came to faith in the God of Israel and who at great danger to herself sheltered the Israeli spies; Deborah, a chief justice, military leader, and prophet; Ruth, an alien from Moab, the hated enemy of Israel, who joined herself to God's people and became an ancestor of Israel's greatest king, David; Hannah, a troubled woman whose prayer for a child was marvelously answered by God; Abigail, a wise and beautiful woman who had to act quickly to overcome the awful consequences of her husband's foolish behavior; Tamar, a desolate woman who was raped by her own half-brother and whose life was ruined but who will shine with honor in the kingdom of God; Esther, a courageous Jewish girl who became a member of a despot's harem. We also look at the portrait in Proverbs 31 of a woman of strength and see in her some of the characteristics that God values in his people.

Turning to the New Testament we study the life of Mary in some depth, asking the question: What should it mean for us that all generations are to call her "blessed"? We also look at several examples from the Gospel records of how Jesus relates to women. Then we turn to the Day of Pentecost and the fulfillment of the prophet's words, "Your daughters shall prophesy" and consider what this should mean today for all God's people. Finally we reflect on the image by which God chooses to describe his church—the bride of Christ—and rejoice in the honor that God shows to all women with this title.

This book is a happy exposition of the dignity and glory that the Lord showers on women. Its aim is to encourage women to delight in their creation, redemption, and calling and to challenge men to honor women as does the Lord himself. My hope is that many men, especially pastors and teachers, will read this book and be challenged by it, in addition to the book giving great encouragement to women. My special prayer is that younger women who are becoming disenchanted with the church and with the Christian faith will be sufficiently encouraged by the book to embrace their faith much more wholeheartedly. I long for men to treat their wives, and women in general, better.

Many women experience discrimination and poor treatment in their churches and in their homes. In conservative circles this is sometimes defended and justified by specious appeals to Scripture. I am thoroughly conservative in my approach to Scripture, but I passionately believe that Scripture teaches our equality and mutual dependence. Some will be troubled that I do not devote a chapter to the so-called "restrictive passages" (1 Corinthians 11 and 14 and 1 Timothy 2) and to the issue of who should be pastors and elders with teaching and ruling authority in the churches. I have taught on this subject in many settings, and if anyone wishes to know my views on this, they can find them in a series of lectures on "Women in Church" and "Women in Society" that are available on Covenant Seminary's website (www.covenantseminary.edu). However, my aim in this book was not to address that issue, a subject on which many volumes have been written, but to look at the far more extensive material in Scripture about God's love and respect for women, material that is often neglected. My prayer is that the Lord will use this book to be an encouragement to both women and men, for we all need to see women through God's eyes.

1

THE FIRST FACE OF EVE:

Eve at Creation

To commence these reflections on women of God, we have to go back to the very beginning, to the origins of the human race. Eve is the name that the first man, Adam, gives the first woman after their expulsion from the Garden of Eden. God drives the two of them from the Garden after they have rebelled against him. But to turn to the shame of their disobedience takes us too far ahead, for the name of the first woman has nothing to do with her temptation or with her and Adam's fall into evil.

We might ask, what's in a name? For those who live in a western society, names do not usually have particular significance, beyond being the parents' choice and sometimes being a name carried down through the generations. But in many cultures around the world names commonly have particular meanings—they tell others something about the specific person who carries the name. This was also true for the cultures of the peoples of the Old Testament. Eve's name means "the mother of all living," and it tells us something about her nature; it captures something of who she is as God created her to be. Revealing a person's nature is what naming is all about in God's Word. Naming also represents something of the significance of the one giving the name.

Eve, then, is the mother, the ancestress, of every human being who has ever lived, apart, of course, from Adam, the first man. We might respond with wonder as to how one woman and one man could have had such a genetic richness that all the diverse traits found across the world could have come from this original pair. But many secular thinkers, people who believe in the evolution of our species, rather than in the creation of humans by God, recognize that we are all descended from one human source. We do not know the exact date of our first mother's existence but God has told us that there was indeed one mother of us all.[1]

For our reflections on the first woman, we need to consider the three faces of Eve—Eve at creation, Eve as rebel against her Creator, and Eve as the recipient of God's promise of redemption. In each of these portraits we learn something about ourselves, for each one of us, female and male, can trace Eve's features in our own lives, so many thousands of years after her life here on earth was finished.

EVE AT CREATION

What do we learn from Genesis 1–2 about Eve as she came from the hand of God?

Eve and Adam are described as "living creatures" (2:7) or "living beings" (NIV) just like all the other "living creatures" (1:20, 24). We are indeed "from the earth," "natural" (1 Corinthians 15:45–49). We, as humans, are creatures with the same physical nature as the other creatures made by God that are all around us. Some may complain, "Surely I am not made of the same basic materials as a monkey, a mouse, or a mosquito!" However, we most certainly are made of the same stuff as monkeys, mice, and mosquitoes, and we should not regard this as a problem, for this is indeed what God made us to be. We bear the likeness of the first woman and the first man taken by God from the earth, and we bear the likeness of all the other creatures of this earth. We are more than animals, but there indeed is a sense in which we bear the same physical nature.

It is because of this fundamental physical similarity that we are able to live on this earth, breathe the air of our atmosphere, and eat what this earth produces. We share a kinship as physical creatures with the other creatures of earth, sea, and sky, and we ought to recognize this kinship (think of Francis of Assisi with his profound understanding of this when he called the animals and the birds of the air his "brothers and sisters").

This kinship is important when we think of our stewardship of the environment, for we are those who are given authority over this earth and over all of its creatures—we are to see all other creatures as living members of God's good creation just like ourselves. Scripture also acknowledges this kinship when all creation, including humans, is called on to offer praise to the Creator. See, for example, Psalm 148, which urges angels, sun and moon and stars, sea creatures and oceans, lightning and hail, snow and clouds, mountains and hills, fruit trees and cedars, wild animals and cattle, small creatures and flying birds, rulers and nations, young men and maidens, old people and children—all the creatures of this universe—to praise the Lord.

So the biblical text draws attention to our similarity to the rest of God's creatures as well as to our uniqueness. Francis Schaeffer used to represent the dual reality of our nature in this way:

FIG. 1-1: MAN'S TWO NATURES

<u>infinite</u>	personal God
finite	<u>personal humans made in God's image</u>
animals	animals
plants	plants
physical structures	physical structures

Eve and Adam were like but also different from all other living creatures; of them alone is it said that *they are made in the image and likeness of God.* Eve, our mother, and Adam, our father, bear the glory of being the crown of creation, the ones who are like their Creator and not merely like their fellow creatures. What does this mean?

The basic meaning of the two parallel expressions *image* and *likeness* is that there is a resemblance of being, a fundamental similarity, between the Creator and his human creatures, a resemblance that is not true of anything else in this creation. Eve and Adam are made as finite and visible/physical copies of the infinite and invisible God. The image, or statue, of a king was set up in a city square to be a constant visible reminder of the king himself and of his governing power to all the dwellers in that city. Just so with Eve and Adam.

Eve and Adam are not lifeless statues, of course, but living, breathing, personal representations of the Ruler of the universe. Eve and Adam are to be constant reminders, visible representatives, of God, the King of creation, to all his other creatures. The Scriptures do not define the precise content of *image* and *likeness* for us. But God's people have always recognized that there are many consequences of this reality of being God's image, and these may be summarized in the following way as we reflect on this traditional understanding, an understanding that came from seeking scriptural statements about the nature of God that are then applied to us his creatures, made to be like him:

Eve and Adam are created for dominion over the other creatures. God is the Sovereign over all creation, and we have a finite and limited sovereignty under him. We are designed to exercise loving and faithful rule over this earth and all of its creatures. We are not to be despots who simply use and abuse our environment for our own willful pleasure but rather those who are to imitate the loving, gracious, and caring rule of God. Psalm 8 teaches that this creational purpose—that a human person is designed to be ruler over all of this creation—is what makes King David declare:

> *You have made him a little lower than the heavenly beings*
> *and crowned him with glory and honor.*
> *You have given him dominion over the works of your hands;*
> *you have put all things under his feet. (vv. 5–6)*

Eve and Adam are created for love and relationship. Scripture draws attention to the personal and relational nature of the image of God. God declares, "Let us make man in our image," and the text adds, "So God created man in his own image, in the image of God he created him; male and female he created them" (Genesis 1:26–27). Eve and Adam are made for a personal relationship as male and female. Just as the three persons of the Trinity love, relate, and fellowship with each other through all eternity, so we as those created in God's image are made for love, relationship, and fellowship with our Creator and with one another. Fundamental to our humanity is that we are made to dwell in families, in community. As Paul would later write, "I bow my knees before the Father, from whom every family in heaven and on earth is named" (Ephesians 3:14–15). Every human person is designed for loving union with God and with other persons who are made in his likeness.

Eve and Adam are created to be like God in righteousness and holiness. We are to mirror the moral nature of our Creator, to walk the way he walks. Behind every commandment of God stands the reality of God's moral beauty: "You shall be holy, for I the LORD your God am holy" (Leviticus 19:2). Consider also the words of Jesus when, after an exposition of moral obligations, he teaches us, "You therefore must be perfect, as your heavenly Father is perfect" (Matthew 5:48).

Eve and Adam are created to be significant. We are designed to willingly and gladly choose to be what God has made us to be and to live in love and in moral beauty as he designed us to live, delightedly reflecting his nature in all we do. We have a kind of limited sovereignty over our own lives, mirroring in a little way the infinite sovereignty of God's divine majesty. We are finite history-makers, under God, the Lord of history.

Eve and Adam are created to think God's thoughts after him. We are made to be rational, to use our minds to the glory of our Creator, as we seek to understand our world and our life here in it, as we turn our thoughts to understand and to treasure all that is right and true.

Eve and Adam are created to be those who use language. We are all like the Word himself—we might say that we are "little words," made to be communicators in words just like our Creator. God is the One who called all worlds into being by his creative word, who sustains and rules over all things by his powerful and law-giving word, who reveals himself by his truth-giving word, who communicates by his life-giving word. We are to use language in imitation of him by exercising the gifts of creative imagination, by understanding and naming the world around us, by revealing ourselves truthfully in all we say and write, by communicating with our Creator and with one another to build trust and to give life to all of our relationships.

These attributes of Eve's and Adam's humanity, and of ours, are basic aspects of how Scripture reflects on our likeness to God. Basically these are the characteristics of what it means to be a person, just as God is truly personal. Each of us shares these characteristics, and yet each of us is different from each other person. Each one of us is unique, just as Eve and Adam were alike and yet each was a different person from the other; and their children in turn were like them, yet different from each of their parents. In this, too, our human life reflects the nature of God in whom there is both unity and diversity.

Eve is as fully God's image-bearer as is Adam. There is therefore complete equality between the first woman and the first man as we reflect on their fundamental nature as persons made to be like their Creator. This full equality means that there is no hierarchy of being between a man and a woman. As those made by God and made to be like God, Eve and Adam are made first of all for eternal personal fellowship with God, for a loving relationship with their designer, a relationship that is intended to endure forever.

This is important for us to remember, for before we start to think about the relationship between female and male we need to recognize that our relationship with God is even more foundational to us than any human relationship. This means also that our relationship with God takes precedence over any human relationship, whether it is a relationship between wife and husband, mother and child, father and child, sister and brother, friend and friend, ruler and subject, employer and worker, teacher and student, or pastor and church member.

Every one of us is answerable first of all to God, for we, each one of us, were made by him and for him, and each one of us will have to give our own account to him. When we answer to him, there will be no other human intermediary between each of us and him. Every woman will stand before God directly, giving her account of herself and her life to him, for she is his image-bearer made for fellowship with him and is therefore answerable to him, just as every man will stand before God giving his account of his life and choices.

But in addition to being made to love God and to know him as their primary characteristic and primary calling, these two, Eve and Adam, are made for each other as their secondary calling. We ought not to use these terms *primary* and *secondary* to suggest that our relationships with each other are secondary in the sense of less significant or as if they could be safely ignored or even set aside, for Scripture teaches us that we cannot properly claim to love God if we do not love our fellow human beings (see 1 John 3:16–18; 4:7–12—we are taught in fact that anyone who says they love God but hates his or her fellow human beings is a liar).

Rather, this language of *primary* and *secondary* reflects the way that Jesus himself speaks when he teaches us about the two great commandments in answer to the question, "Which commandment is the most important of all?" Jesus answered, "The most important is, 'Hear, O Israel: The Lord our God, the Lord is one. And you shall love the Lord your God with all your heart and with all your soul and with all your mind and with all your strength.' The second is this: 'You shall love your neighbor as yourself.' There is no other commandment greater than these" (Mark 12:28–31). Jesus makes it quite clear that while the command to love God is primary, it necessarily carries with it and within it the second command to love our neighbor.

Returning to the account of our origins, Genesis 1 emphasizes our creation as those with a primary relationship upward to our Creator. Genesis 2 focuses on our secondary relationships horizontally with our fellow human persons.

In the second, more detailed account of creation, we learn that *Adam is made before Eve.* He is created first. He then needs to learn that he is alone, in the sense that while he has personal fellowship with God, his Creator, and he has a similarity as a fellow creature with other living beings that God has made, he has not yet met another who is his equal. God, the infinite One to whom he owes his existence, his life, his breath, and his world, is clearly his superior. The animals are brought before him to be named so that he, and we, may learn that no other living creature is like us. This naming of the creatures implies that Adam understands the nature of each creature, and the naming also implies his authority over the creatures as he is the one who can give to each one its appropriate name. As he understands and names them as God's representative, he also understands that none of the other creatures is his equal or is fully like him. None of the other creatures is the image of its Creator.

Then God creates Eve from Adam to be his equal, his helper, and his complement—one similar to Adam, yet corresponding to him in her difference from him. An old English folk song that is often sung at weddings expresses in a graphic way the meaning of the phrase "a helper fit for him."

> *She was not took out of his head, sir,*
> *To reign and triumph over man;*
> *Nor was she took out of his feet, sir,*
> *By man to be trampled upon.*
>
> *But she was took out of his side, sir,*
> *His equal and partner to be.*[2]

Adam cries out with joy, "This at last is bone of my bones and flesh of my flesh" (*Genesis 2:23*). This is the cry of all men and women when they find one who is their equal, their mutual help, one who will be the perfect complement to them. This creational likeness and complementariness is the foundation for monogamous, lifelong marriage; it is at the heart of who we are as women and men made for relationships with one another.

The text also teaches us that *sexuality is God's good gift from creation*, a gift about which there should be no shame. Sadly, the church has not always acknowledged this. The primary purpose of the sexual partnership that God has given to us is not reproduction but rather the expression, the consummation, of love and unity between one man and one woman.[3] Of course, bearing and begetting children is a possible consequence of some of the occasions when a couple comes together sexually; but it is not a probable or even possible consequence of every sexual union. There are times of each cycle when pregnancy will not result from sexual union, and there is a time in every woman's life when ovulation ceases (this is true during the months of pregnancy, and it is true after menopause), but this does not mean that sexual desire or sexual union and fulfillment come to an end. The joy of becoming one flesh is more fundamental to sex than is childbearing.

Any view that regards procreation as primary and that is therefore in principle opposed to any form of birth control fails to do justice to this text about the joy of becoming one flesh and so reflecting the unity of the Trinity and also fails to do justice to the difference between human sexuality and sex among other creatures. When a man and a woman come together, they sometimes hope and pray that they might have a child, but that is not the primary reason they come together. It is their love for each other, their desire for each other, and their delight in each other that is primary and that is basic to sexual union.

In addition to this delight in their physically coming together, *God has made sexual union, as with most other creatures, the means of bringing a new generation into the world.* All of us are the children, the offspring, the descendants of Eve and Adam. All that it means to be human, to be both a creature and to be in God's image, comes to us through the fruit of this original union between Eve and Adam. God has created us so that we beget and bear children truly made in our own likeness—they bear the image of their mother and their father. Out of our greatest experience of unity comes the possibility of diversity, the bringing into the world of a new person, a unique daughter of Eve or son of Adam. This creation of diversity out of our greatest experience of unity is yet another way in which we as human persons reflect the likeness of God—in this case the unity and diversity within the Trinity. As we saw in an earlier section, our families are named after the family of our heavenly Father (Ephesians 3:14–15).

The text in Genesis 2 suggests that *some kind of leadership is given to Adam, for he is created first*, and Eve is created "from" him and "for" him (1 Corinthians 11:8–9). In addition, it is Adam who gives Eve her name, and, as was mentioned earlier, this implies a particular significance or authority in the one who does the naming. It is important to stress here that this structure in the relationship of Eve and Adam does not negate what has already been written about both the woman and the man being equally in the image of God. This leadership of Adam in relationship with Eve, and her corresponding commitment to him, does not mean that their equality is undermined, for Eve and Adam are like the Trinity in which there is a headship of the Father over the Son, and yet there is also a full equality of Godhead (1 Corinthians 11:3; Colossians 1:19; 2:9).

This last point needs to be developed more fully as it is an issue of such contention in our generation. We will reflect on this further after we look at the second and third face of Eve. For now, let us leave Eve and Adam enjoying the wonder of their union of equals—two who see in each other a perfect reflection of the glory of their Maker, two who see in the other a perfect complement to be a lifelong partner and helpmate, two who have the same dignity and yet are delightfully different, two who are designed to fit together and support each other in every way—physically, emotionally, mentally, imaginatively, volitionally, spiritually.

SUGGESTED READINGS AND QUESTIONS

1. Do you struggle with the biblical teaching about our origins? If you do, a fine book by Philip Johnson (*Darwin on Trial*) may be of help to you. Also see the excellent volume *Science and Faith* by John C. Collins.[4]

2. Does the teaching that all races are of one origin and therefore that the people of all races are all equally God's image-bearers go against what you have been taught or what you have heard?

3. Some believers are troubled by the teaching that we are those who *physically* bear the image of God and insist that it has to be

our *spiritual* nature that shows the image and likeness of God. How would you respond to someone who holds such a view?

4. What do you think are some implications of our sharing our physical nature with the other creatures of this earth? Do you find this idea distasteful, and if so, why?

5. What to you is the most wonderful implication of your being made in the image of God?

6. How do you see the equality of Eve and Adam as God's image working itself out in your relationships with men or women (especially in your husband or your wife for those who are married)?

7. What was your experience of equality between the sexes (or lack of it) in the family in which you were raised?

8. How do you see being complementary, the fitting, supporting, and meeting one another's needs of Eve and Adam, working out in your relationships with men or women (especially with your husband or wife for those who are married)?

9. Read Genesis 3:1–24. What changed in the relationship between Eve and Adam in consequence of the Fall? How does sin particularly impact us as men and women according to Genesis 3?

2

THE SECOND FACE OF EVE:

Eve at and after the Fall

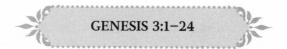

GENESIS 3:1–24

I n our first chapter we learned something of the glory of Eve and what it means to be made in the image of God. The glory that all human beings experience in our lives is one that we inherit from the mother of us all. Though the Scripture does not use this precise expression (it does speak of human persons as rulers of creation), we might say that Eve was the queen of creation, given that position of authority by God when he made her in his likeness and gave her, along with Adam, authority or dominion over everything around them. As we think of ourselves and of all that makes us uniquely human, these are all things that we inherit from Eve, for we all share with her the likeness of God. She is the mother of every characteristic that makes us persons as we reflect in our finiteness the infinite majesty of God, the three-personed Lord.

Apart from dwelling in our minds and hearts on the greatness and glory of God, there is nothing more wonderful in human life than for us to treasure our creation in the image of God or more marvelous than for us to reflect on the glory of our humanness. This is something that those of us who name ourselves Christian believers need truly to cherish, not only in ourselves but also in everyone around us. We sometimes work very hard at seeing faults, and we appear to think it is very biblical to search out the sinfulness of people around us, both the sins of our fellow believers and, in particular, the sins of unbelievers. But that is not what Scripture calls us to do. We are indeed to recognize people's moral failures, especially our own, but we are called first to recognize their glory as persons made in the image of God. With every man and woman we ever encounter we are to ask the question, "Who is this person, Lord, that you are mindful of him or her?" Our response ought to be, "Here is a person crowned with glory and honor" and not, "Here is a worthless sinner."

We need to train ourselves to see the human dignity in the people around us. If we do not do this, we are being disobedient to the command of God's Word and to the example of our Lord and Savior as he met and engaged women and men with such grace. One effect of failing to see and honor the dignity of those around us is that there will be no way we will be able to communicate the good news of the Christian message to them in a way that is obedient to the example of Christ and to the commands of Scripture. If we do not respect people as God's image-bearers, we simply cannot communicate with them effectively and faithfully.[1]

We need to learn to trace that descent from Eve and to delight in what we see of the glory that shines in the image of God in every person around us. Invariably this should be our first impulse: where does this woman or this man or this child demonstrate the image of God? From this reflection on our human glory we turn to what we will call the second face of Eve, the broken, shameful, and sad side of our humanity—Eve at and after the fall.

EVE AT AND AFTER THE FALL

The text for our reflections in this chapter is perhaps the saddest in all of Scripture, for it describes the day when all of human history was permanently changed. We read of God coming to Eve and Adam after their disobedience and saying to Eve, "What is this that you have done?" (Genesis 3:13). God's demanding inquiry expresses for us just how tragic the consequences of sin are. We will seek to determine what leads to the Fall, to reflect on the temptation by Satan and its appeal to Eve, and to ask ourselves about Eve's response, and we will then study the consequences of her choice. As we read Genesis 3, the story seems very simple, but the issues in these simple brushstrokes of the narrative are very profound.

What happens on that day of death? We read that Eve is beguiled by the serpent and disobeys God by taking the forbidden fruit and then sharing it with Adam. These facts sound straightforward enough, but of course it is much more complex than that.

We are told that Satan comes to visit Eve in the form of a serpent, for he is the master of disguise, deceit, and betrayal. Jesus calls him "the father of lies" (John 8:44), and in the same passage he is described as "a murderer from the beginning." His purpose on this occasion is to turn Eve and Adam from their worship of God alone; to turn them from their trust in the Lord as their Creator, Provider, Helper, and Friend; to turn them from their contented knowledge of who they are and to make them dissatisfied; to turn them from their glad acceptance of their status as creatures in God's world and to cause them to become distrustful of God's good intentions toward them.

Eve and Adam have been created to glorify God as their Creator, as their provider, the One on whom they are dependent for existence and for the breath of life, for health, for happiness, and for their own glory. Satan wants to turn them from all this—from their acknowledgment of God as their Creator and from their trust in him as the one who has given and will continue to give them every good thing. He is eager to turn them away from their understanding that it is enough to be creatures in God's world, completely dependent upon their Lord. Instead Satan desires that they join him in his own rebellion against God, the King of heaven. His plan is that they reject God's rule and serve and honor themselves in place of God. In his own revolt against God, Satan seeks to put himself in the place of God, and he is eager to bring down others so that they may join him in his fall from heavenly splendor.

Satan, on this occasion, is not so much calling for Eve and Adam to worship him as he is tempting them to worship themselves, to put themselves in the place of God. This is what he himself has done. This has been his own terrible revolution, his own failed attempt to overthrow the divine majesty and to set himself up in the place of God. And now, in his rage at God for his own folly, not content to be under the sentence of destruction himself, he comes to Eve to try to bring God's new creation down with him. He sees this beautiful world that God has made, and he sees the glory of this first human pair who are made in God's image. He sees their happiness in knowing God, in knowing each other, and in ruling this earth, and he longs to overthrow it all. He burns with longing to take away from them the enjoyment of their life. He seeks to find a way to poison their contented delight in God. He hopes to dispossess them of all their joy so they will share in the disaster that has befallen him.

In desiring that they begin to honor themselves rather than God, his approach is to cast doubt on the word of God and more importantly to cause them to question whether God is really good to them. We all recognize this now as something that is a daily struggle within our own hearts, for Satan's temptation to us today is just the same as it was for Eve and Adam: "Has God really said?" We struggle with, "Can I trust God?" "Does he have in mind what is good for me?" "Are his purposes for me good or are they evil?"

This is precisely the temptation that Satan sets before Eve. He assures Eve that God's threat of judgment will not be fulfilled, that she "will not surely die" if she disobeys God. Instead, what he says to her in essence is, "Rather than dying or being punished by God, you are going to become even more godlike than you already are. You are going to have the wisdom and the knowledge of God himself. You can rival God if you disobey his word. God is, in fact, trying to prevent you from becoming more like himself than you are today. He is depriving you of what is rightfully yours, of your true and full destiny."[2]

Of course, this promise and this charge against God's character are deception, but these clever lies make up the temptation that is set before Eve. What is her response to these false promises and trumped-up accusations? Eve's response, after some reflection, is to doubt God's word, to doubt that his threat of judgment would come true, to doubt God's goodness toward her, and to believe that God is indeed trying to prevent her from achieving her full glory and potential.

As we look into our own hearts, we need to acknowledge that these are very powerful temptations, temptations with which every one of us constantly struggles. It is easy to read this account in a superficial way and say, "What was she doing? How could she respond like that?" But if we examine our own histories of doubting God's goodness, of failing to take his warnings seriously, of trusting our own judgment rather than his, of putting ourselves at the center of the circle of our lives, we might find it more difficult to cast our stones of criticism at Eve. The text describes how she turns Satan's words over in her own mind as she looks at the tree's fruit, as she sees its beauty, its value as food, and its promise of greater wisdom. These are the things that tempt her. We all wrestle with these issues: the importance to us of our outward appearance—"What kind of an impression do I make on those who see me?"; the significance of our daily physical needs being met—"How will I put food on the table?"; the value of being wise and of being seen by others to be wise—"Can I demonstrate how clever and sensible I am so others will think well of me?"

Eve sets these imagined gains against the command of God and against her own knowledge of the goodness of God. Instead she concludes that God is mean-spirited to deprive her of these wonderful gifts, gifts that she is beginning to think are rightfully hers. This, too, is the way all of us think at times. We ask, "Why does God want to deprive me of these legitimate pleasures—pleasures rightfully mine, pleasures he is obligated to give me for my enjoyment?" She sets these purely imaginary gains against God's explicitly known commandment and against her own sure knowledge of the goodness of God.

We need to reflect more deeply on this latter point. Up to this moment, all Eve has ever experienced is a daily reality of many diverse and good gifts from the generous hand of God. This rich provision of God for her life is what Genesis 1–2 are about—the treasures and blessings that God has poured out on this first human pair. What does Eve have to set against this constant beneficence?

Against all that she has seen and enjoyed Eve has to set only the word of Satan, the deceiver, a creature whom she has no reason to trust at all. In contrast she has every reason to trust God. Against this certain knowledge of God's goodness and against his warning of judgment she has her own imagination as to what the future might hold for her if she chooses the deceiver's way. While she, no doubt, rationalizes her disobedience, as we all do, she has no reason to trust the serpent's word, no basis for doubting the love of God, no knowledge to set against what she already was convinced of concerning God's character. And yet she disobeys, and Adam also is persuaded to disobey God along with her (the text simply says, "she also gave some to her husband who was with her, and he ate").

In spite of the reality that the whole weight of evidence is against the way that she chooses, Eve turns her face from God and disobeys him. There is nothing more unreasonable than the choice she makes. But all sin is like this. We all need to admit that this unreasonableness is the nature of any sin, any disobedience against God. There is no excuse for sin. Sin cannot be justified, excused, or explained away. No matter how we hold sin up to the light of rational inquiry, no matter which way we look at sin, sin makes no sense. Sin is absurd. We may ask, "Why did Eve disobey?" or "Why did I turn from God's commandments?" "Why did this woman or this man forsake her or his marriage vows, commit adultery, and wreck her or his beloved children's lives?" We are desperate to be able to give a rational account of sin; we want to give sufficient reasons to show why Eve, or why you or I, make such a choice, but there are none.

We will never, no matter how much we search or however long we reflect, find a sensible or adequate explanation or excuse for sin. Sin by its very nature is against the structure of the universe, and therefore we cannot make sense of it. Sin is against the character of God, the Creator of all things. Sin is opposed to the way God designed the universe to be. Sin is contrary to the life that God created us to live, and it is contrary to our human nature as those made to be like God.

What are the consequences of this disobedience? We can summarize all the consequences of Eve and Adam's sin and refer to all of it as the judgment of God. This is easily said, but what does this judgment mean? How does God's judgment work itself out? We can try to capture it by speaking of the sevenfold effects of sin or the seven-pointed curse, to adapt a phrase of Francis Schaeffer who refers to a four-pointed curse.[3]

THE SEVEN-POINTED CURSE

The first curse of sin is that *God is alienated from Eve and from all of us.* As the righteous, perfect, holy Judge of all reality, whose standard is moral perfection, he can have no dealings with sin or with sinners. His face is turned away from us, as Isaiah expresses it in one passage (Isaiah 59:2), so that he cannot hear us, for he can have fellowship only with what is good and perfect. This is true now, and it is true for all eternity. That is the first and central impact—God's wrath and anger is directed against Eve, against sin, against sinners.

We may not want to think in such a way, but this is clearly what Scripture teaches us in one passage after another. Paul says that we are all "children of wrath," like the rest of our race.[4] That is the reality and the first consequence—the settled anger and enmity of God against sin and against sinners. Some readers will object here and protest, "God hates sin, but he loves sinners!" While this sounds like a pleasant sentiment, it is necessary to remember that it is sinners who will face God's judgment and not simply sin disembodied from the person who committed those sins. It is not a handful of particularly obnoxious sins but rather actual women and men who will "appear before the judgment seat of Christ, so that each one may receive what is due for what he has done in the body, whether good or evil" (2 Corinthians 5:10).

The second curse of her disobedience is that *Eve is alienated from God, and so are we all.* In Genesis 3 we see Eve and Adam trying to hide from God because they no longer love him, because they have disobeyed him, because they have ceased to trust him, because they now doubt him, because they no longer seek the enjoyment of his company, and so they turn away from him. Eve becomes, and we all become, enemies of God, hoping and trying to hide from him our sin and our rebellion. We find ourselves longing to honor ourselves rather than honor him, for the very heart or essence of sin is pride.

At the center of the Genesis account of the Fall is the problem of arrogance, with which we all wrestle—that is, we seek to put ourselves in the place of God. We all find this tension in our hearts every day of our lives. This is still true of us as Christian believers who have bowed before God and who have prayed repeatedly that he will humble us before the infinite power and glory of his divine majesty. We are constantly eager to put our hope and confidence in ourselves rather than in God.

This then is the second consequence of sin: we have become enemies of God. The apostle Paul expresses it this way in Colossians 1: "[we] were alienated and hostile in mind, doing evil deeds" (v. 21). In Romans 3 he writes, "no one understands, no one seeks for God. All have turned aside" (vv. 11–12). The world is not full of people desperately anxious to become Christians. We might wish that it were that way, or we may delude ourselves into thinking that it is indeed that way, but the truth is far different. The truth is that everyone is running away from God.

The reality is as C. S. Lewis said of his own conversion to the acknowledgment of God:

> You must picture me alone in that room in Magdalen, night after night, feeling, whenever my mind lifted even for a second from my work, the steady, unrelenting approach of Him whom I so earnestly desired not to meet. That which I greatly feared had come upon me. In the Trinity Term of 1929 I gave in, and admitted that God was God, and knelt and prayed: perhaps, that night, the most dejected and reluctant convert in all England. I did not see then what is now the most obvious and shining thing; the Divine humility which will accept a convert even on such terms. The Prodigal Son at least walked home on his own feet. But who can

duly adore that Love which will open the high gates to a prodigal who is brought in kicking, struggling, resentful, and darting his eyes in every direction for a chance to escape?[5]

That is the reality. Even when we do come to believe that Christianity is true, that it answers our most important questions and satisfies our deepest needs, we are still reluctant to bow before God and to acknowledge that he is indeed the Lord. It took me more than a year after I was persuaded that Christianity is the truth before I was converted. And even when we have come to know God through Jesus Christ, we still struggle with bowing daily before him. Women and men are not desperately seeking God. Rather, we are alienated from God in our minds and hearts.

The third curse of sin is that *Eve is alienated from herself; and so are we all*, each one from herself or himself. What is meant by this self-alienation? As we look within ourselves, we are aware that there is a disorder within us. We experience shame and even self-loathing because of who we are. We have all awakened in the middle of the night and reflected on things we have done, said, or thought, and even though there is no one else to see us (apart from the Lord), we have simply been overwhelmed with a sense of shame. We find ourselves blushing and sweating in the dark. We see Eve and Adam experiencing this sense of shame—before God, before each other, and even in their own hearts. We experience disgust with ourselves. Paul said of himself, and this was when he had been a believer and an apostle of Christ for many years, "Wretched man that I am! Who will deliver me from this body of death?" (Romans 7:24).[6]

We sometimes observe this self-loathing expressing itself in extreme ways. It is at times present in teenage girls wrestling with problems like anorexia or bulimia. But even when there is not the experience of such extremes of self-hatred, whenever there is any honesty about oneself, we all find ourselves struggling with a sense of dissatisfaction in our life, in our character, in our choices, in our behavior. I find a profound lack of happiness when deep within myself I face the question, who am I? There is no longer any perfect happiness for us in knowing ourselves and having to live with ourselves, either because we do indeed know ourselves or because we are trying desperately to avoid knowing ourselves.

I am not suggesting that every human person is unhappy because every person we meet in this world has an acute sense of sin, for it is possible to harden one's conscience, so that one deceives oneself about one's true inner state. Many people are nauseatingly self-righteous. Many are complacent and self-satisfied. Such attitudes to oneself are profoundly inaccurate and require a constant suppression of the truth about oneself. However, this suppression of self-knowledge is another form of self-alienation.

In addition, many forms of addiction, whether they appear relatively harmless like excessive shopping or inordinate devotion to the beautification of one's home or one's person or whether they are more obviously harmful like sexual obsessions or too much indulgence in alcohol, have beneath them a deep sense of self-alienation. The truth is that whenever we get to know anyone well, we will find some form of enmity with the self.

The fourth curse of sin is that *Eve is alienated from Adam*. In this aspect of the curse we observe the beginning of alienation and of the breakdown of relationships across all human contacts. Each one of us wrestles with this alienation from every other person we meet and even from those we love the most dearly or to whom we are bound the most closely. In the very next chapter of Genesis we find Cain killing his brother Abel because he is jealous and angry. In the account of the curse on Eve and Adam we see described for us how this disintegration even affects those relationships most treasured by us, the tie of marriage—this most precious relationship of all, where two become one. God spells out for Eve and for Adam the particular effects of sin in the relationships between a man and a woman.

The impact of the curse on Adam is to "rule over" his wife (Genesis 3:16), to turn his headship into domination. This is the temptation of men in general, to treat a wife—whom he should regard as his equal and partner—as "his woman," to use her like a servant, to regard her as an object for doing his bidding or for meeting his needs for sex, companionship, food, laundry, a comfortable home, a source of pride before other men.

All of us have some experience of observing or practicing or suffering from this pattern of behavior. The desire to dominate is something against which all men have to wrestle. It is particularly acute in the relationship between a man and a woman—which is why Paul has to challenge husbands to "love your wives, and do not be harsh with them" (Colossians 3:19). We also observe this desire to rule in all other relationships between men and those to whom they relate: fathers and children, sibling rivalries, in the workplace, at play, in the church. In fact, we have to state it as a general principle that wherever there are men, this urge to be first and to dominate will be found.

Of course, it is possible to work against this and to put such sin to death and so experience a deep level of delight in one another rather than to be indulging in constant competition and the need to be superior. But such joy in male relationships is not found without a profound commitment to work against these innate pressures. This is true in the family also, where the apostle Paul reminds fathers, "do not provoke your children, lest they become discouraged" (Colossians 3:21; see also Ephesians 6:4). Men have to resist this desire to "rule over" their children if they long to have a close and permanent relationship of love and friendship with them.

The impact of the curse on Eve with regard to her relationship with Adam is expressed by the text as, "your desire shall be for your husband, and he shall rule over you." A woman's temptation is so to long for a good relationship with a man that she may endure almost anything in order to gain it, even if it is to her own hurt. This inordinate desire seems to be what Genesis is describing. An extreme example of this is wife abuse, where a wife will simply give in to her husband, will submit repeatedly no matter how unreasonable and even absurd are his demands, will subject herself to verbal and even physical abuse. She endures all this in the desperate and thoroughly unlikely hope that forbearance and even greater submission will produce a fruitful change in the relationship. The movie *Sleeping with the Enemy* is a graphic picture of this destructive pattern.

An alternative understanding of the phrase, "your desire shall be for your husband" is to suggest that the woman will long to master her man, to turn her husband into the one who will fulfill all her desires. She may not have physical power, but she will use emotional manipulation to gain her way in the marriage and so "rule over" him. Certainly everyone sees marriages like this, so this is a possible though less likely interpretation of the text since the second half of the curse refers to the rule of the husband. However, it is perhaps a possibility that both of these understandings, inordinate submission and inordinate control, are appropriate ways to interpret the text, for both are perversions of desire for the relationship.

Even here, then, in this most precious relationship, sin brings alienation, tension, and trouble into every close encounter of men and women. And, of course, this alienation and breakdown apparent in marriage is present in every other human relationship. The rest of Scripture spells out for us innumerable examples of this disease of our sin corrupting every relationship we touch.

The fifth curse of sin is that *Eve and Adam are alienated from creation*, the creation they were made to rule. As with the other curses, this affects every one of us. Genesis spells out this loss of dominion by focusing on the difficulty of producing food from the ground. My father-in-law was a farmer, growing peaches, plums, nectarines, persimmons, grapes, kiwis, and other fruit trees all his life, and he like every other farmer in the world could testify to the reality of this curse. Farming is hard work, literally backbreaking work. The farmer is continually facing new difficulties, constantly having to try to figure out how to get the ground, his crops, his machines, his body to accomplish what needs to be done so that the ground will bring forth a harvest, the bills will be paid, and food will be set on the family table.

Whether it is in the area of farming or gardening or whatever—literally producing food from the ground or in any other area of our work—we all experience loss of dominion as we seek to labor in the world in which God has set us. Work in this fallen world is a joy as we use body, mind, heart, and imagination to do fulfilling tasks in seeking to exercise dominion, but work also always has an element of trouble, sorrow, and pain in it. We all experience a sense of frustration at not being able to accomplish what we want to. Things seem to work against us—there is a spanner in the works in every task we try to accomplish. All human beings are faced every day with the impossibility of creating a utopia, for we are confronted daily with our failure to exercise dominion and with our abuse of dominion. Even as we drive through traffic on our way to work or school or play we experience loss of dominion.

The sixth curse of sin is that *Eve is alienated from her own body.* Again, this alienation affects us all. There is a kind of disintegration between body and spirit. At the end we experience this most terribly in death, when body and spirit are torn apart. God did not create us for this tearing apart; rather he created us for a permanent union between body and spirit. However, the consequence of sin is physical death as well as spiritual death.

We experience this disintegration all through our lives as we suffer sickness, pain, and aging. When I turned forty, someone said to me, "If you wake up on your fortieth birthday with no aches, you're in heaven already." We all are familiar with this problem. Sometimes this becomes particularly acute as when a person is diagnosed with Lou Gehrig's disease (ALS). A relative of mine died a few years ago of this terrible sickness after her body had become less and less responsive to her wishes as the years passed—unable to speak, unable to swallow, unable to walk, unable to order her muscles to do the simplest tasks. We all are familiar with such tragedies because this physical brokenness, this physical mortality, is a universal human experience.

Eve, in particular, feels the effects of this in that most marvelous process, the bearing of children. Genesis 3 expresses this very clearly as one of the consequences of sin—the increased pain and trouble of childbearing. Giving birth to a child is still a wonderful gift from God, yet all women know what a struggle, a *labor*, childbirth literally is.

The seventh and final curse of sin is that *Eve and Adam have to live in an environment that itself is under judgment and that experiences alien-*

ation. The earth is cursed because it is their home and the place of their dominion. This earth is the setting in which we have to face the reality of our sin and its bitter fruits every day of our lives. God has not allowed us to live in a utopia where we can hide ourselves from the reality of human sin or of sin's consequences.

This earth is still very lovely; it still declares the glory of God. But it is "subject to futility," as Paul expresses it in Romans 8. The earth resists our attempts at dominion. Nature itself is "red in tooth and claw," as Tennyson put it, and, according to Paul, longs to be "set free from its bondage to decay" (Romans 8:18–22).[7] Nothing can be made perfect here in our present lives, not even this beautiful earth on which we live. God has judged the earth as part of his judgment on our race. The Lord declares that "the earth he has given to the children of man" (Psalm 115:16). Because it is our home, this world is subjected to the curse that we deserve. The earth has been given to us as our dwelling place and as the sphere of our rule, and so it has been subjected to vanity along with us.

These are the seven consequences of sin, and as a result of Eve and Adam's disobedience we see breakdown and alienation coming into every aspect of our human existence. Nothing is untainted by our failure to obey the commandments of God, and in particular by our failure to worship God alone. Each one of us experiences all seven of these curses of sin every day of our lives. This is the reality we all experience as a constant in our present human existence in this world.

SUGGESTED READINGS AND QUESTIONS

1. Do you find it difficult to accept that God is alienated from you by your failure to love him and worship him and by your disobedience to his commandments? Why do you think people, including Christian believers, are reluctant to face the clear teaching of Scripture at this point?

2. Where do you see the second alienation, the alienation between you and God, working itself out in your life? What did it take for God to bring you to bow humbly before him?

3. Where do you see the third alienation, the alienation between you and yourself, working itself out in your life? Are there aspects of your own personality that you secretly dislike? Where are you tempted to harden your own conscience rather than facing up to the reality of your sinful nature?

4. Which of the ways in which Eve was tempted do you think would have been most attractive to you if you were in her situation? Which do you struggle with the most—appearance, physical comforts, or the longing for wisdom?

5. What has been the most difficult area for you with regard to the brokenness of human relationships, particularly in your relationships between women and men, in family life and, if you are married, in your marriage?

6. Where do you see yourself experiencing the loss of dominion?

7. Where do you most observe the alienation within the creation?

8. Read the first promise of the Messiah in Genesis 3:15. What does the text teach us about the promised victory over sin?

9. How does Christ overcome the curse in all its ramifications?

3

THE THIRD FACE OF EVE:

Eve, the Bearer of the Promise of Redemption

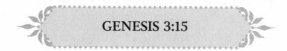

GENESIS 3:15

We saw in Chapter 2 that God is alienated from Eve, from Adam, and from all who sin and rebel against him. At the heart of this rebellion is the refusal to worship God and the insistence on serving and worshipping ourselves instead of our Creator. It is as if we consider ourselves to be gods. Some of the thinkers who have shaped our postmodern world have indeed taught exactly that. The philosopher Nietzsche is an example of such thinking. In a famous passage he writes of the way in which modern western thought has "killed off God," and he insists that our contemporary generations must reach for the noble calling of becoming gods ourselves:

> Do we not feel anything yet of the noise of the grave-diggers who are burying God? Do we not smell anything yet of God's decomposition? Gods too decompose. God is dead. God remains dead. And we have killed him. How shall we, the murderers of all murderers, comfort ourselves? What was holiest and most powerful of all the world yet owned has bled to death under our knives. Who will wipe this blood off us? What water is there for us to cleanse ourselves? What festivals of atonement, what sacred games shall we have to invent? Is not the greatness of this deed too great for

us? Must we not ourselves become gods simply to seem worthy of it? There has never been a greater deed; and whoever will be born after us—for the sake of this deed he will be a part of a higher history than all history hitherto.[1]

While we may be shocked by the passion and clarity with which Nietzsche sets out his views, we need to recognize that his words capture a fundamental truth about the human condition, a truth we might find hard to acknowledge, but it is the only account that makes any sense of our broken situation in this world. The apostle Paul describes our world and human life in a similar way to Nietzsche—just read Romans 1:18–32 to see Paul's summary of our present state.

> [A]lthough they knew God, they did not honor him as God or give thanks to him, but they became futile in their thinking, and their foolish hearts were darkened. Claiming to be wise, they became fools, and exchanged the glory of the immortal God for images resembling mortal man and birds and animals and creeping things. . . . They exchanged the truth about God for a lie and worshiped and served the creature rather than the Creator, who is blessed forever . . . they did not see fit to acknowledge God. (vv. 21–28)

In acknowledging that this is indeed our human situation—that we are rebels against the divine majesty of God and worship ourselves instead of him—we might even say that the miserable tale told in Chapter 2 of this book is good news. This may seem a shocking statement to make, but my point is this: there is a desperate need to have a true understanding of the dilemma in which we find ourselves as human persons.

Only the biblical story, the account of the origin of the seven-pointed curse that brings such daily tragedy into our lives, enables us to say that life as we know it now is *abnormal*. Every other worldview, every other religion, every other account that men and women have made of our world and of our condition, tells us that life as we know it now is *normal*. Sin, sickness, death, suffering, tears, natural disasters—all these have to be seen as "just the way things are" in every other attempt that people have made to try to describe life on this planet.

This is true of all other religions, and it is true of secular philosophies. To declare that our present condition is fundamentally normal, that the world as we experience it now has come like this from the hand of God (for the religious accounts) or has always been this way (for the secular accounts), is to make light of the terrible suffering of this world. To declare that our present condition is fundamentally normal is also to undercut true sorrow and the commitment to bring radical transformation to the human condition.

But the wonder of the biblical account is that it alone is the true story, for it is the story that God tells us about the abnormality of our world and of our human life, and it is because it is the true account revealed to us by God that it describes so accurately the way things are. The biblical narrative is like a glove that is perfectly molded to the hand of reality—it is a perfect fit!

Sometimes non-Christians, and sometimes even our fellow Christian believers, try to tell us that it is naive to read the stories of the early chapters of Genesis as sober history. The protest is loudly made, "That is a belief for another age, an age of less sophistication, an age of ignorance, an age of the absurd power of religion and of religious leaders. We need an understanding of the world that is more real, more scientific, more fitted to deal with the problems and wisdom of the twenty-first century." Our response to such dismissals of our faith in the biblical account of our origins and of the broken reality of our world needs to be confident and courageous.

No other account makes such sense of our world. No other account fits the facts of the sorry record of human evil. No other account gives an adequate explanation of the troubles of our lives. No other account enables us to weep such true tears of sorrow over the tragedies of human existence. No other account enables us to fight against suffering with such conviction that we are not engaged in a hopeless battle against the way things always have been and always will be. No other account urges us to work with confidence and firm hope for the betterment and transformation of our sad lives. Things are not as they originally were; they are not as God made them. God hates sin and all its consequences—and so, therefore, may we, and indeed we must!

I am not saying, of course, that people who follow other religions or people who hold to some secular worldview do not weep over the tragedies of their lives and do not work for the betterment and transformation of this world. Thank God, indeed they do; but their tears and their work go against the basic account of reality that their religion or their philosophy gives. If things are as they always have been, why weep over them, why bother to change them?[2]

This biblical account is one of the reasons I became convinced that Christianity is the truth. As an unbeliever I struggled with three basic questions. 1) What value do I have as a human person if I am just a part of this physical universe—am I really different from any other creature on this earth? 2) Is there any foundation for distinguishing between good and evil? 3) Is there any adequate explanation of the problem of suffering and evil? The first three chapters of the book of Genesis answer all three of these questions. As human persons we have unique value because we are made in the image of God. God's own character is the foundation for an ultimate distinction between good and evil. The biblical account of the Fall gives us the only satisfactory explanation for the problem of suffering and evil.[3]

I am not saying, of course, that the Fall itself is good news. God forbid! The fall of Eve and Adam was a terrible event with tragic and enduring consequences that impact each one of our lives in profound and miserable ways every day we wake up in this world. The true good news comes in the next part of our story.

EVE, THE BEARER OF THE PROMISE OF REDEMPTION

We turn next to ask the question, is there any comfort for us at all in this sorry history of Eve and Adam's disobedience? Was there any comfort for Eve and Adam along with God's words of judgment? God could have, and would have, been right and justified simply to have left Eve and Adam to live and die with the consequences of their sin. That would have been perfectly just. If we want perfect justice from God, there would be nothing else to say after Chapter 2 (both Chapter 2 of this book and the third chapter of the Bible). With perfect justice the story would end with the account of the reality of temptation, the act of disobedience, and the consequences of sin. However, we don't get perfect justice. Thank heaven that we don't! For instead of abandoning Eve and Adam to the choice they had made, God comes with a message of grace and love. This is seen in the text of Genesis 3 in three ways.

First, *God's coming to them, his presence with them in the Garden each day, is in itself an affirmation of his love.* He comes to them to assure them of his continued care, to seek them out and communicate with them rather than leaving them in their disobedience and proud rebellion. God does the same for each one of us. We did not go seeking all over the world to try to find God. Rather, he came and sought each one of us and found us even in our willful turning from him, even in our insistence on going our own way, even in our state of disobedience and proud rebellion. This coming of God to walk with us happens every time God calls someone to put his or her trust in him, just as he comes to Eve and Adam in the Garden.

Second, *God promises that he will put enmity between Eve and Adam and Satan.* This may not seem so good. Who needs the devil as an enemy! However, the point is that God, instead of abandoning us to Satan, has rather declared that we are on his side, that we are enemies against Satan along with God in the battle that rages down through history between the kingdom of God and the kingdom of darkness. God puts enmity between you and me and Satan. There is a natural hatred of the devil in all people, just as everyone loves their children. Sadly, some go against this and consciously choose to worship and serve the devil, just as some choose to hate and mistreat their own children, but all over the world such practices are regarded as abominable wickedness. God has not handed us over or given us up to the powers of darkness; rather he has set us against the forces of Satan, and he has put enmity between those forces and us.

Third, *God gives to Eve the good news of the coming of a deliverer.*

This is the first promise of ultimate redemption that we find in the Scriptures. (One of my colleagues, Michael Williams, calls this promise "the mother promise," for it is the promise of the mother of the Redeemer and the mother of all the other promises that would come later.) God declares that he will send one into the world who will overcome Satan and sin for Eve and for all of us. However, this overcoming of Satan will be at great cost to the Deliverer when he comes. One descended from Eve will crush the serpent's head, but he himself will be bruised, or crushed, in the process.

Why do Christians see this brief prophecy in Genesis 3:15 as such a wonderful promise? God is committing himself, through the coming Seed of Eve, to overcome the seven-pointed curse that is his judgment on our race for our rebellion and disobedience. God promises to heal the seven states of alienation described in our last chapter. This original promise, this mother of all promises, is repeated as other generations come, and with each repetition the outlines and details of this initial picture of redemption, this *proto-evangelion*, this first proclamation of the gospel, are filled in.

As the prophecies of the Messiah unfold, so we see in greater detail a portrait of his life and work, and that portrait shows the Messiah's goal in coming into this world as being the full restoration of all that was lost, the healing of every alienation that has come into our lives as a result of Eve and Adam's sin.[4]

First, *the Seed of Eve will face the wrath of his Father, the just anger of God, against our sin.* He will appease this wrath and propitiate the universal Judge by bearing all of our sin, disobedience, and punishment himself. He will be condemned for our failures though he himself is perfectly good. How will he accomplish this amazing work? Though he is the eternal Son, the Word, the agent of creation and revelation, the second person of the triune God, he will also become the Seed of Eve. He will be born of a woman, and he will be born under the Law—that is, he will be born as an Israelite.

The people of Israel were a nation chosen by God and a nation, therefore, that had committed itself as a people to keep covenant with God and to obey his commandments. The Seed of Eve is to be born as one committed to keeping God's Law. This is true both because of his membership in the human race, a race that is called by virtue of our being human to live in obedience to our Creator, and also because of his birth as an Israelite—this people who have bound themselves to live honoring God's every word. As a man in whom the whole fullness of deity will dwell, he will live a life of complete and glad obedience to all of God's commandments in Eve's place and in Adam's place, in your place and in my place. This descendant of Eve will be crushed—he will be put to death bearing God's just penalty for our disobedience and rebellion. In his perfect life and sacrificial death he will reconcile our heavenly Father to us and overcome that first and most terrible alienation between our Creator and us, his creatures.

Second, *the Seed of Eve will bring new life to Eve and to Adam and to each of us*, so that they and we are no longer alienated from God. He will pour his love into Eve's heart, into Adam's heart, into our hearts so that they and we will freely and gladly love God. He will free Eve and Adam from their sins and each of us from our sins by his own sacrificial death, so that not only the condemnation due to sin but the guilty conscience before God that Eve and Adam had and that we all rightly have will be cleansed and given liberty.

This freedom of the conscience and the renewal of our inner being enabled Eve and Adam, and enables us, to want to know and to love God. Eve and Adam could cry to their Creator, and we can cry to him: "Daddy"—"Father"—"I love you." With confidence we can call God our Father because the Seed of Eve, a member of our own race, Eve and Adam's descendant, and our elder brother, leads them and leads us into the presence of his Father and assures us that Eve and Adam are loved and that we are loved—that we are loved even as he, the Beloved Son, is loved. Once again Eve and Adam could have, and we can now have, complete and unlimited access to the throne of God. This free entry into heaven's counsels is available when Eve and Adam come, and when we come, in the name of their descendant, their son, our representative—for he is the one who shares our humanity, the one who shared our struggles, and he is also the one who resisted temptation and sin, even though it cost him his life.

Third, *the Seed of Eve, in bearing Eve's sin, in setting her free from sin's condemnation, and in renewing her, enables Eve to love herself;* he enables Adam to love himself; and he enables you and me to love ourselves. Eve no longer needs to feel worthless because she gave in to the tempter. I no longer need to feel overwhelmed with guilt and shame, for even if my heart condemns me, his love is greater than my heart (cf. 1 John 3:20).

I look inside myself and find that whenever I try to do right, there is a principle, a deep-seated law of my soul, that commits me to want to do wrong and to resist what is good and true and beautiful. However, I can know now that this insistent sinner is part of the "old me," not the "new me" that belongs to God and that longs to love God and to walk in his ways. Of course, this "new me" is never perfectly realized in this life, but there is within each one of us who belong to Christ the glimmerings of a newness that he has created in us by the power of his Spirit. So I may conclude with Paul that it is no longer I, no longer my true self, but rather the sin that dwells within me that has this ongoing commitment to evil. The new me, the true me with a new name,[5] that Eve's seed is creating in me will one day be the only me, and on that day I will obtain the glorious liberty of being a child of God, a sister or brother of Christ, who will only desire what is good.

Fourth, *the Seed of Eve has died to reconcile Eve to Adam and to restore all broken relationships in her life*—and in all of our lives. My elder brother, the Seed of Eve, has died to reconcile me to other people, to overcome every barrier that exists between me and anyone else. He calls me to love my wife as he has loved me, and he empowers me so that I am enabled to do this. He calls me to love my children and, in this love, to imitate my heavenly Father, the Father from whom every family in heaven and on earth derives its name. He calls me to friendships that mirror the perfect love that he showed to John, his beloved disciple.

In every relationship I have he calls me to be a servant, as he has served me, whether at home, at work, or in the wider society. He calls me to be reconciled across all barriers of gender, race, social status, or whatever other barrier there might be, for he is my peace who has made the two one and destroyed the barriers, the walls of enmity between any hostile individuals or hostile social groups of people, by his death on the cross. This is one of the glorious mysteries of the good news that our representative died to bring us—the mystery of formerly hostile groups of people becoming united and loving each other. (A mystery in Scripture is something that we could not know without God revealing it to us, something we could not experience without God's work, the resolution of problems that we could never resolve apart from God's marvelous intervention.) The greatest mystery of all is that we who were God's enemies now have the privilege of knowing the one who became man and who became sin for us so that we might be at peace with God. But this greatest mystery carries within it the additional mystery that through his love we are able to love one another across every social barrier erected by sinful humanity. He longs to make the angels marvel by showing them, wherever his love enters human hearts, what new delight in one another and what self-giving there can be between those who were formerly alienated from each other.[6]

Fifth, *the Seed of Eve restores Eve's and Adam's, and our, dominion over creation.* He enables us first to have dominion over ourselves and our sinful passions, and then he calls us and enables us to begin to restore dominion over every aspect of our lives, for there is not one square inch of which he does not say, "This is mine."[7] We begin to see this renewal of our dominion as we acknowledge Jesus Christ as Lord, as the one who has the right to rule over us in all of life, and as, submitting to his authority, we begin to seek to serve him in all we do.

He longs for us to be his salt and light to bring new life to this world, to restrain its evil, to push back the darkness, and to overcome the consequences of the Fall. He wants our lives to be the firstfruits of the new creation, outposts of his kingdom, "pilot plants," as Francis Schaeffer used to say, of the new day that will come to the whole world when Christ descends from heaven to claim the kingdoms of this world as his own.

Sixth, *the Seed of Eve promises Eve and Adam, and their children (us), that the separation of body and spirit, the coming of death into human experience, will not be permanent.* Even now we begin to see the first

The Third Face of Eve

glimpses of the healing of the separation between the body and the spirit that the curse has brought into our lives. Our mortality is most certainly ever with us, the corruptible nature of our flesh, for in this life "our outer self is wasting away" (2 Corinthians 4:16). Yet one day we will be made completely new, and our bodies will be raised immortal and incorruptible.

However, even now our bodies are the Lord's, and the Lord is for the body,[8] and so we take pleasure in the gifts of food and drink, sexuality and marriage, creation all around us, and the physical well-being of ourselves and others.[9] In the years of Jesus' ministry on this earth we see some promising signs of the kingdom to come and the ultimate restoration of the body as he heals every kind of sickness and disease, as he casts out demons that bring such suffering to those they possess, and as he even raises the dead. We work at setting back the effects of the fall by honoring the healing arts. Hospitals and hospitality, where we see comfort, care, and healing for the human person—body and spirit—have been one of the marks of the church of Jesus Christ from the earliest centuries.

Our elder brother, the Seed of Eve, invites us to sit and eat at his table now, in this present age, as he calls us to intimate fellowship with him and as we partake of the bread and wine that represent to us his body and blood offered up for us, that proclaim his death and life to us, and that nourish us spiritually with his life. He also invites us to sit at his table and to be served by him at the consummation of his kingdom at the wedding feast he is preparing for us all. He calls us, in turn, to welcome friends, neighbors, and strangers to our tables so they can share in our enjoyment of his good gifts to us. This is the central meaning of all our exercise of hospitality— that is, celebrating the hospitality of Christ so liberally shown to us and inviting others in need to enjoy with us the firstfruits of the hospitality that we will enjoy forever.

It is for this reason that practicing hospitality is a command given to all Christians—it is not an optional extra for some who feel called to it or for a few who seem to have the gift of hospitality. Rather, it is basic to any Christian understanding of what God has done for us in Jesus Christ and our call to show that same generous love to others.

In addition to these daily expressions of delight in the renewal of the gifts of the physical creation, we may even see, from time to time, like "arrows of glory from heaven,"[10] the miraculous healing of someone suffering with severe illness. There are, of course, many examples of such healings in the ministry of Jesus, and there are a considerable number in the accounts of the ministry of the apostles. We also find a few cases of such miraculous healing at other moments of history scattered throughout the Old Testament record. Such signs of the coming kingdom can be found in clusters during times of great events in the unfolding of God's reign of redemption.

In the New Testament the apostle James commands us to pray for those who are sick, anoint them with oil, and lay hands on them. Believers have been assured all through the twenty centuries of the history of the church that God does, from time to time, intervene to bring healing to his people. However, in even the most dramatic cases we know that the healed person will have to die one day, like everyone else, and wait with them in Paradise for the final resurrection of their body. This was true for Lazarus who was commanded by Jesus to come out of his grave and was raised up from the state of death. But Lazarus had to die again. Only at the return of Christ will the tearing apart of body and soul be completely overcome.

Seventh, *the Seed of Eve promises Eve and Adam, and he promises us, that the judgment on this earth will one day be removed.* So we await with eager anticipation the lifting of the curse from creation. We may know with confidence that there will one day be a renewed earth with no more thorns and thistles to infest the ground, no more violence of any kind. The lion will even lie down with the lamb, and the little child will be able to play with snakes. A time is coming when there will be nothing to bring harm or hurt in this world. One day there will be, as Jesus declares, the regeneration of all things, for the earth itself will be made new (see 2 Peter 3:13; Revelation 21:1–5). Every one of the seven points of the curse will be finally and fully overcome.

Even now while we live in this valley of tears, we know that God loves us with a perfect love through his Son, our elder brother. The first of our alienations is fully resolved—God's love for us is complete. He could not love us any more fully than he already does. In giving Christ for us he has given us the greatest gift imaginable. That inestimable gift will one day bring about Christ's return in glory and the full establishment of his kingdom. We know that we have to wait for that last day of this age for the resurrection of our bodies and for the renewal of the earth and the utter removal of the seventh point of the curse. But what of the other five alienations? What can we expect now, in this life?

Francis Schaeffer used to say there should be substantial healing in the life of the Christian—not complete, not perfect, but substantial. In each of the other five areas of the curse we should begin to see the firstfruits of the victory of the Seed of Eve: a growing confidence in our being loved by God, and a growth in loving him; a growing acceptance of ourselves and a delight in the renewing work of his Spirit within us; a readiness to love one another more fully as the days go by and to extend that love to more and more people and so to break down one barrier after another; an increasing commitment to offer our lives in every area to the lordship of Christ; a steady confidence that though our bodies will decay, yet he will not leave us unclothed but will swallow up our mortality with life, and with this a growing delight in the good gifts of God that we are to share with others in anticipation of the glory that will one day be ours.

Even a little advance in these five areas will indeed bring substantial healing in this life. This all-pervasive salvation is what that first promise in Genesis 3:15 opens up to us—a window into the inheritance and the joy prepared for us by our heavenly Father and won for us by Jesus, the second Adam.

One of the great wonders of this promise is that in his kindness, mercy, and gentleness God tells the woman Eve—the one who listened to Satan's deceitful lies—that she is the one through whom this deliverer will come into the world. It is through the process of bearing children, which is in itself God's wonderful design for bringing new human lives into this world, that God has promised there will be new life—new life in the ultimate and eternal sense. Salvation itself is going to come about through the process of bearing children. Indeed, a woman will bear the child who will eventually conquer Satan the deceiver.

The gift God gives to Eve, and to most women, the gift of being able to bear children, is a constant source of hope and a herald of promise. This hope and promise is at the heart of the life of every daughter of Eve from the Fall until today and onward from now till the end of this age. Women have this gift of being able to bring children into the world, children who remind us of who we are, those made in the image of God. We see in little children our glory, both in the general sense of their being God's image, like us, and in the particular sense of their inheriting some of the individual gifts and abilities that God has given us.

But sadly they are also like us, in that they bear in themselves the image of ourselves as sinners. In our children we see the shame of what it means to be a sinner in the general sense that they too are born with the inclination to sin. We also see our shame in the particular sense that our children inherit our particular faults and failings. Our children are truly our likeness, both for good and for ill.

However, despite this reality of seeing our shame paraded before us in our children, even more we see the glory of who God made us to be as we see a new person come into this world. Every newborn child is a sign of hope. God has not abandoned our race to sin but has rather committed himself to the constant renewal of our life and of his likeness in our race.

In addition, it is through this "ordinary" means of bearing children that God promised to bring about redemption for the human race. The very means that brings survival to our sinful race is the means that God has ordained to defeat our own worst failures and follies. In the coming of every new life into the world we see, like a candle shining in the darkness, the steadily burning light of that promise of redemption. This is why Paul says in his first letter to Timothy, in that passage that is sometimes considered so strange and difficult to understand, "she [the woman] will be saved through childbearing" (1 Timothy 2:15). These words are literally true. Salvation has come into the world through the bearing of children. Every birth of a child before the birth of the Seed of Eve, Jesus, was a sign of the one who was to come. Every birth of a child after the birth of Jesus is a reminder of the way God has brought about our salvation.[11]

All the many years through the story of the Old Testament we see the line of hope, the herald of salvation to come, as we trace the histories of individuals, descended from Eve, who are ancestors of the Messiah. This is one of the central themes of the Bible, perhaps *the* central theme of the Old Testament, the promise of a child who will come.

This is why Eve cries out with joy at the birth of her firstborn, "I have gotten a man with the help of the LORD" (Genesis 4:1). Eve knows that God is going to fulfill his promise to her to redeem the world. Of course, Cain was not the one, but the point is that bearing children became the source of hope, the reminder of God's commitment to the human race that he would one day bring redemption through a Seed of Eve.

SEED OF EVE
Seed of Eve, we worship you
Promised from the Fall;
The serpent's head, once bruised by you,
Now conquer in us all.

Abraham's child, God's only Son,
You died upon the tree;
Now come to us, Lord, dwell in us
From sin to set us free.

Judah's blessing, royal lion,
The scepter is your own!
From every nation, Lord, we come;
Now make our hearts your home.

Jacob's star, whom wise men found
As you in manger lay;

Now rise for us, shine bright in us,
And turn our dark to day.

Virgin's child, Immanuel,
Mighty God, now come
And comfort us with love divine,
And be to us our home.

Root of Jesse, David's son,
Lord of earth and sea,
All creatures await the peace you bring;
Now grant us victory.

Lamb of God, rejected one,
Servant suffering;
We praise you now who shed your blood,
Our perfect offering.

For all these names, dear Jesus Christ,
Ourselves and lives we bring;
Now help us love and honor you,
Our Savior and our King.

Lord, help us love and honor you
Our Savior and our King.[12]

SUGGESTED READINGS AND QUESTIONS

1. Have you thought of the words to the serpent, "I will put enmity between you and the woman, and between your offspring and her offspring" as words that are an encouragement to us? How would you express in your own words the comfort it is to know that you are on God's side of a great battle against the powers of evil?

2. Have you believed in God's promise that his Son, who is also the Son of Eve, has fought your battle against Satan and done all that is necessary to restore you to a full and perfect relationship with your heavenly Father?

3. How would you describe the way that God has brought you to love and serve him, so that you are no longer an enemy of God in your thinking and in your heart? Do you identify with C. S. Lewis's words, "I gave in, and admitted that God was God, and knelt and prayed: perhaps, that night, the most dejected and reluctant convert"?

4. Where do you see the greatest challenge in your own life to becoming a person who is renewed in your own inner being? Do you find it difficult to love yourself?

5. What testimony can you give of God bringing reconciliation between you and other people? Think of examples both at the personal level of a relationship that was broken but that you have committed yourself to restore and at the social level. What are the cultural barriers that separate you from others, and what are you doing to try to overcome these?

6. Where do you see your dominion beginning to be restored over your own personal life, over your daily work, and over creation?

7. What do you most look forward to as you wait eagerly for the renewal of all things when Jesus comes to establish his kingdom?

8. If you are the mother or father of a child, did you reflect about the way God has brought redemption into our world as you conceived (or fathered), carried, and gave birth (or watched your wife giving birth) to your baby?

9. Read some of the passages that teach us about marriage and what the marriage of a wife and husband who love Christ should look like (Ephesians 5:18–33; 1 Corinthians 13:1–7).

4

SARAH:

The Mother of All Who Believe

GENESIS 11:27–23:20

For our second portrait we go forward many years to the time of Sarah and Abraham. In terms of the calendar of human history we are looking at the period between twenty-four hundred and about two thousand years before the coming of Christ.

MAKE-BELIEVE OR HISTORY?

As we read the story of Sarah and Abraham, many elements in the accounts seem strange to us and come from a world that appears alien to ours. So we wonder (if we are honest about our doubts) whether this story can possibly be a true history of their lives. What are some of the culturally strange practices that confront us when we consider these texts from Genesis? Some of the more obvious examples are:

• Sarah is the half-sister of Abraham, and yet the two marry (11:29–31; 20:12). Later on in the biblical record such marriage practice is declared incestuous. The Levitical codes—codes that govern most Western cultures to this day—set out the allowed relationships for marriage (Leviticus 18:6–18; 20:17; Deuteronomy 27:20, 22–23); and marrying the daughter of one's father's second wife is prohibited in these laws. Such marriage practice is problematic for us, though we should note that this ignorance of the Mosaic legislation is an argument for the antiquity of the story (that is, this account comes from a period of history considerably earlier than the time of Moses) and of this section of the Genesis text.

• We twice read of Sarah being passed off by Abraham as his sister rather than Abraham acknowledging boldly that she is his wife (12:10–20; 20:1–18). This deception and failure by Abraham is deeply offensive to us. A new Christian I know, when she first read this account, said, "Abraham is a total jerk! Why would God devote so much of his Word to this man's life? And why should we be asked to regard him as a hero of the faith?"

• We find the barren Sarah proposing that Abraham try to build a family by taking a servant girl as a concubine to beget children for her and Abraham (16:1–12). Such behavior is hard for us to credit or even to understand.

• When we read the story of the hospitality of Abraham and Sarah to the three strangers who come by at an inconvenient time of day, their behavior seems to us not simply very generous but far outside the range of most of our experience (18:1–15). Which of us would invite complete strangers into our home and prepare a lavish meal for them? The story of this meal is presented to us as if there were nothing unusual at all about it; rather such hospitality is seen as normal practice.

• We read the account of Abimelech giving Abraham gifts after he had taken Sarah into his harem, and we wonder, "What is going on!" (20:1–18).

• We ask ourselves why the buying of the burial plot for Sarah from the Hittites is recorded in such detail (23:1–20).

Some of these accounts simply appear culturally bizarre to us; others seem to be morally questionable. But before we consider the moral and spiritual issues involved in these passages, it is important to notice that each of these accounts sets the story of Sarah and Abraham into real history.

It is these strange stories that reveal the customs of the peoples from whom Sarah and Abraham came and among whom they lived—Hittites, Egyptians, Canaanites, and others. One hundred years ago historians knew almost nothing about the Hittites; indeed for many centuries the only known mention of their existence was in the biblical text. Today there is a vast amount of knowledge available about the Hittites and about the other peoples inhabiting the land in which Sarah and Abraham were nomads, and we learn that all the details of their history recorded in these texts fit perfectly with what has been discovered about these peoples.

Set in their historical and cultural context, Sarah and Abraham are not behaving in a bizarre manner; rather they are showing us that they were children of their time. The record of archaeological research and historical exploration has been like this repeatedly. Things that were difficult for the modern reader to understand have become more meaningful and clear with every new discovery. In addition, all genuine historical and archaeological research has given support to the veracity of the biblical records.

One little detail that is interesting is the name of Sarah herself and of others who are mentioned as the story of Sarah and Abraham begins. The names Terah, Sarai, Milcah, and Laban all suggest that these were a people who worshipped the moon, and there was indeed a cult of moon worship "prominent in Ur and Haran."[1]

THE CHILD OF THE PROMISE

The major theme of the history of Sarah is the fulfillment of the promise made to Eve. Sarah's name when we first encounter her is Sarai, and we will refer to her throughout this study either as Sarai or Sarah according to where we are in the story line; it is the same with Abram and Abraham, for both their names are changed by the Lord at the appropriate point in their history. So for the present they will be Sarai and Abram.

Right from the beginning of her story we are informed that "Sarai was barren; she had no child" (11:30). God had said to Eve that eventually a seed of the first woman would deliver her descendants (and Eve and Adam themselves) from the power of sin and Satan. This hope becomes the theme of Genesis. Whose names will be found in the line of promise? How will God fulfill his commitment, the covenant of deliverance that he made so graciously with Eve? Who will the women (and men) be through whom God will send the Deliverer? When Sarai is introduced to us, our immediate assumption is that she will not be in this line of promise, for she is barren and childless. Gordon Wenham writes:

With stark brevity the bitterness of the childless wife is summed up. Digressions within a genealogy are of special significance, and this is no exception. The whole Abraham cycle is an eloquent witness to the desperate desire for children in primitive society (and in every other society too!). Without children the man had no one to perpetuate his name and the wife enjoyed little prestige and much frustration, for she had no alternative career to motherhood. Further, in old age, childless couples had no children to care for them, and after death, none to carry out the funerary rites regarded as vital to the soul's well-being in the afterlife. This traditional motif is given an additional piquancy in the Abraham stories in that this barren couple are repeatedly promised a child by God, but there is great delay in the fulfillment of the promise.[2]

Despite this declaration of Sarai's being barren and childless, the text leads us very quickly to the call of Sarai and Abram and God's promises to them (Genesis 12:1–3).

In the promises he makes to them we see God taking another major step forward in his desire to bring redemption to the human race. God calls Sarai and Abram to himself, so that they might have fellowship with him and so that they might become the mother and father of the people of Israel. He also calls them to leave their country, their people, and their family and to travel to another land that he will show them. In this first encounter God makes a series of promises to Sarai and Abram.

- "I will give you—Sarai and Abram—many descendants, and these descendants will become a great nation" (Genesis 12:2; 13:16; 15:5). In fact, Abram is promised that many nations will arise from his descendants (17:6).
- "I will give you—Sarai and Abram—and your descendants a land, the land of Canaan" (Genesis 12:1, 5–9; 13:3–18; 15:13–16, 18–19; 17:8). We should notice here that the land would not be taken from the people, the Canaanites, who were living in the land at that time until their iniquity was complete and their judgment deserved. God makes it very clear that he always does what is right and good. So even though he has chosen the descendants of Sarai and Abram to be his treasured people, he is not prepared to treat other nations unjustly for the sake of those he calls to

himself. Only when their judgment will be fully just will he take their land from them and give it to the people of the promise.

• "I will bless you—Sarai and Abram—with personal fellowship with me" (Genesis 12:2; 15:1). This promise of personal fellowship with God is the very heart of the covenant. This is God's great longing, a desire to have intimate fellowship with those he created for himself but who had rebelled against him.

• "Sarai and Abram, I will bless your descendants with fellowship with me, for they will be in a covenant relationship with me as a demonstration of my love to them" (Genesis 17:7–8). "You and they are to live by faith in me, a faith that will be accounted to you, and to them, as righteousness" (Genesis 15:6). "You and your descendants are to keep the covenant I make with you, for those who rebel against me and against my covenant with you will be cut off from the people who belong to me" (Genesis 17:9–14). This covenant involved circumcision for the males, an outward sign that always had an inner and spiritual meaning—a meaning of trust in the Lord rather than in oneself, of commitment to the Lord to serve him, to follow him, and to obey him rather than to serve, follow, and obey anyone or anything else.

• "I will make you—Sarai and Abram—and your descendants after you a blessing to the nations" (Genesis 12:2–3). "In addition those nations who curse you will be cursed." Sarai and Abram and their descendants were called to be bearers of God's truth and salvation to the world. They were to be priests for the world, interceding with God for the nations (consider Abraham's praying for Sodom and Gomorrah in Genesis 18), living in righteousness that would draw the nations to God, and declaring the praises of God who had called them to follow him (Genesis 14:17–24).

• "I will give to you—Sarai and Abram—a particular descendant who will bring salvation to all nations" (Genesis 22:14–18). The Seed of Eve is now revealed to be the Seed of Sarai and Abram.

From this point in the book of Genesis onward, the Old Testament becomes the history of the people that God raised up as descendants of Sarai and Abram. This does not mean that the nation of Israel itself is the central theme of the Old Testament; it would be more appropriate to say that the faithfulness of God and his promise to redeem people through the Seed of Eve is the central theme of the whole Old Testament. Another way to express this same point is to acknowledge that grace is the very heart of all that transpires in this account of Abraham and Sarah and in the origins and history of the nation of Israel.

The whole story of Sarai and Abram unfolded in these accounts in Genesis is also a story of tests of faith. Will Sarai (and Abram) trust God's promises, and will they believe him and yield themselves to his purposes, and will they be content to let him fulfill his promises in his time? Or will they seek to take their lives and future into their own hands and design their own means of trying to bring about the fulfillment of his promises at times of their choosing?

These, of course, are the questions that we all face. Will we do the Lord's work in the Lord's way?[3] Will we put our trust in him or in our own plans and abilities? Will we yield ourselves to the Lord and to his sovereign purposes, or will we try to take our histories into our own hands?

In seeking to answer these questions about the tests of faith in the lives of Sarai and Abram, we will look at a series of events in their story, beginning with their journey to Egypt shortly after their arrival in the land of Canaan. They have followed God's call from their original home in Ur of the Chaldees in Mesopotamia (somewhere in modern Iraq) and are now living as nomads (like present-day Bedouins). They set up their tents first in Shechem, then near Bethel, then toward the Negeb. The text tells us that in each place of their temporary abode Abram built an altar to worship the Lord.

FOLLY IN EGYPT (GENESIS 12:10–20)

As Sarai and Abram move from one campsite to another, they take their family and large household (if this is an appropriate word for people who live in tents) or retinue with them. There would have been several hundred people in their encampment, and this number grows as God blesses them and as Sarai and Abram increase in wealth. They travel first southward and then to the southwest to move with their household to Egypt because there is a severe famine in the land of Canaan.

Why Egypt? we might ask. The hill country of Canaan is subject to periodic drought, whereas the Nile valley in Egypt is almost always fertile because of the constant supply of water in the River Nile, making irrigation of the land that is close to the river possible. So, to save their household (from drought in the land of promise!) they settle for a time in Egypt.

Even before they arrive in Egypt they run into a problem. Abram, lacking in courage and in self-sacrificing love for his wife, foresees difficulties. Sarai is very beautiful, and Abram, fearing for his life (20:11), despite the promise of God's protection, proposes to her that she should pretend to be his sister (partly true, for she is his half-sister).

It is easy, of course, for us living at a different time and in a different culture to judge Abram for his fear and cowardice. We must assume, however, without excusing him, that there was a serious likelihood that a powerful ruler like Pharaoh would have killed Abram and taken Sarai as one of his wives. We may not have to face such problems, though many wealthy and powerful men today do not scruple to seduce married women. So perhaps our own culture is not as different as we might wish to think! (Consider, for example, the former practices of Saddam Hussein and his sons or perhaps the behavior of some prominent western political leaders.)

What we can assess more readily than this cultural setting is the very obvious lack of trust in God's promises and the cowardly element present in Abram's proposal to Sarai. All of us can, if we are honest about our own hearts, relate easily to his lack of faith and to his cowardice. Sarai's reply to Abram (and her private view of this request!) is not recorded, but we must assume that she goes along with his proposal. She must have loved and honored him—despite his cowardice—because her beauty would probably have saved her life. If she so desired, she could easily have betrayed Abram to Pharaoh and presumably lived a very comfortable life without her fearful and untrusting husband.

When they arrive in Egypt, her beauty is indeed brought to Pharaoh's attention, and she is taken into his harem and made one of his wives. Now we come to one of the divine ironies in this story. Despite his lack of faith Abraham's ruse makes him wealthy, for he is well treated as the brother of this beautiful woman; but his ruse also brings God's judgment on the house of Pharaoh. Pharaoh shows an appropriate fear of God (this is not a commended form of evangelism!) and sends Abram and Sarai off with great wealth.

This is a story in which God shows both Sarai and Abram that he will deliver them and that he will keep his promises to them, despite Abram's fear and lack of faith. The response of any new believer or any skeptical unbeliever to this story may well be one of amazement: "What a wretch Abram is to treat his wife this way!" It is more refreshing, and more appropriate, to read the text and respond like this than to pretend that everything about Abram's life is a wonderful example of faith, courage, and righteousness!

SARAI'S LACK OF FAITH (GENESIS 16)

Our second account of Sarai brings us to a point several years further along in their history. God has repeated his promise to bless them and to give them a son through whom numerous descendants will come. The text of Genesis 16 finds Sarai trying to find a way to help accomplish God's purposes. She reasons that God is not fulfilling his promises, so she will find a way to do his work for him.

Already in the previous narrative (chapter 15) we read of Abram's proposal to God to resolve their problem of childlessness and the problem of God's not seeming to keep his promise. Abram's plan is to make Eliezer of Damascus, a trusted servant of his household, his heir (this was apparently a cultural practice in such circumstances of childlessness). "You have given me no offspring, and a member of my household will be my heir," Abram tells God (15:3). God rejects this plan and assures him that the promise of a vast number of descendants will be fulfilled: "'This man shall not be your heir; your very own son shall be your heir.' And he brought him outside and said, 'Look toward heaven, and number the stars, if you are able to number them.' Then he said to him, 'So shall your offspring be.' And he believed the LORD, and he counted it to him as righteousness" (15:4–6).

We are not told Sarai's response when Abram passed on to her God's reaffirmation of his promise. We do not know whether she believes the promise at this time, or whether it was as the years went by that both she and Abram begin to doubt the Lord. One day we can ask her this question, and, without shame, knowing in full the forgiveness of God, she will be able to tell us in detail the story of her times of trust and her times of doubt.

What we do know is that as time passes and no child is conceived, Sarai takes her turn to try to make sure that God's promise will be fulfilled (16:1–4). Sarai has her own plans, as God seems slow to get on with his plans and keep his word. In fact she tells Abram, "The LORD has prevented me from bearing children" (16:2). She blames God for her infertility, but rather than rushing to judgment, we might want to sympathize with her at this point in her life. She is about seventy-six years old by this time, and in addition to her having always been barren, she is now long past childbearing age.

Her resolution to the problem is to propose to adopt another cultural custom, just as Abram had in the previous narrative. Her plan is that Abram should sleep with her servant Hagar. In the Code of Hammurabi there is just such a provision in cases of childlessness (Law 146), and there were similar customs among other peoples of that day.[4] It is quite possible that Hagar became a member of their household on their earlier trip to Egypt, as we are told explicitly that Pharaoh had given them male and female servants (12:16).

Whether Abram justified his readiness to accede to Sarai's proposal as an expression of his belief in God's promises, we are not told explicitly. He could have tried to persuade himself that Sarai's plan would still give him children from his own body and that this was what God had promised. However, there is a linguistic parallel between this passage ("Abram listened to the voice of Sarai," 16:2) and God's rebuke of Adam after the fall ("Because you listened to the voice of your wife and have eaten of the tree," 3:17). This linguistic parallel suggests that Abram's obedience to Sarai's proposal was disobedience to God's words and a failure to live by faith in God's promises. So, in his unbelief and disobedience Abram agrees to Sarai's plan, and as a result Hagar conceives a child. Abram is eighty-six years old at the time of the birth of Ishmael.

Not surprisingly, Hagar, the Egyptian put forward by Sarai to have a child in her place, becomes proud of herself and of the fact that she becomes so quickly pregnant. In addition, she despises her mistress Sarai. The word for "contempt" (v. 4) is very strong. It is the same word that is translated "dishonor" in the account of the first promises of God to Abram: "him who dishonors you I will curse" (12:3). Hagar treats Sarai with contempt. It does not take much imagination to reflect on how easily such contempt—and the resulting distress for the barren one—can come in a home with one "wife" who is fertile and one who is not.

Sarai's first reaction is anger with Abram: "May the wrong done to me be on you!" (v. 5). The NIV renders this, "You are responsible for the wrong I am suffering. . . . May the LORD judge between you and me." Her words are not the most pious words, nor are they completely fair (after all, this was her idea, not Abram's), though they are thoroughly understandable! Her own ongoing sorrow, caused by her many years of unfulfilled hopes for children, is quite naturally compounded by her newfound knowledge that Abram is fertile and so is Hagar, but she herself is not.

Abram's response to her anger and bitterness is to tell Sarai she can do whatever she desires with Hagar and, of course, with the child she is carrying in her womb. Abram, in effect, returns Hagar to the status of Sarai's slave: "you are simply a temporary concubine, a mistress for a brief time, but not a wife!"

Neither Sarai nor Abram come well out of this story. Abram abandons Hagar and his own child that Hagar has conceived. Sarai reveals a cruel streak and mistreats Hagar so badly that she runs away. The one beautiful element of this story is that God intervenes to rescue Hagar and her unborn son and reveals himself to her, and at God's bidding she returns to serve Sarai and responds to God in faith: "she called the name of the LORD who spoke to her, 'You are a God of seeing' [margin], for she said, 'Truly here I have seen him who looks after me'" (16:13–14). We must presume that God also used Hagar's deliverance and return and the birth of her son Ishmael as a means of reminding Sarai to trust him and to believe his promises. Presumably Abram also learns something about trusting God rather than trying any more of his own and Sarai's plans to accomplish God's work for him.

SARAI'S LAUGHTER (GENESIS 18)

God repeats his promise to Abram that he will indeed have many descendants despite the long delay in the fulfillment of the promise. God also initiates the covenant of circumcision with the males of Abram's household (17:1–27). In addition God reassures Abram that the promise is to be fulfilled through Sarai, who is to be renamed Sarah ("princess"). Sarah is the one who is to be the mother of nations, the founder of dynasties of kings. Abram ("exalted father") is to be renamed Abraham ("father of many").

Abraham's response is to laugh at God's words: "Shall a child be born to a man who is a hundred years old? Shall Sarah, who is ninety years old, bear a child?" (17:17). He protests to God that he already has a son, Ishmael, and asks that Ishmael be the seed of the promise. We learn from this that Abraham had continued to believe (at least secretly and with a part of his heart) that Sarah's Hagar plan had been a good one and that it had indeed been the means of fulfilling the promise of descendants. God, however, insists that Sarah is to bear the son of the promise, the son God has in mind for them. It is possible that Abraham's heart is moved by this repeated assurance to trust God's word, for Abraham's action in having himself and the males in his family circumcised appears to be an expression of faith.

This incredible promise of their having a son in their old age is repeated later, on the occasion when the Lord appears to Abraham and Sarah in the form of three men visiting their tent (18:1–21). On this occasion the Lord makes, for the first time, a specific promise that Sarah will bear a son at a particular time—his promise will be fulfilled within a year of this visit (v. 10). Abraham makes no protest on this occasion, but it is clear that Sarah is not persuaded, for Sarah's response is incredulous laughter: "Sarah was listening at the tent door behind him. Now Abraham and Sarah were old, advanced in years. The way of women had ceased to be with Sarah. So Sarah laughed to herself, saying, 'After I am worn out, and my lord is old, shall I have pleasure?'" (vv. 10–12). Sarah laughs in mocking disbelief and then lies about her incredulous laughter to the angel of the Lord to try to cover up her shame and unbelief. Should we be shocked by the continuing lack of belief in the promises of God? Not if we know our own hearts and how slow we are to believe the promises to us of God's love and faithfulness.

We should probably assume that this angel of the Lord is a christophany, an appearance of the second person of the Trinity, for Christ is the eternal Son and Word of God, the one who makes God known.

FOLLY IN GERAR (GENESIS 20:1–18)

Once more we see Abraham displaying a lack of faith in God's promise of protection. As they pursue their nomadic life, Abraham's household and retinue journey south to Gerar in the direction of the Negeb—the desert on the way from Canaan toward Egypt. Gerar lies southeast of Gaza and was at that time the territory of Abimelech, a Philistine king. This land is not far from the Gaza Strip, so constantly in the news at the present time in the ongoing conflicts between Israel and the Palestinians. Once more Abraham fears for his life and tries to pass Sarah off as his sister. This plan of Abraham's must have involved many members of his household in carrying out the deception as well as requiring the involvement of Sarah herself. One lie invariably leads to others.

At the remarkable resolution of this encounter with Abimelech we hear a full account of how Abraham had required Sarah to say she was his sister when they were first called by God from Ur to the land of Canaan: "When God caused me to wander from my father's house, I said to her, 'This is the kindness you must do me: at every place to which we come, say of me, He is my brother'" (20:10–13). This was the shameful pledge he exacted from his wife and that he asked her to abide by at various points along the way of their life together.

What can we say of Abraham's behavior, in addition to our distress at the obvious and repeated betrayal of his wife Sarah? Once more we see Abraham showing a lack of trust in God's protection. Once more we see God protecting Sarah from her husband's lack of faith and from his cowardice toward her. Once more we see God persevering in keeping his promises to Sarah and Abraham despite the failure of trust in him. Once more we see God's patience and faithfulness and his commitment to his covenant people, even when, as in this instance, they display less integrity than those among whom they live.

Abimelech emerges from this story as a man of integrity and righteousness. He is eager to clear his name with God. He gives Abraham gifts despite the way he has been treated, and he even desires to demonstrate publicly that Sarah's reputation is not tarnished in any way (20:16). Yet it is Abraham who is "a prophet" and a priest, the one who has to pray for God's judgment to be withheld from Abimelech and from his people (v. 7).

There are many remarkable details in this account of Sarah and Abraham's sojourn in Gerar. Perhaps the most extraordinary is the continuing grace that God shows to Sarah and to Abraham. He even demonstrates to them his power to give life and to withhold it when he closes and then opens the wombs of the women of Abimelech's household.

THE FULFILLING OF THE PROMISE (GENESIS 21:1–13)

At last, when God has delivered them repeatedly from their foolish attempts to fix their problems, when he has proven his commitment to them over and over, when all their efforts to find their own way out of their troubles have been exhausted, when their unbelief has been repeatedly demonstrated and finally overcome, at last Isaac is born, a miracle child indeed, as Sarah is far past the age of childbearing ("Sarah's womb was also dead," Romans 4:19, NIV). Isaac's name means "laughter," for the laughter of their disbelief is turned to the laughter of joy. "Sarah said, 'God has made laughter for me; everyone who hears will laugh over me.' And she said, 'Who would have said to Abraham that Sarah would nurse children? Yet I have borne him a son in his old age'" (Genesis 21:6–7).

Yet again, even in her time of joy and the fulfillment of her longings, we read that Sarah would not endure the presence of

Hagar and her child Ishmael, so she has Abraham send them away. She is clearly anxious about the inheritance of her son, Isaac, and she is jealous of anything that might come to her slave's child. But God again intervenes on behalf of Hagar and her son Ishmael.

SOME CONCLUDING THOUGHTS

There are many shocking elements in this history of Sarah and Abraham, but through it all we find a wonderful account of the triumph of God's purposes and also a very sobering account of the vessels of clay through whom his promises are fulfilled. It is also a story of how God brings two people to himself and how he slowly, gently, and surely sanctifies them despite their sin, their folly, and their unbelief.

All women who believe, who imitate Sarah's gentle and submissive spirit, who do what is right and "do not fear," are described by the apostle Peter as Sarah's "children" (1 Peter 3:6). In like manner Abraham is set before us as an example—we are all said to be his children, and we are urged to imitate his faith. When we think of the repeated failures in their lives and the lack of faith apparent in so many of their actions, we should find it encouraging that they are set before us as examples.

It may be shocking to some to say that we should be encouraged by having Sarah and Abraham set before us as examples by God's Word. But if we find it offensive that Sarah and Abraham are given as models of faith and righteousness for us to imitate, then we need to ask ourselves how well we know our own hearts and how accurately we remember the history of our own ongoing lack of belief in the promises of God to us. The truth is that we are all like Sarah and Abraham in our unbelief and in our disobedience. The fact is that the story of each one of us is a story of God's faithfulness and of God's persevering with us despite our failure to trust him and to cling firmly to his amazing grace.

SUGGESTED READINGS AND QUESTIONS

1. Were you shocked by any part of the story of Sarah? Does the realism of the Bible about human sin present you with problems?

2. In most teaching and preaching that I have ever heard on the life of Abraham and Sarah, people usually choose to preach on the parts of the story that throw a better light on Abraham. I imagine your experience has been similar to mine. We usually hear about his faith in being ready to sacrifice Isaac or his prayers for Sodom but not much about his lack of faith. Why do you think this happens?

3. Why do you think that many preachers, if they do focus on aspects of this story that show the problems, seem more ready to refer to those passages where we see Sarah's failures than the weaknesses and failures of Abraham? I have heard sermons on Sarah's cruelty to Hagar, for example, but not on Abraham's cowardice and lack of faith in Egypt and Gerar.

4. Where do you find yourself most in sympathy with Sarah's and Abraham's finding it so hard to believe the promises of God?

5. You are one of Sarah's daughters (1 Peter 3:6) or one of Abraham's sons (Romans 4:11–12) or one of his offspring (Galatians 3:28–29). What aspects of their character or parts of their story would you like to be able to model yourself after or to emulate?

6. Do you find it helpful to discover that some of the more difficult and strange aspects of biblical stories are actually signs of the historical reliability of the text?

7. For our next chapter read the story of Tamar in Genesis 38.

5

TAMAR:
A Righteous Woman

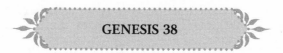
GENESIS 38

S ome of the elements of the history of Sarah and Abraham's struggle to walk in faith before the Lord are challenging for us to read; but the life of our next woman of God will stretch us even more. The account of Tamar's life presents us with a particularly difficult history lesson. If you have never read this passage of Scripture before and you are encountering it in this chapter for the first time, you may find it shocking. Even if we are familiar with it, there are many troubling aspects to this biblical story. However, in my experience this is not one of the passages of Scripture with which most Christians are very familiar.

Many evangelical and conservative Christians make rules about which books, DVDs, television shows, and music it is "righteous" for Christians, especially young people, to read, view, or hear.[1] The story of Tamar would be on the banned list of many Christian magazines, TV shows, youth ministries, and churches! I have yet to hear a sermon preached upon this passage.

So it is with some concern and trepidation that I have included a chapter on Tamar in this book, but this story is part of God's inerrant Word, and, like all the rest of Scripture, has been written for our enlightenment and growth. This chapter was one of the most difficult to write as I was unable to find any particularly helpful commentaries dealing directly with the issues raised in the history of Tamar's life. As the story deals with subjects that are rarely discussed, I need to make it clear that my thoughts on Genesis 38 are suggestions rather than convictions of which I am certain. I am not pretending that I have clear insight as to how to deal with this story. But it has, without question, been "written for our instruction," as the apostle Paul reminds us (Romans 15:4), and we need to learn to wrestle with passages that are not easy to read or understand.

I have given as the title to our study, "Tamar: A Righteous Woman." This is how the text in Genesis 38 refers to her (quoting Judah), and many generations later at the end of the book of Ruth we are reminded of Tamar, for Ruth is compared to her: "may your house [the house of Boaz] be like the house of Perez, whom Tamar bore to Judah" (Ruth 4:12). No one would have any doubt that Ruth was a righteous woman, and yet Tamar is also held up for our admiration as another mother of Israel.

HISTORICAL SETTING

What is the historical setting in which this account of Tamar's life comes? The previous chapter tells a story with which we are much more familiar, a story about rivalry and jealousy between the twelve sons of Jacob. Judah, along with his brothers, has been involved in the terrible crimes of kidnapping, threatening to kill, and then selling his younger brother Joseph into slavery to a caravan of passing Midianites. The brothers then smear the blood of a slaughtered goat on Joseph's coat. They take it home to Jacob to show to their father, and they tell him that his favorite son is dead, presumably killed by a wild animal. That is the previous chapter—and again, it is not a pleasant story, but it is one with which every Christian and every Sunday school child is familiar. Reading that chapter we learn that Judah had behaved a little better than Joseph's other brothers, but his behavior is not to be commended.

Sometime after these events Judah leaves his family to settle down near a Canaanite friend named Hirah at some distance from his home (38:1). The text does not tell us why he leaves, whether it is because his conscience is full of guilt toward his father, Jacob, who is inconsolable about Joseph's fate or whether it is because Judah is becoming sickened by his brothers' behavior. Some of them were brutally and viciously violent men, as we learn from the account of their wickedness to Joseph.

That this was not an isolated incident becomes apparent when we read the story about Dinah, their sister, and the manner in which they deceived and then killed a whole community of men after making a "pious" proposal to them (Genesis 34). Their father Jacob says of Simeon and Levi, the ringleaders of this abominable slaughter, "You have brought trouble on me by making me stink to the inhabitants of the land" (34:30).

For whatever reason, Judah moves away from his family and is able to build more friendly relationships with his neighbors. In this new situation Judah marries a Canaanite woman and establishes his household near his Canaanite friends. Judah's union with his wife, Shua, produces three sons—Er, Onan, and Shelah. This is how the story begins.

Years pass by, for the main part of the story of Tamar takes place twenty or more years after Judah's marriage. Judah is still living far away from the rest of his father's household. His sons come to maturity one by one. So he fulfills his responsibility as a father by finding a wife for his eldest son, Er. The wife Judah finds for his firstborn is a Canaanite, just as he had found a Canaanite wife for himself. The name of his new daughter-in-law is Tamar.

At this point we might want to ask the question, should Judah have taken Canaanite wives for himself and his son? Strictly speaking the answer to this question is no, for God's Word calls his people to marry fellow Israelites. However, this story, like many other biblical stories, teaches us that God is faithful to his people and to his promises to them even when they appear to ignore his commands.

There are many other examples of this in the Scriptures, though preachers do not often draw attention to these aspects of the biblical records, perhaps because so many sermons present biblical characters as heroes of the faith, godly examples for us in all they do. Some of those who marry non-Israelite women are Joseph, who marries an Egyptian and Moses, the giver of the Law, who marries a Midianite or Cushite. In addition there is the story of Ruth, who is a forbidden marriage partner because she is a Moabitess. It is probable that Ruth, just as is likely with the wife of Joseph and the wife of Moses, was not a true believer at the point of her first marriage. Elimelech, Ruth's father-in-law, gets wives for his sons while he is living in Moab, just as Judah does when he is living among the Canaanites (but we will look at this story in a later chapter). Another very clear example is that of Esther marrying King Xerxes (which we will also examine in a later chapter).

What can we conclude from this ignoring of God's words about marriage? God is always far more kind to us than we deserve. His love and his faithfulness to his covenant with his people endure despite our weaknesses and sin, and this particular area of disobedience is one of the most common, both in the record of Scripture and in the lives of believers throughout the history of the Christian church. All of us, if we are honest, have to acknowledge that we have members of our families or friends, or even some of us, who have married people who are not believers. This is one of the most common realities that we see in the church today and throughout history. The Bible is quite realistic about the weaknesses of God's people. But it also teaches us the wonderful truth that God's loving-kindness triumphs over those weaknesses.

God is always kinder than we deserve. The history of the whole Old Testament and the history of the church demonstrate to us the triumph of the faithfulness of the loving-kindness of God despite the failures of his people. Acknowledging this does not give us a license to disobey God's words about marrying within the faith. But recognizing this reality reminds us that the most basic and wonderful of all truths is the repeated story of the persevering, forgiving, and ever-loving kindness of God.

Back to our story: Tamar becomes joined by marriage to the eldest son of Judah. Though we don't know about the particular wickedness in which Er, the firstborn, indulged, we may assume that his sin was serious because he is punished with death. Though God is indeed faithful, kind, and persevering in his love to people who are invariably sinners, there are, of course, times when he steps in and judges particularly heinous sins, sometimes as a direct punishment for the individual and sometimes also as a warning to his people.[2]

The next part of this story, just as with aspects of the story of Sarah, introduces some culturally alien practices to us. To understand the account in Genesis 38 we need to understand what is called the law of levirate marriage. This law stated that Judah's responsibility was to provide his second son, Onan, as *levir* (a husband's brother) to Tamar. After his elder brother's death, Onan was required by this law to marry Tamar and to beget children in the name of his brother Er, in order to keep alive the name and the inheritance of the elder brother.

Onan, however, is reluctant to fulfill his responsibility. In a later chapter in this book (the story of Naomi and Ruth) we will discover that Naomi's closest relative, whose obligation it was to redeem Naomi's land, to marry Ruth, and to raise up children in the name of the dead man, would not agree to fulfill his responsibility because he thought it might damage his own inheritance. In a similar vein, in this story of Judah and Tamar, Onan does not wish to be a second son who sees his own child by Tamar become the head of the clan, the inheritor of Judah's estate, and ultimately his own tribal lord, a son to whom Onan might one day be in submission. Such a son, fathered by Onan, would carry on Er's name, not his biological father's name.

We must presume that Onan desires to be the one to inherit and to be the head of Judah's clan when Judah dies. So whenever Onan sleeps with Tamar, he either ensures he has premature ejaculation or withdraws before ejaculation so he spills his semen on the ground. His refusal to fulfill the responsibility of the *levir* by practicing *coitus interruptus* not just once but several times brings the judgment of God down on him. So he dies also, leaving Tamar twice widowed and with no son and heir. We learn from this judgment on Onan that God requires people to fulfill their familial and cultural obligations, even if those obligations are not a permanent part of God's moral law for his people in every age and in every culture.

JUDAH'S RESPONSE TO HIS DOUBLE TRAGEDY

What should happen next, now that Judah has lost his two older sons and Tamar has been widowed for a second time? The point of the story is that it is Judah's clear responsibility before God to promise his third son, Shelah, to Tamar to be the *levir* for her, to beget a son for Er, so that this son can become the inheritor of the family's wealth, property, and name.

Just as God has bound himself to his people in a solemn covenant, so his people are to bind themselves to one another in solemn covenants. For us marriage is still understood, at least by most Christians, to be just such a solemn and binding covenant. For Judah and for Shelah the law of the *levir* was just as binding before God as is marriage for us. So the obligation of both Judah and Shelah is to try to ensure that the name and the line of the eldest son be continued. As Shelah is still too young to marry, Judah sends Tamar back to her own father's household to live as a widow. At this juncture in the account it is clear that Judah has no intention of fulfilling his covenant obligation to Tamar.

What is happening in Judah's mind as he tries to justify his failure to fulfill his covenantal obligations? Judah apparently begins to think of Tamar as a woman who is cursed, and he fears some tragedy will happen to his youngest son, Shelah. This reaction is common in many cultures when a woman survives her husband. She is regarded as the reason for her husband's dying before her, particularly if he dies while he is young or in his prime. In Hindu India in the practice of suttee the surviving wife in such a case was expected to honor her husband by being burned to death on his funeral pyre.[3]

What does Judah do? When he reflects on the death of his two older sons, rather than acknowledging that his sons are responsible for their guilt (and maybe wondering about his own responsibility as a father of such sons), he plans to be unfaithful to his obligations to Tamar and to disobey God's requirement of him to give his youngest son to Tamar. Judah sends Tamar back to her father's house, even though there is nothing in the account to suggest that Tamar was in any way a poor wife, a difficult daughter-in-law, or in some way deserving of the tragedy that had befallen her.

Those of us who are parents may secretly feel some sympathy with Judah, for none of us finds it easy to acknowledge either our own or our children's guilt—and for many of us it may be more difficult to face up to the guilt of one of our children than it is to face our own guilt and shame. But no matter how much we may sympathize with Judah in his tragedy, and how difficult it is for us to deal with our own or our children's moral failings, we are required by God's Word to see Judah's behavior as morally reprehensible.

TAMAR'S PREDICAMENT

This challenge to our moral sensibilities brings us to the next shocking installment in the story. It is important that we try to understand the predicament of Tamar before we decide to pass judgment on her reaction to the unfaithfulness of Judah. She is faced with her responsibility to God and to her dead husband, and we should remember that this is a responsibility given to her by God's Law. She has been in two marriages neither of which can have been particularly happy or fulfilling—since God judged these two men so severely, we must assume they were not exactly ideal husbands!

Tamar has experienced the loss of her first husband, Er, who would have been the family head. She has been betrayed by Onan's refusal to fulfill his marital obligation to her and so has lost a second husband. She has been cast out from the family in which she ought to occupy a place of honor as the widow of the eldest son. It is her father-in-law, Judah, the head of the family, who has treated her so poorly. She has lost her status as the intended mother of the future head and heir of the household. She faces the prospect of an empty life, for everyone in the communities around must know that Judah regards her as cursed and has therefore sent her away from her home. Her future seems to be bleak, for it is most unlikely that anyone will marry such a despised, rejected, and cursed woman or give a son to her in marriage. She has the prospect of a life of shame, dishonor, and childlessness in a culture that values women primarily for the children they bear.

After some time has passed, Tamar hears that Judah's wife has died (38:12), and knowing him well enough to realize that he is not a man devoted to chastity and that in his loneliness he will continue to be sexually active, she decides to take advantage of the situation.

TAMAR'S DESPERATE MEASURES

Tamar removes her widow's clothes (in many societies, for the rest of their lives widows have to wear clothes that reveal their status to everyone else, unless and until they marry again). She then disguises herself as a prostitute. We might want to ask such questions as, how is it possible for her to get away with this? or, why is she not immediately recognized? The answer is that Tamar lived in a culture where all women covered their faces in public, so her disguise could conceal her well. She sits down at a crossroads, a place she knows Judah will pass on his way to the sheepshearing.

Tamar, knowing her Canaanite culture well, disguises herself as a shrine prostitute. This means that she dresses up as if she were one of the women who serve at the shrine of a pagan goddess such as Astarte, known to the Canaanites as Ashtaroth. Such shrine prostitutes would give themselves for sex with men as a religious act in a fertility rite. Many pagan religions have fertility rites as a part of their religious services. The worshipers act out in sexual intercourse their hopes for divine blessing on the fertility of their land and their crops. In a later chapter we will see that the sons of Eli treated the women who served at the entrance to the tent of meeting as if they were shrine prostitutes (1 Samuel 2:22).

On his way to the sheepshearing Judah sees a woman whom he takes to be a prostitute and asks her for sex. He has sex with her, but not before Tamar manages to get a pledge from Judah that he will pay her for her sexual services with a young goat. This was a substantial payment because a prostitute's time and body could cost as little as a loaf of bread. Tamar pretends to ensure she will be paid by demanding a pledge from Judah. The pledge she secures is his seal, the cord on which the seal hangs around his neck, and his wooden staff wrapped with leather. She demands her security with great care.

The head of a family would wear on a cord around his neck a

small cylinder of fired clay or carved stone inscribed with his name or with some other mark of his identity. This seal was then used to roll the mark of his identity onto a tablet of wet clay or onto the clay ball attached to a papyrus scroll. The seal and staff would have been particular to Judah and therefore immediately identifiable. She demands the cord on which the seal hangs so that Judah might not at some later date be able to say that the cord broke and he lost the seal by accident. She demands the staff as well in order that she might double her security. No one would lose both their seal and staff by the side of the road!

Judah's willingness to make such a substantial promise of payment to a prostitute and to give such a pledge to a woman whose character he knows nothing about perhaps tells us something about his lack of control of his passions, his sexual appetite, and also the weakness of his moral standards.

Judah sends his Canaanite friend, Hirah, to pay the prostitute with the young goat he has promised. He is at least a man of honor who wants to pay his debt, though we should not think too highly of him—he needs his seal and staff returned! The people living nearby respond that they know of no shrine prostitute there at any time. It is evident from this response that Tamar must have hidden herself until she saw Judah coming to the crossroads where she met him. Judah realizes that he cannot have his friends and household members continue inquiring everywhere for his prostitute as such questions will make him a public laughingstock! Many men pay prostitutes for sex, but very few openly advertise such behavior! Tamar has been clever in her strategy.

THE DENOUEMENT

Three months later Judah is informed that his daughter-in-law is pregnant. The conclusion of everyone is that she must have been guilty of immorality—after all she is a widow and not a married woman. Judah's response is typical of many men's double standard with regard to sexuality: "Bring her out, and let her be burned" (38:24). The Bible is very frank about this attitude four thousand years ago, and many men think the same way today—they believe they can be unfaithful while they are married or promiscuous before marriage, but they demand a wife who is chaste before marriage and faithful during marriage. Men in many societies have double standards—one for women, another for themselves.

This appalling response by Judah helps us understand why Tamar obtained these particular pledges from him. As she is being taken out to be burned, she sends a message to Judah along with the pledges that Judah had given her: "By the man to whom these belong, I am pregnant. Please identify whose these are, the signet and the cord and the staff" (v. 25). Clearly we must imagine this appeal and confrontation as taking place in public, for there is no opportunity for Judah simply to conceal the evidence. He openly recognizes the pledges as his own and then makes his remarkable admission, "She is more righteous than I" (v. 26).

What is righteousness in this context? How can we look at this story and say that Tamar has been "righteous"? After all, she pretended to be a prostitute and had sex with her own father-in-law! How can such behavior be considered righteous in any way?

We can suggest as an answer to these difficult questions the following proposal. Tamar's righteousness is her commitment to honor her obligations to God, the covenant she has made before the Lord to her husband. Her desire is to be faithful to her promise to her dead husband. She steadfastly holds to the importance of carrying on his name. She has made a covenant with Judah's family to fulfill her obligations as a wife and a daughter. She, quite rightly, sees that her first human calling is to honor the family obligations she has made. She desires to do what is "righteous," that is, what is in keeping with the relationships to which she has committed herself before God.

In addition to her righteous sense of family responsibility, we also, I think, need to acknowledge that this was an act of faith on Tamar's part, in that sense similar to Abraham's act of faith in being prepared to kill his son as a sacrifice (an act that also offends our moral sense!). In addition, just like Abraham's, hers is an act of faith honored by God. Where others in this story die because of their sin and unbelief, in contrast we see that God honors Tamar by blessing her obedience of faith. Tamar bears two sons, one of whom, Perez, is in the line of promise, the line of David, the line of Christ (Matthew 1:3). Our Savior, the Lion of Judah, is a descendant of Tamar, a woman who was more faithful in her sense of responsibility to God, to his law, and to her family than was Judah himself.

At the heart of righteousness is the commitment to proving oneself true in relationships. Righteousness is not simply obedience to the letter of a body of laws. The text does not tell us that what Tamar did was a good thing or an honest thing, but it should be clear to us that God's Word, Holy Scripture, looks at the intention of her heart in seeking to fulfill her responsibilities to the covenant promises she had made.

The contrast that Judah draws is between her behavior and his. He has not been righteous. He has not been faithful to his obligations to his oldest son or to his son's widow, Tamar. He has refused to be righteous. In fact, Judah has treated Tamar abominably, and he knows it and acknowledges it. Unlike Judah, Tamar commits herself to being faithful to her obligations, and God honors her commitment despite the reality of sin that is involved in it.

This story of Tamar is a very challenging story, but it is also a very encouraging story. When we read the Bible, when we read the stories of the people whom God loves, the people whom he honors, the people to whom he fulfills his promises, the people for whom he keeps his covenant, the people for whom he does his acts of righteousness—when we read the stories of these people, we discover that the people God loves and honors are not absolutely pure people. They are sinners. They are broken people. They are weak people who sometimes disobey the commandments of God. They are people who come up with plans that it is impossible to commend wholly. But God loves his people despite their failures.

We have already reflected on the story of Sarah and Abraham. They are held up to us in the Scriptures as primary examples of faith. And yet when we read their story, we see that they struggled to believe God's promises; we see that they tried to find ways of their own to fulfill the plans of God. They sometimes lacked faith in all kinds of serious ways; yet they are examples to us of people who had faith, people for whom God cared, people whom God loved, people through whom God fulfilled his promises. Because of God's commitment to such sinners as Sarah and Abraham, we who are also such sinners are called children of Sarah, children of Abraham.

In the same way in this story of Tamar we see that God is faithful to his people. God is working out his acts of salvation in her history even though she, like you and me, is weak and sinful, even though she, like you and me, makes choices that are far from ideal. If we are honest, we have to recognize that all believers are like this. Every one of us needs to look at our own heart and see there the reality of how far from perfection we are, how far we fall short of the goodness, the kindness, the perfection, and the loving mercy of God. All of us can look back in our lives and see ways in which we have been like Sarah, like Abraham, like Tamar, like Judah, and yet all of us can see how faithful God has been to us.

The story of Tamar is a shocking story, but events like these in her story happen every day in all of our cities, in every country on the face of this earth. Some of the people involved in these shocking events are Christian believers, and yet God does not abandon them. Each one of us who reads Tamar's story knows that we have made choices and done things to other people that have been seriously wrong, and yet God has not turned away from us. The truth is that God has no other people to love and to honor—and to forgive— than people who are sinners.

The history of Tamar is very challenging to us, but one day we are going to see Tamar in the kingdom to come. We will meet her, and she will occupy a place of honor. She will be presented to us (or perhaps we will be presented to her) as an ancestress of Christ. God gave her this place in his grace and love, despite her sin, and honored her as one who was more righteous than Judah, as one who was faithful to her sense of obligation. We are not asked by the Word of God to approve of her deception, her disguise, her acting the part of a prostitute; but we are asked by the Word of God to honor her faithfulness, her readiness to fulfill her obligations, her righteousness. And one day we will have the opportunity to honor her to her face.

SUGGESTED READINGS AND QUESTIONS

1. Are you attracted to the teaching that Christians should never watch movies, TV shows, and DVDs or read books that contain explicit scenes of sexually unfaithful behavior, violence, etc.? What are your reasons for your views either for or against such rules?

2. If you answered yes to the first question, how would you justify reading or viewing a representation of the story of Tamar or of Genesis 34 with its rape of Dinah and brutally violent revenge by some of Jacob's sons? At what age do you think it would be appropriate to include the reading and study of these biblical stories with children, either at home or in Sunday school?

3. What is your response to the statement that righteousness is not about observing a set of rules, of holding to legality, or even simply about keeping a written code of morality, but that righteousness is, at its heart, a matter of proving oneself true in relationships?

4. Read 1 Samuel 12:7–8; Jeremiah 23:5–6; 33:14–16; Psalm 72:1–4. In these passages we read about the Lord's righteousness. What are we taught in them about the nature of God's righteousness?

5. What does righteousness in our relationship with God mean? Or to put it another way, what claims upon our conduct and choices does our relationship with God bring?

6. What relationships are you in that confront you with claims upon your conduct and choices? In particular, in which relationships have you made binding promises or commitments?

7. Do you understand that those claims (the claims of your relationship with God and with others) are more important than what you may perceive to be your own personal happiness? How is this different from the thinking of the society in which we live?

8. Read Joshua 2 and 6:15–25, the story of Rahab.

6

RAHAB:
Deliverer of the Spies

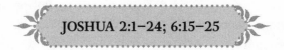
JOSHUA 2:1–24; 6:15–25

Our reflections on the story of Tamar saw us wrestling with the issue of Tamar's disguising herself as a prostitute so she could fulfill her obligation to bear children in her dead husband's name. This was her commitment to her dead husband and to the family of which she had become a part by her marriage. Her motivation for her action was faith in the Lord and her sense of what was appropriate faithfulness to the memory of her husband.

Tamar was in a difficult situation. Faced with the failure of Judah to fulfill his responsibilities as head of the family (by giving her his youngest son to be her husband), she took matters into her own hands, and greatly to our surprise, she is declared righteous for her action. God's righteousness is his faithful commitment to act on our behalf, his gracious commitment to fulfill his covenant responsibilities toward us. Tamar acted to fulfill her covenantal commitment, for Tamar had become a part of God's people, identifying with their faith and with their covenantal responsibilities.

Our present chapter brings us to another history that presents us with challenges—the account of Rahab, a prostitute in the city of Jericho. In beginning our reflections, we need to recognize that despite the footnote that many of us may have in our Bibles in reference to this text (an NIV footnote has "possibly *an innkeeper*" as an alternative translation for 2:1), there is no reason to doubt that Rahab was indeed, up until the time of the history recounted in our text, a prostitute. "Prostitute" is the most appropriate translation of the Hebrew word used of Rahab, and "prostitute" is how Rahab is described in the New Testament (James 2:25).

We do not need to shrink back from this reality as if it were improper in some way for God to choose a prostitute to be the means of delivering his people. I will never forget Francis Schaeffer preaching on this story and declaring, "We are all prostitutes. We are all harlots. Each one of us is a whore in the idolatry of our hearts."[1] Whenever we fail to trust in God, when we put our confidence in anything rather than in him, we are indeed prostitutes. The covenant that God has made with us binds us to him just as in a marriage bond; so when we are faithless, we become adulterers or whores.

THE SETTING

The story of Rahab recounted in the book of Joshua is an amazing, intensely exciting story. John Grisham and Tom Clancy have written nothing that is more dramatic! It is a story filled with danger, intrigue, and betrayal. What is the historical situation in which the story of Rahab unfolds? The people of Israel have spent the previous forty years sojourning and journeying back and forth through the wilderness, enduring the Lord's judgment for their disobedience and unfaithfulness to him.

The book of Joshua begins with the encampment of Joshua and the Israelites on the east side of the Jordan, on the very border of the land that God had promised to Abraham, Isaac, and Jacob. God's promise to the patriarchs, given many hundreds of years earlier, is about to be fulfilled. The people of Israel have been delivered from their slavery in Egypt with extraordinary demonstrations of God's power. They are about to see him work in the same miraculous way to bring them into the Promised Land.

Forty years earlier they had crossed the Red Sea, and very soon now they will cross the Jordan River. God will bring them across the Jordan, just as he did at the Red Sea, with a demonstration of his authority over the forces of nature. The pagan peoples who inhabited Canaan and the countries around it thought about the physical universe as a theater for their gods. Nature was, for the pagans, the stage on which the unseen deities, who stood behind the forces of sea and land, sky and weather, seasons and fertility, displayed their arbitrary power. Many of the miracles recounted in the historical books of the Old Testament must be seen against the background of these pagan religious beliefs.

God demonstrates, by his holding back the Jordan, that this world is his creation, that the forces of nature obey his ordering word and are subject to his intervention. He is the Lord of heaven and earth, of sea and dry land, of mountains and hills, of forest and desert, of weather and seasons, of fertility and harvest. God's miracles have an apologetic or evangelistic purpose. His desire is to show the pagan peoples of Canaan and their neighbors that their religious understanding is wrong. The gods they worship are no gods at all. There is only one true God, and he acts into this universe, a universe that he governs faithfully and justly.

In our own time we face different false understandings of the world of nature. For many of our contemporaries the universe is a closed natural system governed entirely by physical laws. Our response as Christians has to be that the universe is not a closed natural system; rather it is a lawfully ordered system upheld by its Creator and open to his action at any time. The physical laws of the universe are simply descriptions of the orderly way that God rules the world.

For a growing number of others among our contemporaries, this world is Gaia or Mother Earth. New Age thinking has much in common with a pagan understanding of nature similar to that of the Canaanites or with a pantheistic view of nature in which impersonal spiritual power is seen as undergirding, controlling, and infusing the whole physical universe. Our response as Christians needs to be the declaration of the existence of the personal and infinite Creator and Sustainer of all reality.

God intervenes in the world of nature by holding back the

Jordan so that his people may cross safely on the dry riverbed. This miracle demonstrates the truth of the Israelites' claim that they worship the one true God, the Lord of heaven and earth. God encourages his people's faith by the miracles he does on their behalf. He also reveals his glory to the pagan Canaanites and their neighbors by displaying his power over the forces of nature and his supreme authority over the gods the Canaanites worshipped.

Before the Israelites cross the Jordan they are camped near the town of Shittim (see Numbers 25:1). Shittim is the city where some of the Israelites had become involved in temple prostitution with their pagan neighbors a few years earlier at the instigation of the false prophet Balaam.[2] Joshua, as the leader of the army, is planning his strategy for the conquest of the land. He knows that God has declared that he will go with his people and that he will fight for them, but as a military leader Joshua knows he needs to understand the layout of the land to be conquered.

Joshua sends two spies ahead secretly, for he has no wish to repeat the disastrous spying expedition that had taken place forty years before. On that occasion the spies (with the exception of Joshua and Caleb) had given such an alarming account of the land of Canaan and its inhabitants that the people of Israel had refused to cross the Jordan and enter the land because of their fear. This time Joshua's spying mission is secret, lest their report should be too alarming and also for the protection of the spies on their mission into Canaan. They are military spies—they cannot go openly.

The two spies are sent to look over the land. They are to see how the Canaanite people have responded to the accounts of the miracles the Lord has done to deliver Israel from Egypt and from its enemies during the nation's sojourn in the wilderness. The spies have a particular charge—they are to bring back a report on any preparations for war in the city of Jericho, the first major city the people will come to after the crossing of the Jordan and the first military center from which Joshua can expect serious resistance. The city of Jericho was about two days journey west of the Jordan River. So the spies are only gone for a week, or at the most two weeks, before they return to give their report to Joshua. But their journey of reconnaissance is dangerous. All the neighboring peoples have heard about what has happened as the Israelites have made their way from Egypt.

What God had done for his chosen people had been done openly, for the whole world to see. In fact there are several points in the accounts at which God draws specific attention to his desire to defeat the gods of the nations and to bring people from the nations to a believing knowledge of him as the one true God.[3] The faith of the Israelites and the faith of those from the nations who came to know God—and our faith today—is based on the acts of God in history. People trust God because of the wonderful things that he does in history on their behalf.

The peoples of Palestine and of the surrounding lands are, of course, aware of the movements of the people of Israel at the time of the events of this incident in the life of Rahab. There were about two million Israelites wandering through the wilderness for forty years, so their journeys were no secret! The Canaanites have heard that the God of Israel is planning to bring his people into the land of Palestine and that he is intending to give the Israelites this land. News of this has traveled before Israel in all its movements.

JERICHO

The spies, in obedience to Joshua's instruction, make their way to Jericho. Once in Jericho they hide out in the house of a prostitute, thinking they will be safe from observation there. The spies do not go to an inn where everyone is exchanging news, where everyone is interested in everyone else's business, particularly the business of travelers and visitors with different accents. (This is another reason why it is absurd to suggest that Rahab was an innkeeper.) In a brothel people are secretive; they are not exchanging names and news or making inquiries of strangers. Prostitution is, by its very nature, a private institution! However, the spies are observed entering the brothel by some of the city's inhabitants. It is probable that their speech betrays their alien status, and the king is informed that spies from Israel are present in his city "to search out the land" (Joshua 2:2).

Palestine at this time was made up of many city-states, each with its own ruler. This is how the land had remained for many centuries (it had been true since long before the time of Abraham). Jericho was a typical walled city of the time, built with the intention of being impregnable. In response to the warning, the king sends his men to Rahab's house. His men are to demand that she hand the spies over for arrest. The king, of course, is anxious to ensure that these spies not betray his city into enemy hands. We should presume that the spies would have been killed so that they could not report back to their commander, Joshua, the leader of the enemy forces.

RAHAB'S RESPONSE

The king's men make their way to Rahab's house and ask that the spies be handed over so that they cannot betray the city, its people, and their land. Rahab, however, has already prepared for just such an eventuality. She has hidden the spies on her roof under bundles of flax (drying stalks three to four feet long—Jericho was in a fertile valley at this time with productive fields of grain, flax, and other crops). Rahab acknowledges to the king's men that the spies had come to her house, but in addition to this true word she tells a series of lies. She sends the king's men off to the city gate to chase the spies, though she adds that she does not know which way they went after they headed for the gate just before dark.

Rahab's lies are carefully thought out and cleverly worded (Joshua 2:4–5). She communicates that she noticed that the two men behaved suspiciously. She urges the inquirers to hurry after the spies so they can catch up with them. She pretends to be an upright citizen who is on the side of her city and of the king and his men. The king's men believe Rahab and follow her directions. The gate is immediately locked to prevent the spies from leaving in case they might still be in the city. The pursuers (as they think of themselves) follow what they presume is the path of the spies all the way to the Jordan River—usually a two-day journey to the east, but their hurried pace would have gotten them to the Jordan in a day to a day and a half.

After her successful foray into deceit and lies, Rahab then explains her actions to the spies and also gives them advice on how to avoid capture by the king's men (2:16). By this time it is after dark, and as her house is built on the city wall she lets them down by a rope so they can safely escape from the city. She tells them that nearby are hills, perhaps with caves, where they can hide safely and wait until the king's men return from their pursuit and their search. Rahab advises them well. We can imagine how grateful the two spies were for her courageous actions, her wise advice, and her clever and bold-faced lies.

Rahab asks for and is promised safety for herself and all her family, with the added understanding that they are all to take shelter in her house at the time of the Israelite attack. It is a large extended family that will be protected. The spies swear on oath in the name of the Lord that she and her household will be saved if she places the scarlet cord (used to let them down the city wall) in her window to mark out her house. In the name of Yahweh (v. 14), God's personal name as the covenant-keeping God, they swear their lives in exchange for hers should they prove faithless to their promises. Rahab's obligation, in turn, is to continue to keep silent about the spies and their whereabouts (vv. 20–21).

UNDERSTANDING RAHAB'S BEHAVIOR

How are we to understand Rahab's behavior? What is her motivation? Can we ever justify lies? These and many other such questions spring to our minds when we read this account.

Perhaps, first, we need to recognize the breadth and depth of Rahab's actions. She does not simply tell a few lies. She risks her life by taking the spies into her house and by protecting them rather than handing them over. She plans and executes a bold scheme to bring them to safety. She has no guarantee, apart from their oath, that they will do what they have promised. Unlike Tamar there is no pledge that she can hold in keeping so that she might ensure her safety when the crisis comes. These men she hides and helps escape are her nation's enemies, and she betrays her own people and disobeys her own king in order to save the spies. She sides with the Israelites—a people who are alien to her—against her own people.

She tells several serious lies, but in addition she fails to honor her ruler and to obey him (these are commands of God and matters of conscience, not simply issues of loyalty and fear of punishment—see Romans 13:1–7 and 1 Peter 2:13–17). Later, after she helps the spies escape, she conceals the truth about their whereabouts in order to keep her word that she will not hand them over to her king. Of course, it is possible that someone may have seen her hiding the spies or helping them escape. It is possible that someone in her household could reveal what has taken place. The course of action she chooses is very dangerous. It is probable that she became involved in telling further lies. She gives the spies advice as to how long and where they should hide. Her desire in doing this is to help them get back to their commander and to their people, Israel. She is perfectly aware that all she is doing has as its purpose the aiding of these spies, their commander, and their army, so that they will be successful in their plan to attack her own city and its people.

Again, Rahab is not simply telling a few lies. Her choice is a serious matter that will help bring about the destruction of the city of Jericho. Everyone in the story knows that this is the issue at stake. We need to understand her courage and the risk that she is taking and her willingness to turn away from her own king and from her own people to side with the Israelites.

This brings us to the second issue and to the heart of the matter. What is Rahab's motivation? Why does she make such choices, and why does she take such a dangerous and treacherous course of action? This is the most important question. It is made very clear in the text that her motivation is her newfound faith in the God of Israel. The Lord is the one in whom she has put her trust. She is already a believer.

It is also clear that it is God's providence that brings the spies to her house. It is not an accident that the spies and Rahab are thrown together. The result of this divine appointment is the saving of the lives of the Israelite spies and the saving of the lives of Rahab, her household, and her extended family.

Rahab's story is a wonderful account of the grace and mercy of God. The Lord has intervened in her life. Her response is to make a beautiful profession of faith, one similar in wording to the faith demanded of the Israelites (compare Deuteronomy 4:39 and Joshua 2:11). She acknowledges God as the God of the whole earth, not simply as a more powerful tribal deity. She uses God's own personal name—"the LORD" (Yahweh; vv. 8–13) as she confesses her belief in him.

We may want to ask, how did Rahab come to faith? The text answers this question for us. It is the news of all that the Lord has done in delivering his people that has drawn her to faith in him. (See Exodus 9:9–16; 15:14–16; 18:9–11 for accounts of God's desire to use the events of Israel's deliverance as a means of drawing people from the nations to faith in himself.) Rahab speaks about the response of her people—they are afraid because of the extraordinary things that God has done for Israel.

She acknowledges that the God of Israel is the one true God, the God of heaven above and of the earth below; that he is the Creator of the universe, the Ruler of history, that he is the one who intervenes in history to redeem his people. Her faith is genuine (Hebrews 11:31), and her faith is not stillborn but is expressed in acts that the apostle James declares to be righteous (James 2:25).

It is indeed one of God's intentions, as he brings his people out of Egypt and into the Promised Land, to draw people from other nations unto himself. Several Scriptures refer to this, for example, in the account of Jethro, Moses' father-in-law, coming to faith.[4] So it is with this account of Rahab. God uses his acts in history to call her to saving faith. Scripture refers to her as a heroine of faith, as one who pleased God and one in whom God delighted.

Rahab's righteous acts, the acts for which she is commended, are the very acts that involve her in lying, in hiding the spies, in disobeying her king, and in betraying her own people.

We need, of course, to address the issue of Rahab's lying. Is lying ever right? People give different responses to this question. Some will say that it is her motivation of faith rather than her lies that are commended. Others will simply comment that God saves sinners, and, of course, her lying was sin.

But we need to think more deeply about this than simply saying, "Yes, Rahab disobeyed the Ninth Commandment." Another biblical example of lying is the courage of the Hebrew midwives (Exodus 1:19) who lie to protect the newborn babies from Pharaoh. Another, similar to Rahab's story, is the account of Jonathan lying to and disobeying his father and his king, Saul, to protect the life of David, his friend.[5]

All undercover members of the police, all spies or intelligence agents, all resistance fighters, have to lie to protect their own lives, to protect the lives of others, and for the sake of the cause or country to which they have committed themselves. Lying and deceit are a fundamental part of their work. If they don't lie but rather reveal the identities of fellow agents, they are deemed people of absolute dishonor and faithlessness, of being traitors in a truly damaging way.

In wartime (and Rahab is living in wartime) there has to be constant concealing of the truth and outright lying and falsehood. Consider people involved in making false papers for Jews being rescued from the Nazis during World War II or numerous other examples when people speak and act in order to save people from unrighteous enemies. In many situations the call to protect human life makes concealment of the truth a necessity—in fact makes such concealment and lying an act of righteousness. (Think of the film *Schindler's List*. Oscar Schindler is accounted a "righteous Gentile" by the Jewish people. Think also of the film *Life Is Beautiful*.)

Consider the present struggle against terrorism connected with Islamic radicals and in particular Al Qaeda and its leader Osama bin Laden. Reflect on how necessary it is for our governments to have agents who infiltrate groups that plan bombings and other terrorist acts. We should pray for such men and women, and we should regard their work as not only dangerous but also righteous, though it will certainly involve lying and deceit.

In a more mundane setting, even at the level of family life there are many occasions when we all conceal truth and tell half-truths out of love for our children and out of love for one another. A child wakes up, feeling sick, at 3 A.M. and comes crying to get you out of bed. Do you tell him exactly how you feel? I hope not. You conceal what you feel because you love him. This is true in our marriages as well. We must not always say what we feel. If we do, we will destroy a marriage very rapidly. We are required to be faithful to our commitment to love our husband or wife rather than to the feelings and words that may be in our heads or in our hearts at a particular moment.

In addition, for each one of us extreme situations may arise in which we are called upon to protect people by lying. We can all imagine circumstances in which we would lie to a criminal or to a deranged person without any compunction. In wartime, too, we can readily imagine lying to protect people from evil. In such situations I do not think it is sufficient to say that such lies are necessary or justifiable sins. Rather, I think we need to see such lies as truly virtuous acts. If we are not prepared to recognize this, I think we raise doubts about the sinlessness of Christ, who, Scripture insists, was tempted in every way like we are, yet was without sin. Would we want to argue that Jesus faced none of these difficult situations—situations like believers in wartime or responding to evil or deranged people? I think not. So we do better, I believe, to regard these lies and deceptions as righteous acts.[6]

There are times when we must speak the truth, but other times when it would be clearly wrong to do so. There are times when the statement of truth is unrighteous, pharisaical, and cowardly. My speech is to be ruled by the law of love on behalf of my neighbor. Rahab's speech and actions are ruled by the desire to honor God, by her commitment to love her neighbors (the spies), and by her casting her lot with the people of God (a people who as yet have no land of their own).

We should also notice that human authority is never absolute—and that is why it is good, faithful, and honoring to God for Rahab to disobey her king. Each one of us is accountable to God first rather than to any human authority. This is true in marriage, in the family (consider Jesus at twelve years old), at work, in the church, and in the state.[7]

THE OUTCOME

A few days later the time comes for Jericho to be destroyed. As we read about the terrible events of the total destruction of Jericho, before we respond with distress, questions, and outrage, we need to notice who is at the head of Joshua's army. It is Christ who is the actual leader of the army of Israel. Christ is coming in judgment against the unbelief, idolatry, and wickedness of the people of Canaan. This account of Christ as the captain of the Lord's host is a picture of him as he will be when he leads the army of God on the day of final reckoning on this earth (compare Joshua 5:13–15 and Revelation 19:11–16).

Many of the events of Israel's story are pictures in history of our ultimate redemption, of God's deliverance of us out of the slavery of sin into the promised land of his kingdom. Sometimes these accounts of deliverance involve the destruction of God's enemies in the process. The overthrowing of Jericho is a picture of what God will do in the future through Christ to every nation of our world.

This, therefore, is one of the reasons that Jericho is utterly destroyed, given up to "the ban" (1 Chronicles 2:7, NIV). Men, women, children, and animals too are utterly destroyed (Joshua 6:21). This is a very sobering account for us to read, for it is a picture of what will happen at the close of the age. What is different about this occasion, compared to the destruction of Sodom and Gomorrah, is that on this occasion God used his people as his instruments to bring about his terrible judgment on the wickedness of the city of Jericho in Canaan.

This terrible destruction is both the revelation of his judgment on the Canaanites and a lesson to his people concerning the consequences that will come from unrepented sin. The wickedness of the Canaanites at this time is termed "full" (Genesis 15:16, NIV, KJV). And because of this fullness of iniquity, God calls on his people to "utterly destroy" them (Deuteronomy 20:17, KJV). This utter destruction is a terrible lesson to those who have to carry out the sentence, a lesson about the awful seriousness of sin, a lesson that Israel is intended to remember throughout its history, a lesson to which God appeals continually throughout the rest of the Old Testament, saying in essence: "remember what I did to the people who inhabited this land" (see, for example, Leviticus 18:24–30; Psalm 106:34–41; Ezekiel 15:5–12).

On a happier note the story ends with Rahab and all her household being saved, just as the spies had promised. Rahab, her household, her family, and their animals are the only living things in the city of Jericho that are spared from utter destruction. She and her family become part of God's people.

Just as in the story of Ruth and in the story of Tamar, Rahab marries into the line of Judah. She becomes an ancestress of Boaz. Ultimately Rahab is one of those whom God honors by making her an ancestress of Christ (Matthew 1:5). Rahab, the prostitute, through her faith and through her acts of righteousness in sheltering the spies, lying and deceiving, and disobeying her ruler has been incorporated into the line of Christ. We may justly call her one of the great grandmothers of our faith and one of the great grandmothers of the Lord himself.

SUGGESTED READINGS AND QUESTIONS

1. Why do you think some of our Bible translators (and preachers) seem reluctant to acknowledge that Rahab was a prostitute? Does it bother you that God chose to use such a woman for the deliverance of his people and for the advancement of his purposes of salvation?

2. What has been your response in the past to Rahab's lies and deception? Are you persuaded by my comments about lying and truth in this chapter?

3. Do you have relatives or friends who have ever been involved in a situation of war or in any kind of undercover police work or intelligence operations for their country? What do you think of the half-truths, the concealment, the lying in which they have to

participate as a fundamental part of their work? Do you think their work is a sin?

4. Do you think that Christians should gladly serve in such settings, or should believers avoid any jobs where lying will be necessary—for example, seeking to infiltrate terrorist organizations and trying to uncover their plans for future terrorist acts like those of 9/11? We hear every month of such plans being foiled by the work of undercover agents. Are you thankful for their work? If you do think it is necessary for Christians to avoid such jobs, do you think it is right for Christians to live so comfortably with the security and protection that such intelligence work provides for us all?

5. How would you deal with a situation in which to protect someone's life you were called on to conceal the truth or to tell lies? For whom would you be prepared to lie in order to save him or her or them from harm?

6. What everyday situations do you find yourself in that bring you to concealment or telling half-truths and even falsehoods to protect the feelings of other people, or in order that you might be true to the love you have in your heart for them rather than to the sinful feelings that are also in your heart?

7. What is your response to the idea of "the ban," devoting the inhabitants of Jericho to the Lord by slaughtering them all? How is this different from the destruction of Sodom and Gomorrah? Which is easier to accept, and why?

8. Had you understood before reading this chapter that it was Christ who led the army against Jericho? When you think about the utter destruction of Jericho, are you troubled that Christ himself was the captain of the attacking army?

9. Do you see the parallels between the destruction of Jericho and Christ's leading his army to destroy his enemies at the end of this age and then leading his victorious people into the true Promised Land, the land of which Canaan is only a picture?

10. Do you see the relationship between the deliverance and salvation of God's people and the judgment and destruction of his enemies? Why is it necessary for salvation always also to involve judgment?

11. Read the account of Deborah's life in Judges 4–5. What do you admire in the acts and words of the women recorded in those chapters?

7

DEBORAH:

Courage under Fire

JUDGES 4–5

In our reflection on the life of Rahab we learned three main lessons. First, we saw the hand of God at work in his people's history. We saw how God delights in taking care of the people he calls to himself. God watched over the lives of the spies sent out under the command of Joshua. He protected them by bringing them, through his providential guidance, into the house of Rahab. In addition the Lord demonstrated his loving concern for the Canaanite prostitute, Rahab, who had put her trust in him, by bringing her and the spies together so that they might be each other's help and deliverance. God provided gracious protection for Rahab and for the spies in a time of great danger.

In addition, we learned that God reached out to save Rahab and her family despite their Canaanite nationality (these, after all, were the people to be judged by God because the cup of their iniquity was full) and despite Rahab's previous way of life as a prostitute. God incorporated Rahab, her household, and her extended family into his people so that they too became part of the people of God. The story of Rahab is then a story about the merciful acts of the God who is eager to save.

We also learned of the faith and courage of Rahab as she sheltered the spies in a situation of impending war and great personal danger. She cared for them in her own home at the risk of her life. Rahab took her stand with the people of God and against her own people and her rulers, just as we will see in the story of Ruth, though in the case of Rahab her decision to cast her lot with the people of God was daring and life-endangering because it was profoundly unpatriotic. She had put her hope in the Lord of heaven and earth, the faithful covenant-keeping God, and her faith was richly rewarded.

THE SETTING OF DEBORAH'S STORY

Our present chapter brings us to another story of courage in a time of trouble and war. What is the historical context of Deborah's story? The date is sometime before 1200 b.c., so perhaps a little more than two hundred years after the time of Rahab and about one hundred years before the time of Ruth. The people of Israel are settled in the land of Palestine, but their life in the Land of Promise is anything but settled.

The people's life is unsettled and troubled politically because their life is unsettled and troubled spiritually. The period covered by the book of Judges is a time covering several centuries, an extended time of apostasy, a time when the great majority of the covenant people have turned away from God. After the death of Joshua, a generation grew up that looked away from the Lord and forgot what he had done for his people Israel (Judges 2:10–15). They failed to put their trust in the Lord and to be thankful to him and turned instead to the worship of other gods.

This is a time in history when we see the children of Israel experiencing the curses they had pronounced upon themselves before they entered the land of Canaan. They had made a formal declaration of loyalty to God, and they had bound themselves to love and obey him. They had publicly acknowledged as a nation that if they or their descendants should prove unfaithful to the Lord, in consequence they would be subject to every imaginable kind of trouble and suffering (see Deuteronomy 27–30 for the account of this formal ceremony of blessing and cursing). The people of Israel had brought these curses down upon themselves by forsaking the one true God and by worshiping other gods, the gods of the peoples among whom they lived. The result of their abandoning their covenant with God was that for the greater part of this time of the judges they were in deep political and social distress.

Many judgments, predicted in Deuteronomy, were experienced by Israel during this sad time. One particular judgment that came on them for turning away from God was that God gave them up to enemies who attacked them, enemies from the nations around them.

A recurring refrain of the book of Judges is that Israel was defeated by its enemies and then harshly ruled by them, until God called a judge to deliver them (2:16–19). This brief description gives us a definition of the judges: the judges were those whom God raised up to rescue his people from their enemies. Whenever God raised up a judge for Israel, God committed himself to that judge, and he then saved the people of Israel from the hands of their enemies as long as that judge lived. The Lord showed compassion to his people as they groaned in distress under those who oppressed them, and he delivered them through a judge.

But after each judge died, the nation turned back to its evil ways. This repeated cycle of events could stand as a summary of the book of Judges: a period of apostasy, disobedience, and the worship of false gods, followed by a period of oppression by their enemies, followed by a time of crying out to God for deliverance, followed by God's showing mercy to them and raising up a judge to save them, followed by a time of peace and prosperity, followed by a time of apostasy and disobedience, and so on.

Before we condemn Israel too severely, as if we who read the book of Judges would never have behaved as they did, we need to acknowledge that this pattern of the history of Israel recorded in the book of Judges is an examination of the problems of the individual human heart and is a summary of the history of every nation that has ever lived on this earth.

The story of Deborah is set in just such a time. Judges 3 describes the judges Othniel and Ehud who, in the generations immediately preceding the time of Deborah, led God's people and who with God's help delivered the nation from its enemies. Yet, despite God's provision for them in these two wonderful deliverances and in the periods of peace that followed, the people turned back to their disobedient ways once more.

GIFTED BY GOD

Judges 4 opens with the account of the people's reversion to apostasy. On this occasion God's judgment is to give Israel up to the oppression of Jabin, a king from the northern part of the land of Canaan. Jabin's kingdom seems to have covered the area of Israel northwest, west, and southwest of the Sea of Galilee. That is this area where the tribes of Naphtali, Zebulun, and Issachar dwelled after the period of settlement in the land. The military commander of Jabin was Sisera, a man known for his cruelty and for his nine hundred chariots with wheels rimmed with iron. Sisera had the latest technology in terms of military hardware.

To understand how severe a time of misery and enslavement this was, we can read Judges 5–7. Travel on the roads was so dangerous that few used them. "Travelers took to winding paths" (5:6, NIV) through the hills to try to find safe passage through the land. The villages in the fertile plains of Jezreel were abandoned, and "village life . . . ceased" (v. 7, NIV). This means, of course, that this was also a time of economic hardship as the fields of the fertile valley were no longer worked.

Why had this severe oppression and economic misery come about? The text gives us the answer: the people worshipped other gods in place of the Lord. When enemies attacked Israel's cities, no one had the courage to come forward and to fight against the invaders to try to repel them. When Jabin and Sisera with his armies overran their towns, no one resisted them. It was a time of no confidence in the Lord, a time of cowardice and fear, and consequently a terrible time for the people.

What does God do for his people during this time of unbelief, idolatry, wickedness, fear, and distress? God's response is to raise up a deliverer, and on this occasion his provision for the people is Deborah. How is Deborah described in the biblical text?

First, Deborah is described as a *prophetess*. Two other women in the Old Testament—Miriam (Moses' sister, Exodus 15:20) and Huldah (in the time of Jeremiah and Josiah, 2 Kings 22:14–20)—are also described as being prophetesses. Sometimes preachers will say that God only used a prophetess when the men were all living in unbelief. It is important for us to acknowledge that Deborah, Miriam, and Huldah were not called to be prophetesses simply because there were no men available. After all, Miriam prophesied during the time of Moses, and Huldah prophesied during the life of Jeremiah. God himself chose to give this gift of prophecy to Deborah, to Miriam, and to Huldah. These women were given the gift of revealing the word of God to his people. God called each one of them to speak for him—to make known what he would do for his people, to reveal the future, to call the people to repentance, and to summon them to serve and follow the Lord.

This office of prophetess was a teaching ministry, a warning ministry, and an encouraging ministry. It was also an authoritative office. The prophetess or prophet spoke with the authority of God himself. Considering the great span of millennia recorded in the Old Testament, we recognize that this office was given only to a few chosen individuals who were called to be God's spokesmen and spokeswomen and whose names were then written down for us in the pages of Scripture.

The time in which we live after the coming of Christ is a different time in the history of God's saving work. The gift of prophecy is a different gift today. The book of Acts teaches us that believers, both female and male, are given the gift of prophecy, and the apostle Paul urges all believers to desire the gift of prophecy (1 Corinthians 14:1). This general giving of the gift of prophecy is one of the marks of this age, the age of the giving of the Spirit to all women and to all men after the completed work of the death and resurrection of Christ (see Acts 2:17–18, and see Chapter 20 in this book).

Prophecy today is no longer an authoritative gift as it was in the time of the Old Testament; all of us, women and men, are now called to speak for one another's strengthening, encouragement, and comfort (see 1 Corinthians 14:3). All believers are asked to commit themselves to the building up of fellow believers. Prophecy, in this sense, is a gift and calling for all believers. Prophecy is a gift that all of us are to earnestly seek to exercise, so that we may encourage and comfort our fellow believers, both female and male.

The gift that Deborah has is somewhat different from the gift of prophecy today. Hers is a gift of speaking with absolute authority. Deborah speaks God's word to the people, his inspired, infallible, and authoritative word, the word that has authority over all people both then and ever since. This prophetic gift of the woman Deborah has authority over you and over me today.

In addition, Deborah is a *judge*. The New International Version in Judges 4:4 says that Deborah was "*leading*" Israel, but it would be more accurate to translate the Hebrew word in this text as "Deborah was *judging* Israel," as in the ESV and as the NIV does in every other place in the book of Judges where this word is used to describe the one raised up by God to deliver the nation of Israel from her enemies. Deborah is the supreme justice of Israel. She is described as holding court in the hill country of Ephraim, to the west of the Jordan, and in the area south of the Valley of Jezreel, north of Bethel. Later in the biblical text we read that a judge like Samuel travels around the land considering cases that come to him from the lower courts and then passing judgment on these cases for the people. We do not know if this is true of Deborah or whether she only considered the cases brought to her in this one place, the hill country of Ephraim.

The judge is the one to whom the people come for the resolution of their disputes when the lower courts are unable to reach a satisfactory verdict (Deuteronomy 17:8–11; Judges 4:5). Every clan had its own kind of court, with elders governing the communities (commanders of tens, fifties, hundreds, and thousands; see Deuteronomy 1:9–18). Israel had, in effect, a series of courts from the local, to the district, to the regional, and finally up to the national level. So Deborah is the supreme justice whom God has appointed.

But the judge is more than just the head of the judiciary. The judge is also the political leader or ruler of the people, raised up by God when the people are experiencing times of oppression from their enemies. The judge is to be the one who calls the people back to the worship of God and back to obedience to his command-ments. The judge is to be the rallying point of opposition to those who oppress the people of Israel. Deborah, then, is the judicial and political leader of the nation at this time. There were no kings in Israel at this period of history; a judge was the closest office to that of a king.

Deborah is also a *warrior*. She is clearly called by God to be Israel's military leader. As the military leader she sends for Barak (from Kedesh to the far northwest of the land, up beyond the Sea of Galilee, even north of Lake Huleh) to command the army of the Israelites against Sisera. Deborah, however, is the one who gives the military strategy devised by the Lord. It is very clear from the text that it is Deborah who tells Barak where to go to engage the enemy in battle, it is Deborah who tells Barak whom he should call up for the troops, and it is Deborah who gives the battle plan.

When Barak is informed of the battle plan, he refuses to go unless Deborah goes with the army. I have heard preachers saying that Deborah only goes with him because he is lacking in cour-age and virtue. However, this misses the point of the biblical text. Barak clearly sees her as God's leader for that time and knows that she could inspire the soldiers to fight courageously for the Lord and for his people. His words to Deborah, "If you will go with me, I will go, but if you will not go with me, I will not go" (4:8), quite purposely echo words that people sometimes utter to God, and her reply echoes the words of the Lord to his people: "I will surely go with you." This echoing of such words is not accidental but rather emphasizes the exalted status of Deborah as the one chosen by God to lead the people. It is certainly true that Deborah rebukes Barak, presumably for his failure to believe that God could use him for this task. Even so, it is quite clear from the text that Deborah is the one whom God has raised up. Deborah, then, is a military leader.

Finally, Deborah is a *poet and singer*. She is the composer of the song recorded in Judges 5 that she and Barak sing to celebrate

Israel's victory (see vv. 7, 12). This poem is full of wonderful images and powerful rhythms (see, for example, vv. 12–14, 19–22, 24–27). It was originally sung with musical accompaniment. Be sure to read it aloud so you can hear the rhythm and power of the poetry, for this comes through even in translation. One day we can learn the melody that was composed for the original singing of this song— and whether Deborah was also a composer and instrumentalist.

Note the very first words: "That the leaders took the lead in Israel, that the people offered themselves willingly, bless the LORD!" God is to be blessed for raising up a woman to lead Israel, and God is to be blessed for the people's willingly following this woman as their leader. Notice the terrible irony of the words that describe Sisera's mother waiting for her son's victorious return (vv. 28–30).

These, then, are the gifts and callings that God gives to Deborah— prophet, judge, military leader, poet and singer.

THE BATTLE AND THE VICTORY

The battle and the victory are described both in prose and in poetry, though more detail is given in the poetic recounting. Deborah and Barak summon the people from the various tribes to participate in the coming battle against their oppressors. Judges 5:2 describes how good it is when leaders lead and when the people willingly offer themselves to serve—that is, when they don't have to be conscripted for military action.

Verses 13–18 of the poem detail the names of the tribes that volunteered for the battle. The poem also gives a list of those who refused to come to the aid of their fellow Israelites. Some came from Ephraim, Benjamin, Makir (part of Manasseh), and Issachar. Those from Zebulun and Naphtali are singled out for their courage, as soldiers from these tribes were especially brave in risking their lives. It is their land in particular that is under the oppressive rule of Jabin, so they are fighting directly for their homes and families. Those from Reuben, Dan, Asher, and the other part of Manasseh refuse to fight. The Reubenites discuss the call-up at length but do nothing. Judah and Simeon, the two most southern tribes, are not mentioned in either of the lists, possibly because they were involved with their own battle against the Philistines at this time in their history.

On the enemy side there is Sisera with his chariots, and there is also an alliance of Canaanite kings with their armies (5:19). This, then is a major battle, not a tiny local skirmish. In preparation for the conflict Deborah tells Barak to gather his forces together on Mount Tabor (4:6); from there they are to come down the mountain slopes to fight against Sisera's forces.

The outcome of the battle is a total victory for Deborah and Barak's forces. The reason for this is not just that Deborah is a good military strategist, but primarily, of course, because the Lord fights on the side of Israel (4:15), so that there are no surviving warriors from Sisera's army. The whole army appears to have been destroyed. How could there be such a total defeat of this powerful army with its vastly superior military hardware?

From the description in the poem it seems that God brings a violent thunderstorm with lightning, hail, and torrential rain (5:20–21), making the latest military technology—the iron-wheeled chariots—totally useless. (For similar instances of terrain and weather changing the conditions of battle, consider the Battle of Agincourt and the way in which the rain negated the huge military advantage of the French;[1] or for a contemporary example think of the loss of the rescue helicopters that President Carter sent on a mission to Iran that were caught in a sandstorm.)

Deborah's battle with Sisera's forces is joined in the fertile valley of Jezreel, between Megiddo and Tanach. The fleeing army of Sisera heads north and is overwhelmed in the floodwaters of the Kishon River, a river that flows from the slopes of Mount Tabor and out to the Mediterranean near Mount Carmel. On this occasion, because of the storm the Lord sends, the river is swollen and raging, and the chariots of the retreating army become mired along with most of the soldiers.

One other point to notice here that is helpful for interpreting later passages of Scripture is to reflect on some of the metaphorical language Deborah uses in describing this victory. In particular, see the reference to the stars in Judges 5:20—"From heaven the stars fought, from their courses they fought against Sisera." Deborah uses the language of warfare in the heavens to describe the conquest over Sisera and his army. This is one of the earliest occurrences of this particular metaphor of heavenly warfare in any scriptural passage. But from the time of Deborah onward this becomes a part of the language of God's people as they seek to describe his deliverance of his people and his defeat of their enemies. Here are a few examples of the occurrence of such images—some of them are used to describe actual historical events when God gives deliverance to his people over particular enemies, and others look forward to the end of history when God will bring about the final salvation of believers from all that opposes him and them. A final example of this comes in John's account of the sixth seal in Revelation 6:12–15, which I will quote first.

> When he opened the sixth seal, I looked, and behold, there was a great earthquake, and the sun became black as sackcloth, the full moon became like blood, and the stars of the sky fell to the earth as the fig tree sheds its winter fruit when shaken by a gale. The sky vanished like a scroll that is being rolled up, and every mountain and island was removed from its place. Then the kings of the earth and the great ones and the generals . . . hid themselves.

John is using the metaphorical language of a tradition that begins with Deborah's song of triumph and became a part of the way biblical writers refer to God's power over the nations and spiritual forces. Here are other examples of this pattern:

> *For the stars of the heavens and their constellations*
>   *will not give their light;*
> *the sun will be dark at its rising,*
>   *and the moon will not shed its light.*
> *I will punish the world for its evil,*
>   *and the wicked for their iniquity;*
> *I will put an end to the pomp of the arrogant,*
>   *and lay low the pompous pride of the ruthless.*
> *I will make people more rare than fine gold,*
>   *and mankind than the gold of Ophir.*

Therefore I will make the heavens tremble,
    and the earth will be shaken out of its place,
at the wrath of the Lord of hosts
    in the day of his fierce anger. (Isaiah 13:10–13)
All the host of heaven shall rot away,
    and the skies roll up like a scroll.
All their host shall fall,
    as leaves fall from the vine,
    like leaves falling from the fig tree. (Isaiah 34:4)

Jesus puts the above two passages together:

Immediately after the tribulation of those days the sun will be darkened, and the moon will not give its light, and the stars will fall from heaven, and the powers of the heavens will be shaken. (Matthew 24:29; Mark 13:24–25)

Consider also:

I clothe the heavens with blackness
    and make sackcloth their covering. (Isaiah 50:3)
The earth quakes before them;
    the heavens tremble.
The sun and the moon are darkened,
    and the stars withdraw their shining.
The Lord utters his voice
    before his army,
for his camp is exceedingly great;
    he who executes his word is powerful.
For the day of the Lord is great and very awesome;
    who can endure it? (Joel 2:10–11)

And I will show wonders in the heavens and on the earth, blood and fire and columns of smoke. The sun shall be turned to darkness, and the moon to blood, before the great and awesome day of the Lord comes. (Joel 2:30–31)

This passage from Joel is quoted on the Day of Pentecost (Acts 2:19–20).

He stood and measured the earth;
*   he looked and shook the nations;*
then the eternal mountains were scattered;
*   the everlasting hills sank low.*
*   His were the everlasting ways. (Habakkuk 3:6)*

The mountains quake before him;
*   the hills melt;*
the earth heaves before him,
*   the world and all who dwell in it.*
Who can stand before his indignation?
*   Who can endure the heat of his anger?*
His wrath is poured out like fire,
*   and the rocks are broken into pieces by him. (Nahum 1:5–6)*

For thus says the LORD of hosts: Yet once more, in a little while, I will shake the heavens and the earth and the sea and the dry land. And I will shake all nations, so that the treasures of all nations shall come in, and I will fill this house with glory, says the LORD of hosts. (Haggai 2:6–7)

But who can endure the day of his coming, and who can stand when he appears? . . . [when] the great and awesome day of the LORD comes. (Malachi 3:2; 4:5)

These passages are just a few of the more obvious texts where the imagery of the sixth seal appears. If you want other examples of the use of such imagery, you could look—for a beginning—at Psalm 68:7–8; Isaiah 24:19–23; Jeremiah 4:23–28; Ezekiel 32:6–8; Joel 3:15–16; Amos 8:8–9; Habakkuk 3:6–12; Zephaniah 1:14–18. The point here is simply this: the language John chooses to describe the final judgment of God involves the choice of images used repeatedly throughout biblical writing from the time of Deborah onward. The passages quoted above each mention some of the following aspects of God's judgment:

- The darkening or loss of the light of the sun
- The loss of light or the blood-red color of the moon
- The loss of light or falling or fighting of the stars

• The shaking, darkening, or removal of the heavens
• The shaking of the earth or the mountains

Several of these passages tie this time of cataclysm to the day of the Lord or the day of his anger. They also all relate this cataclysmic time to the judgment of the nations and of their rulers. In the quoted texts sometimes it is Babylon, sometimes Edom, sometimes Egypt, sometimes Israel's enemies, sometimes Israel, sometimes the whole earth that is judged.

Deborah's poetic gifts and particular metaphors becoming a wellspring for later biblical writers should cause us to rejoice in the gift and calling that God gave to Deborah. It should also help us to think more carefully about how we are to interpret Jesus' language about the end of the age in the passages quoted above:

> Immediately after the tribulation of those days the sun will be darkened, and the moon will not give its light, and the stars will fall from heaven, and the powers of the heavens will be shaken. (Matthew 24:29; Mark 13:24–25)

We should also think carefully about how we are to interpret the book of Revelation when it uses this tradition of metaphor in, for example, Revelation 6 (quoted above).

Many present-day interpreters insist on a woodenly literal interpretation of passages like these quoted from the Gospels and from Revelation. But, of course, no one is completely literal, however much they claim to be. It is evident, for example, that if the stars literally fell to earth, the earth would be totally destroyed by just one of them! So Hal Lindsey, one of the "literalists," proposes that the falling stars are actually Russian bombs. Hal Lindsey also thinks that Revelation 6:13 is describing the "first nuclear exchange."[2] This is also the view of Ray Stedman who believes that the sixth seal describes a "nuclear winter."[3] We might describe this approach as using contemporary equivalence metaphors that could, of course, have had no meaning to those who originally read the book of Revelation. Such an approach is totally unnecessary, for the original readers of the Gospels and of Revelation would have been quite at home with these metaphors because they are so commonly used in the Scriptures, from the time of Deborah onward.

This little excursus on the long life of Deborah's poetic images brings us back to the battle she describes and the manner in which God brings victory. The iron-rimmed chariots bog down in the water-logged ground, and Sisera is forced to flee for his life. We are then presented with a very dramatic account of his demise. He arrives at the tent of Heber, looking for rest and safety from his pursuers. Heber is a Kenite (the Kenites were descendants of Moses' Midianite brother-in-law and were not Israelites). At this time there is apparently a treaty of friendship between their peoples (the peoples of the Kenites and the Canaanite tribe to which Sisera belongs).

Jael, Heber's wife, welcomes him royally (5:25). Sisera, exhausted, goes into her tent to rest, asking her to conceal his whereabouts from Barak and the pursuing forces. She waits until he is asleep and then kills him efficiently with the weapons at hand, a tent peg and a mallet. Her deed is celebrated in Deborah's song as a deed of courage, heroism, and faith, a deed that brings praise from fellow believers and also brings the blessing of God.

Here is another woman who is not an Israelite but who identifies herself with the people of God and who, in the service of God and against his enemies, acts with great courage. We need to remember that this is wartime and that Sisera is a ruthless tyrant. He would have gladly raped and murdered any woman he considered an enemy (see 5:30—"Have they not found and divided the spoil?—a womb or two for every man"—and this is his own mother speaking!). Jael, of course, is not privy to all the details of the outcome of the war; so we need to see her scheme and the determination to carry it through as particularly courageous.

Jael is blessed by the Lord as the one whom God uses to destroy this wicked and ruthless man, while the people of Meroz (a village near the battle whose people refuse to help the Lord's army) are cursed by "the angel of the LORD" (5:23). There is a contrast here in the Song of Deborah between the curses and blessings given by the angel of the Lord. We should assume, most probably, that "the angel of the LORD" is Christ, the one who appears to the Lord's people and who goes with Deborah's forces as the leader of the army of the Lord.

As Deborah reflects on the battle and the victory, she does so in words that declare the course and outcome of the conflict to be an awesome revelation of God's glory.

> *So may all your enemies perish, O LORD!*
> *But your friends be like the sun as he rises in his might. (v. 31)*

Deborah's words in Judges 5:4–5 are purposeful echoes of two very significant occasions in Israel's life, occasions on which we hear of God's special revelation of himself.

> *LORD, when you went out from Seir,*
> *when you marched from the region of Edom,*
> *the earth trembled*
> *and the heavens dropped,*
> *yes, the clouds dropped water.*
> *The mountains quaked before the LORD,*
> *even Sinai before the LORD, the God of Israel.*

One occasion comes when God speaks to the people on Mount Sinai (Exodus 19), and the other recalls the last words of Moses when he blesses the people at the end of his life (Deuteronomy 33:1–2).

Later in the Scriptures, Deborah's and Barak's victory is celebrated as one of the greatest historical victories that God gave his people (Psalm 83). The consequence of the victory is peace and security for all the people of Israel, rich and poor, high and low (Judges 5:10–11, 31). Once again the people are able to come down from the hills and are able to settle in their homes, dwell in their villages, and pasture their flocks in the fertile plains. This is a great victory and a great deliverance.

Deborah's prayer ends with some wonderful words, a passionate cry for justice and for the flourishing of those who love the Lord: "But [may] your friends be like the sun as he rises in his might." Here is a prayer for yourself, your children, and your friends.

This account of Deborah's life is at its heart a celebration of victory, a celebration of God's delivering his people, and a celebration of his raising up a woman of tremendous faith, a woman of wise and just leadership, a woman of courage and strength. This is the story of Deborah.

SUGGESTED READINGS AND QUESTIONS

1. Does it present problems to you that God called a woman to be his prophetess and to speak his word to the people, and if it does, why? We need to remember that the sovereign God was quite capable of calling a man to this task if he had so desired. Remember that other prophetesses exercised their calling at a time when there were male prophets—Miriam during the time of Moses, Huldah during the time of Jeremiah.

2. Do you see the difference between the gift of prophecy in the Old Testament and in the New Testament? Do you agree with the definition of New Testament prophecy given in this chapter? Are you committed to praying for the gift of prophecy and earnestly desiring to prophesy? According to the apostle Paul you should be! Do you think there have been occasions in your life when you have exercised the gift of prophecy?

3. Deborah was a judicial and political leader. Does this present problems to you, and if so, why? God teaches us in his Word that men are given headship in the family and in the church, which is the family and household of God; but the Word does not teach that all men have headship over all women in all circumstances. Thus, Deborah is a judge and a ruler. Would it bother you if a Deborah were to become your President, governor, mayor, senator, member of Congress, or Supreme Court Justice? If it would bother you, why would it bother you?

4. It is sobering, painful, and difficult to read about the total destruction of armies. Why do you think that God sometimes brings about this kind of severe judgment?

5. What would you do if you found yourself in a situation like Jael, with a ruthless murderer or criminal coming to your door? (Remember that if you refused him entry, he would probably take your life.) Notice again that, just as with Rahab, Jael's course of action requires deception.

6. Which parts of Deborah's poem do you most enjoy?

7. Do you have a problem with the Scriptures including the kind of dramatic irony that is present in Deborah's poem (Judges 5:28–30)?

8. How do you respond to the point made about Deborah using the metaphor of the stars falling and then this becoming part of the way the biblical writers, from then until the book of Revelation, speak about the destruction of God's enemies by the use of such dramatic images? Have you been attracted to "literal interpretations" of prophecy? Do you need to rethink such an approach?

9. Read the book of Ruth for our study of Naomi and Ruth in the next two chapters.

8

NAOMI AND RUTH:

A Picture of Godliness

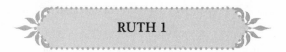

RUTH 1

Deborah was a woman of great courage, a military and political leader in a difficult time. She was also a prophet who spoke God's word to the people of God. We see in her story how God is at work in the history of his people as he raises up women (Deborah and Jael) and men (Barak) to help his people, to answer their needs, and to deliver them in times of trouble.

The confidence that God is always at work to deliver his people was the source of Deborah's hope, her courage, and her commitment to serve the Lord faithfully. The Lord desires that this same confidence should be the motivating power to give us hope, courage, and faithfulness in serving him today. When we consider the lives of Christians—whether it is the needs of individuals, the troubles in families, the struggles of churches, or any other kind of challenges facing God's people all across this earth, scattered among the nations—we know that God has promised to build his kingdom. God is always active among those who love him, always seeking a people out to draw them to himself, always committed to caring for them, always eager to safeguard them against all their enemies. He is ceaselessly working to establish his reign in his people's lives and, through them, into all the world. In the best of times and in the worst of times God is building his church, just as Christ promised.

For these next two chapters we turn to a time that is the worst of times, just as when the story of Deborah begins. Our study will be the story recorded in the book of Ruth. The German poet Goethe called this story the most beautiful short story in the world, the loveliest short story that has ever been written.

We need to set the story of Ruth in the context of the primary story that the Old Testament tells. Just as with Eve and Adam, so also Sarah and Abraham were given God's commitment that they would bear the child through whom his covenant of love would be fulfilled. They were told they would be the parents of the child of the promise, that from their descendants would come the One who would bring blessing to all the nations. God also encouraged Sarah and Abraham by telling them that the blessing would come not only in the future at the time of the Messiah's entry into this world—the Christ, the ultimate child of the promise—but that they themselves and their descendants as they worshipped God would be a blessing to all the nations.

The Old Testament is a missionary book. Christians often forget this because we have been taught to turn for the missionary mandate to those texts we know as "The Great Commission"—Matthew 28:18–20 and Acts 1:6–8. These passages contain Jesus' charge to his church to go out to all the nations with the gospel. But the Great Commission does not begin with this command to the apostles. The Lord promised Israel, the Old Testament people of God, that they would be a light to the nations; and they were charged by him to be his witnesses to the nations, his priests for the nations, and a blessing to all the nations.[1]

For our present study we turn to an account of one such story of blessing, in which someone from another nation, the nation of the Moabites, became part of the people of God. We read in the story of Ruth about how the missionary purpose that God had in mind when he called Sarah and Abraham was fulfilled in the life of one particular person. So the story of Ruth, the Moabitess, is first the story of that missionary purpose, the story of how God's promise of the blessing that Sarah and Abraham and their descendants would be to all the nations was fulfilled in the life of this one individual and her family.

HISTORICAL AND GEOGRAPHICAL SETTING OF THE STORY OF RUTH AND NAOMI

When and where does this story take place? As with the story of Deborah, the account of the life of Naomi and the life of Ruth is set in the time of the judges. The time of the judges runs from the time of Joshua up to the time of the monarchy under the first king, Saul. This particular story is set at the end of the twelfth century B.C. and the beginning of the eleventh century, a little more than thirty-one hundred years ago.

As to location, the story takes place in two places. It is set in the town of Bethlehem, which was at that time a fairly substantial town in Judah, just about five miles south of the present-day city of Jerusalem, on the west side of the Dead Sea. And it is also set in the country of Moab. Moab was a country just to the east of the Dead Sea, only about fifty miles (as the crow flies) southeastward from Bethlehem.

What do we know about the people of Moab? The Old Testament tells us that they were descendants of Lot, Abraham's nephew. Though the Israelites and Moabites were closely related, there was no alliance or friendly relationship between these close neighbors and kindred. In fact, Israel was forbidden by God to make a treaty of friendship with the Moabites. A law in the Books of Moses says that no Moabite was to be admitted to the congregation of Israel to the tenth generation (Deuteronomy 23:3–6). Why does God speak like this to the Israelites about the Moabites? The Scriptures give us several reasons.

• The Moabites had refused to come to the aid of the Israelites as they fled from Egypt, after they had crossed the Red Sea. The Moabites did not fight the people of Israel, but they refused to give them any help at all when they were in desperate need.
• In addition, the king of the Moabites had hired the false prophet Balaam to pronounce a curse on the nation of Israel. We remember how

God thwarted that purpose of King Balak and how Balaam pronounced a blessing instead, including one of the most interesting prophesies about the Messiah. Balaam predicted that "a star shall come out of Jacob, and a scepter shall rise out of Israel" (Numbers 24:17). This is probably the prophecy that the wise men were aware of as they followed the star seeking to find the Christ Child.[2]

• Later the Moabites were involved in temple and ritual prostitution, which was part of the religion of the Moabites on the east side of the Dead Sea and of the Canaanite peoples on the west side of the Dead Sea. Ritual religious prostitution of both men and women was a regular part of the pagan religions. The reason for this was that, like many other pagan religions throughout history, these were fertility religions. So they would practice religious prostitution in the temples of Baal (the main Canaanite god) or of Chemosh (the main Moabite god). They hoped that as they acted out these fertility rites, the gods would see and hear and respond by blessing their crops. In these religious sexual couplings, they played out in human drama what they believed the gods would do to bring fertility to their land. So the Moabites were a pagan people, and therefore they were a threat to the worship of the one true God by the people of Israel. After the failure of Balaam's attempt to curse Israel, he had sought to subvert the Israelites' faith by encouraging them to join in this practice of ritual prostitution (Numbers 25:1–5; 31:15-16).

• The particular god that the Moabites worshipped was Chemosh, and that worship sometimes involved human sacrifice. Several times in the Old Testament they are referred to as "the people of Chemosh," and Chemosh is referred to as "the abomination of Moab" (1 Kings 11:7). There is one particularly terrible story of how one of the Moabite kings sacrificed his firstborn son and heir as an offering to Chemosh. He sacrificed his son on the city wall in view of his army because his battle with Israel was going against Moab (2 Kings 3:26–27). The Moabites were so filled with passion as a result of this sacrifice that the Israelites withdrew from the fierceness of the battle. Pagan practice can indeed fill people with passionate zeal. As an example of this, when I visited India in the late 1980s, a widow had just recently sacrificed herself on her husband's funeral pyre. Millions of people had traveled to her village to honor her as soon as they heard the news of her "noble" self-sacrifice.

There were, then, several reasons why God had forbidden any kind of close relationship between the people of Israel and the people of Moab.

We have said that the events of Ruth's life take place at the end of the twelfth century B.C. What do we know of this period of history? If we turn to the very last verse of the book of Judges (21:25) we read, "Everyone did what was right in his own eyes." This is the way Judges ends. The time of the judges was a terrible time. It was a time of constant upheaval for the people in the land of Palestine. There was almost constant warfare. These were times of occupation by the nations around them, times during which the people of Israel were ruled harshly. For example, there had been one period of eighteen years when the Israelites were oppressed under the rule of the Moabites (Judges 3:12–14), and then Israel, in turn, ruled over Moab for a time (Judges 3:30). This history of conflict gives an additional explanation as to why there was little friendship between these two peoples.

The history of the years leading up to the time of Ruth is a history of the people turning away from God, of unbelief and of idolatry among God's people, of disobedience and rebellion against the Lord and against his commandments. When we read the book of Judges, we see an overwhelming picture of human sin and unbelief and unfaithfulness to God. It was a time of abandoning the worship of God and ignoring his Law—and because of this it was a time of continual political, social, and economic crisis. This is the big picture, the backdrop, against which the book of Ruth is set.

The book of Ruth gives us another picture, a miniature held up against the backdrop of faithlessness; but this is a portrait of faithfulness. In it we read about the faithfulness of two women and one man—Naomi, Ruth, and Boaz. We read a history in this book of three people who honored and loved God, who were faithful to him, and who obeyed his word despite the pattern of life in the culture around them. It is a story of three people who were faithful when the culture around them was characterized by faithlessness to God and faithlessness between people.

But the book of Ruth is also the story of someone from another nation, a hated nation, becoming part of God's people and displaying a faithfulness that was missing from the lives of most Israelites. Before we look in more detail at the life of Ruth, we need to pause and reflect on our own time and the parallels between our time and hers.

How would our time be described by a historian looking at the big picture of events in our culture? If we asked future historians—if we could move a century or two ahead of the time in which we live—I think they might describe our time in a similar way. Today people live autonomously; that is, they live as a law to themselves. Everyone is doing what is right in his or her own eyes.

Think of some of the expressions that are used constantly on television—in commercials, in soap operas, on talk shows—the expressions that are part of the language of the culture. This is a time when everyone is trying to "live for yourself and nobody else," to "be all you can be," to "just do it," to "live to the max," to "be free," to "be a rebel." The ideal is to pursue life, liberty, and happiness as I define these for myself; no one else has the authority to tell another person how to live. One recent morning, while listening to the radio, I heard a discussion on the news about whether there should be laws that limit the moral choices of individuals. Those opposing the "imposition" of any such laws declared that "it is offensive" to make laws for the lives of others because those individuals and families will have already thought about the issues for themselves and will have already decided what is "right in their own eyes."

The novelist Tom Wolfe has assessed the past few decades as a time of ever-increasing freedom. The sixties he defined as the decade of freedom from sexual norms, the seventies as the decade of freedom for narcissism (the freedom to love oneself), the eighties as the decade of freedom from moral norms about money and business ethics, the nineties as the decade of the final freedom, freedom from religion. Wolfe argues that each of these decades also saw an increase in the "freedom claimed" during the previous decades, so that, for example, sexual freedom is now far greater than it was in the sixties, and so also with the freedom to love oneself or to ignore business ethics.[3]

A friend of one of my sons visited a church—for the first time in his life—and told my son afterward how astonished he was by the pastor speaking as if he expected everyone to believe his words and to do what he said. He thought this "unbelievably arrogant!" This brief anecdote underlines the widespread assumption that people think it is their right to do as they see fit. Such personal autonomy, being a law to oneself, is the goal and the downfall for many individuals, marriages, families, churches, businesses, and other social institutions in our culture.

The demand for personal autonomy is perhaps the greatest moral challenge that we Christians face, both in seeking to impact the society in which we live but also in terms of ourselves. Will we submit to God, will we do as he sees fit, or will we do what we feel is right in our own eyes? It is probably true to say that this insistence on boundless personal freedom is the greatest god, the greatest idol, in every western society. We don't worship the vile god Chemosh, nor do we sacrifice our children to him. However, we worship just as vile a god—unlimited freedom—and we sacrifice our children, our marriages, our families, our churches, our business ethics, and many other things to this vile god.

This is the big picture, both in the time of Ruth and now, three thousand years later. In such a time as this, what miniatures contrast with this backdrop? What stories are there in our nation, in our city, in our churches, on our campuses that are parallels to the story of Ruth, Naomi, and Boaz? What stories are there of people who are committed to serving God, stories of people being faithful, stories of people loving God and walking in his ways, stories of people living for others and living for God in a time when everyone around us is doing what they see fit?

This is the background to our story, and perhaps this little excursus on our own time will help us relate to the history of Ruth so long ago, for when we read her story it is full of customs that are radically different from the customs of the times in which we live. We will need to look closely, for example, at the custom of levirate marriage, by which when someone dies childless, his brother or close relative is required to marry the widow to raise up children for the family name. This is a strange idea to us. But many Old Testament stories, like this one and also the story of Tamar, have such requirements at their center.

Another custom that we will need to look at is that of the kinsman-redeemer. As in the case of Boaz, the kinsman-redeemer redeems or buys back the property of someone, in this case that of Naomi and her sons. This is to us a strange custom, but we need to understand it and try to get past its strangeness so that we might see the beautiful elements of faithfulness, kindness, love, and mercy in this story of Ruth.

This outline of the time and this short summary account of two customs we need to understand give us the broad setting of the story of Naomi and Ruth. What about the immediate setting—how does their story begin?

THE IMMEDIATE SETTING

In Ruth 1 we read that Elimelech takes his wife, Naomi, and his sons, Mahlon and Chilion, and moves to Moab because there is famine in and around Bethlehem. Elimelech's name means "God is king." Despite the beautiful name that he himself has, we do not know what the sons' names mean, for Elimelech gives his two sons Canaanite names rather than Israelite names. This might be an indication of his own personal lack of faith in the one true God and his own version of doing what was right in his own eyes, for names were of great importance in that culture and revealed parents' hopes and aspirations for their children as well as revealing their beliefs. Remember how Abraham and Sarah called their son Isaac because God had brought "laughter" to them in their old age, or think of Leah calling her son "Judah" and saying, "I will praise the Lord."

What caused the famine that led Elimelech and his family to leave Bethlehem and move to Moab? We do not know if the famine was caused by poor weather, drought, or some other natural disaster. One possibility is that God sent a pestilence of some kind or withheld the rain only from the people of Israel as a judgment upon them for their unbelief, idolatry, and disobedience. When we read Deuteronomy 28 we see that the curses the people called down on themselves if they failed to keep the covenant included the possibility of drought, pestilence, or some other disaster.

However, another possibility is that the famine was caused by the constant upheavals and unsettled political times in Israel. We know there was no central authority in Israel at this time, and so the tribes and clans each went their own way. War, occupation, or the anarchy of civil disorder can destroy an agricultural economy rapidly. Think of the turmoil in Bosnia during the early and middle nineties, when economies ground almost to a halt, when people could not grow their crops, when there was famine even though the ground itself was fertile and the weather fair.

So Elimelech leaves Bethlehem, stricken by famine, even though the city lies in one of the most fertile areas in Palestine, and he, his wife Naomi, and their family move just fifty miles away to Moab where there is no famine. In Moab their sons, Mahlon and Chilion, marry Moabite women, Ruth and Orpah.

TRAGEDY

Tragedy occurs in Moab as all three men die early deaths. Naomi and her daughters-in-law are left bereft. In most present-day western societies, widows have laws to protect them, and they also have property rights. But it has not always been so. In Britain, for example—and it was probably the same in the United States—just two centuries ago widows rarely inherited family property (consider the example of the Bennett family in Jane Austen's *Pride and Prejudice* or the example of the mother and daughters in *Sense and Sensibility*). In many societies, past and present, if the husband dies, the inheritance goes to the eldest son, or if there is no son, then to a near male relative. In the time of our story, widows had no property rights, no status or honor, and very little protection against the unscrupulous. This continues to be a problem in our own time, for there are many, including even some pastors, who prey on widows.[4]

In Old Testament times, and in most other times and places, if a husband dies, widows are left both with their personal bereavement and in desperate practical need. It is because of the common mistreatment of widows that there is such powerful denunciation in the Scriptures against such abuse. In consequence of this widespread problem, there are many demands from the prophets that widows be treated well. Much is said by God to the rulers about their obligation to defend the needs of widows and orphans, for they had no other advocate.[5] If a widow had no sons, she was, almost always, in a disastrous position. This is Naomi's situation as she is left with only her two daughters-in-law—three widows together.

NAOMI'S RESPONSE

What is Naomi's response? She decides to return to her own people and to the town where she has relatives. The members of her family belong to the clan of Ephrathites from the tribe of Judah. She goes back with the hope that her relatives will be of some assistance to her, particularly with the hope that someone may redeem her husband's property, property that he presumably had abandoned when the family left for Moab. Naomi hears that the Lord has returned to his people, that he has shown favor to them and has given them deliverance from their time of judgment and famine. So she sets out for home after ten years away.

Naomi pours out her bitterness of spirit against the Lord (1:13, 20–21). She expresses this bitterness both to her daughters-in-law and to the other women when she returns to Bethlehem. To her daughters-in-law she says, "It is exceedingly bitter to me for your sake that the hand of the LORD has gone out against me." To the women in Bethlehem she says, "Do not call me Naomi ["pleasant"]; call me Mara ["bitter"], for the Almighty has dealt very bitterly with me. I went away full, and the LORD has brought me back empty. Why call me Naomi, when the LORD has testified against me and the Almighty has brought calamity upon me?"

What are we to think of such open expressions of bitterness of spirit? Should we assume that she is sinning or that she is revealing that her heart is full of unbelief? I do not think we should respond this way. Naomi's words appear to be simply honest expressions of her feelings rather than words betraying unbelief.

Scripture everywhere encourages us to be honest about our distress in the face of disaster and to express our grief or bitterness of spirit. If anyone doubts this, they should read Lamentations 3, Psalm 10, or Jeremiah 12 or 20. We must not overlook the rightness of expressing grief to God. Jeremiah felt free to express his pain, but it is because he pours out his soul so freely that he is also able to come to a sense of God's love to him and care for him. If we read Lamentations 3, for example, we will discover that this passage has both some of the most pain-filled and some of the most comforting words in all of Scripture.[6] It is not more spiritual to pretend that we are not angry and bitter or to suppress our distress when awful things happen in our lives. The apostle Paul tells us that he was "so utterly burdened beyond [his] strength that [he] despaired of life itself" (2 Corinthians 1:8).

So Naomi's open expression of bitterness is not a sign of lack of faith. Indeed, as we read the text in the book of Ruth it seems clear that Naomi is a believer. She believes in the providence of God, in God's rule over her own personal history as well as over the history of the nation. We should also notice Naomi's prayer for her daughters-in-law in 1:8–9, a prayer in which she is seeking a blessing from God for them.

Knowing that remarriage is the only solution for a widow at that time and in that society, Naomi urges Ruth and Orpah to stay in Moab. She urges her daughters-in-law to return to their families, find new husbands, and make a life for themselves among their own people rather than coming with her to Israel where there is such hatred of Moabites. She reminds them that she is most unlikely to be bearing more sons (because of her age and the improbability of anyone marrying her)—sons that either Ruth or Orpah might marry—and she adds that they almost certainly would not wait all the intervening years for her sons to come to maturity even if she should find a husband that very night and conceive more sons immediately.

RUTH'S DECISION AND ITS CONSEQUENCES

This urging of the two younger women to go back to their own families brings a dramatic shift in the story. To understand what happens more adequately we need to think a little about family at that time. When the Old Testament talks about family, it is describing a much larger family than the way our societies usually think about families today. The Old Testament stories tell us about extended families, families that include several generations and other relatives—not simply parents, children, and grandparents but also cousins, nephews, nieces; families that include servants and other household members, perhaps even some aliens from other countries who have become part of a particular family.

In response to Naomi's urging, Ruth commits herself to Naomi and to Naomi's extended family back in Bethlehem and to Naomi's people, Israel. Despite her mother-in-law's repeated insistence on Ruth's leaving, despite the turning back of her sister-in-law, Orpah, to go to her own mother's home, despite the call of her own people, her own culture, and the religion of her childhood, Ruth commits herself to stay with her mother-in-law. This commitment is expressed in some of the most beautiful words, and some of the best-known words, in all of Scripture.

> Do not urge me to leave you or to return from following you. For where you go I will go, and where you lodge I will lodge. Your people shall be my people, and your God my God. Where you die I will die, and there will I be buried. May the LORD do so to me and more also if anything but death parts me from you. (1:16–17)

It is clear from these words that Ruth, the Moabitess, has been influenced by the faith of Naomi, and so she pledges herself to join her mother-in-law in her travels, to become one with Naomi's people, to put her faith in Naomi's God, to be with Naomi until death, and to share the same burial place. She pledges her whole being, for she has become a believer.

People of many cultures at that time were almost always tied to the religions of their people. A parallel today might be a Muslim who risks hatred, exile, and even death if he or she leaves Islam and becomes a Christian.[7] But in this story there is the additional matter of national identity, and this too was bound up with a people's religion. For Ruth to transfer her allegiance, her devotion, to the God of Israel is a huge step. She is turning her back on the gods of Moab.

She is turning her back on her own family and her own nation. She will be an outcast to her own people. She makes this choice with no certainty that she will be welcomed in Bethlehem. She is going to an alien place and to an alien people, to a place where people may not look kindly on her, a place where she has very little likelihood of finding someone who will marry her and provide for her. But without regard for all the uncertainty ahead and without regard for all that she is leaving, Ruth commits herself to go with Naomi.

Ruth adds that she will be buried with Naomi. Extended families had their own burial plot. Abraham, for example, purchased a burial plot for Sarah, and their family used that burial plot for generations. Ruth promises that she will give herself to Naomi to be part of her family in sickness and in health, in life and in death. She even makes this remarkable promise with an oath, calling down the Lord's judgment on herself if she should turn away from her word. She asks God to witness the oath that she has taken.

THE RETURN

Their return to Bethlehem causes a wave of interest, excitement, and admiration. This does not seem to be at all what Ruth was expecting, but it is what happened. The whole town is stirred. Naomi had been gone for ten years. The women of the town ask, "Is this Naomi?" As we have learned, names in the Old Testament were intended to mean something, to tell you something about the person. As mentioned before, the name Naomi means "pleasant," "lovely," or "delightful." But now Naomi urges the other women when they recognize her to call her Mara ("bitter") rather than Naomi. Her life has been a tragedy. She has no idea of how God is going to care for her and for Ruth. She has no expectation that her life might become pleasant again. However, she knows that God's hand has been at work in her life, even though that has meant misfortune for her.

THE TURNING POINT

The extraordinary choice Ruth makes becomes the pivotal moment of the story, the turning point where things begin to change. It is here that God steps in to bless them, for we see their situation being dramatically transformed in the days immediately following their homecoming. Everyone in the town hears about Ruth's decision to love and honor her mother-in-law, to leave her own people and serve the God of Israel (2:6, 11–12; 3:11). They are surprised to see a Moabite among them; so they ask questions and are eager to hear the story. They learn that she is prepared to be with her mother-in-law regardless of the consequences in her own life.

One example of this widespread knowledge of their misfortune and of Ruth's choice is recorded in our text. A few days after their return we find Ruth gleaning grain to feed herself and Naomi. When the landowner, Boaz, sees Ruth gleaning in his field, he asks who this young woman is, and he is told that she is the Moabite who returned with Naomi.

Later Boaz tells Ruth that he knows all about how she left her homeland and how she helped Naomi. And he calls down a blessing on her, asking the Lord to repay her for what she has done:

> All that you have done for your mother-in-law since the death of your husband has been fully told to me, and how you left your father and mother and your native land and came to a people that you did not know before. The LORD repay you for what you have done, and a full reward be given you by the LORD, the God of Israel, under whose wings you have come to take refuge! (2:11–12)

What is particularly remarkable about Boaz's words is that they echo the words of Genesis 12:1, which recount God's call to Sarah and Abraham to leave their homeland and their family and to journey to a foreign country and settle there. These words about the call of the first mother and father of Israel are applied by Boaz to this young Moabite—she, he declares, is a true daughter and worthy successor of Sarah and Abraham. These are wonderful words from Boaz, expressing his faith in the Lord and his great admiration for Ruth. He commends her for her faith and for her noble character. Others in the community who are believers also speak with admiration of Ruth for the choice that she has made (see 4:14–15).

The rest of the story tells how God, in his providence, brings his rich blessing on Ruth, on this woman who has joined herself to the children of Sarah and Abraham. This is a blessing the Lord holds out to all who are Sarah and Abraham's descendants, to all who are heirs according to the promise. This is the blessing that Boaz prays for Ruth in 2:11–12. This is the promise to every woman or man from among the nations who joins herself or himself to God's people. The Lord will richly reward us and repay us when we commit ourselves to serve him. This is a story about God's blessing for the children of Sarah and Abraham, their children from every nation under heaven.

SUGGESTED READINGS AND QUESTIONS

1. How have you found Boaz's words to be true in your life, that God is a faithful and sheltering God under whose wings you have taken refuge (2:12)?

2. Have you ever had to make choices like Ruth's—that is, to choose one family over another, one people over another, one land over another, one road to travel over another, one God over another? What were the deciding issues for you, the issues that helped you make your choice?

3. Does it disturb you that Naomi talked so openly about her bitterness? (It is clear that she expressed this to God as well as to other people.) If you find her words difficult to accept as appropriate, perhaps you should read Lamentations 3. Are you able to weep freely and even be angry or pour out the bitterness of your heart when trouble comes into your life? Have you felt free to express your distress to the Lord and to others when tragedy strikes, or have you kept your feelings bottled up or even believed that it would be unspiritual to be so honest about what you feel?

4. Ruth swore a solemn oath when she made her promise to go with Naomi. Have you ever sworn a solemn oath or made a vow in God's name (the same thing)? Most of us make such vows when we get married or when we are ordained to ministry. Some of us have made such oaths privately, just between ourselves and the Lord. Did

you understand just how serious an undertaking you were making, how serious it is to take an oath or make a solemn promise to the Lord or to another person?

5. One of the wonderful things about the book of Ruth is the weaving together in history of human choice and the sovereign plans of God. Where do you see this in the story of Ruth?

6. Where do you see in your own personal or family history the weaving together of the sovereign plans of God and your human choices?

7. Read Ruth 2–4 for our next study. Which elements of the story seem strange to you? Which elements of the story are beautiful to you?

9

NAOMI AND RUTH:
A Portrait of Redemption

RUTH 2–4

In the last chapter we saw Ruth casting her lot in with her mother-in-law to go with Naomi as she returned to Bethlehem. This dramatic, life-changing decision meant leaving her family, her own people, her language, her own culture, and her religion. She commits herself to serving the one true God, the Lord of heaven and earth, the God who has made a covenant with his people Israel. This means, for all practical purposes, that Ruth commits herself to becoming a member not only of Naomi's family and community but also of the people of Israel, if they will accept her.

Not surprisingly Ruth seems to have some fear about that acceptance. Shortly after her arrival in Bethlehem she is amazed by the kindness with which Boaz treats her. But God loves to honor those who choose to give themselves to serve him and to be part of his people. It is not that we deserve the things that are done for us by God or that Ruth deserves the things that are done for her in the days following her arrival in Bethlehem. Rather, God delights to give gifts and rewards to his people in ways that are far beyond what we deserve or what we expect. God smiles on Ruth, and so for Ruth everything about her life is going to change, and we will see the beginning of those changes in this study.

The two women, Naomi and Ruth, have now made their way to Bethlehem, Naomi's hometown. When they arrive, Naomi's old friends recognize her and welcome her, and the whole community is abuzz with the news of Ruth's choice to come to Judea with her mother-in-law. This response is extraordinary and in itself tells us something about the people of Bethlehem and about the presence of true faith in Bethlehem, even though for the nation as a whole this is the time when everyone is doing as they see fit rather than delighting in obedience to the commandments given by God.

The people of Bethlehem are filled with excitement by Naomi's return and by the news they hear about Ruth's decision to leave her own people, to leave her country, to leave her family, and to abandon the pagan worship of Chemosh. They are moved by her decision to be kind and faithful to Naomi and to give herself to the service of the Lord. Think how delighted we are when we hear of someone's life turning around, when we hear that someone has put away their former life of self-centeredness, drug abuse, broken commitments, and we hear that now this person has put his or her trust in Christ, is repairing those broken relationships, is now serving others, and is working hard so that he or she might give to people in need. We know how joyful we are when we see such a transformation; so we can understand how the people of Bethlehem are filled with gladness when they hear about the commitments that Ruth has made.

GOD'S PROVIDENCE

As we read this happy account of Ruth and Naomi's arrival in Bethlehem and of the glad welcome they receive, we need to observe that underneath the surface of the story line there is an unstated story also being told, and that hidden story is the theme of the providence of God. God cares for his people, and he is at work in their history, but often his work goes on behind the scenes. We make our choices; events happen to us day by day; much of what takes place in our lives seems to us to be quite by chance or random. But in everything God's unseen hand is at work.

In the book of Ruth the text uses the language of chance when it speaks of Ruth gleaning in Boaz's field—"as it turned out" (2:3, NIV) or "she happened to come to the part of the field belonging to Boaz" (ESV). However, God is at work in the events of Ruth and Naomi's lives, whether through the choices they make or in the happenstance things that occur. Behind the scenes God's hand is guiding the lives of Ruth and Naomi because he loves to care for those who make him their refuge.

Naomi and Ruth, in the providence of God, a particular providence of which they are as yet unaware, arrive during the time of the barley harvest (2:17). The barley fields ripen first in the cycle of yearly harvests. The wheat harvest comes several weeks later. But, you may be thinking, what does this note on the annual harvests have to do with Ruth and Naomi and the providence of God? To understand how beautiful this story of God's care for Ruth and Naomi is, we need to reflect on their situation. As widows coming back to Bethlehem, they have no resources, no means of making a living. They are going to be completely dependent on the readiness of their neighbors to obey God's laws about the treatment of widows. Moses gave many compassionate laws of God—laws about kindness to widows, orphans, and aliens—to the people of Israel; but in most of the nation through most of its history these laws were ignored rather than observed. So, for Ruth and Naomi their well-being depends upon how the people of Bethlehem feel about obeying these laws.

GLEANING IN BOAZ'S FIELDS

Naomi and Ruth return in desperate circumstances. As we saw in the last chapter, in that society and in most societies throughout most of history, widows had no means of making a livelihood. To put bread on the table, both for herself and for her mother-in-law, Ruth goes gleaning behind the harvesters in a field where she hopes that the owners will treat her favorably. This was an agrarian society—every family had land, and every family farmed. Each family had been granted an allotment of land by the Lord when Israel first entered the land of Canaan.

The law of Moses required that widows, orphans, the poor, and aliens be allowed to gather what they could find after the harvesters had gone through the fields and had made their first cutting and gathering of the grain (Leviticus 19:9–10; 23:22; Deuteronomy 24:19–22). They were forbidden to reap the fields a second time to harvest what was missed on the first cutting, and in addition the harvesters were forbidden to harvest the corners of their fields. These laws are beautiful in their requirement of generosity to those in need, and it is worth quoting several of them in full.

> When you reap the harvest of your land, you shall not reap your field right up to its edge, neither shall you gather the gleanings after your harvest. And you shall not strip your vineyard bare, neither shall you gather the fallen grapes of your vineyard. You shall leave them for the poor and for the sojourner: I am the Lord your God. (Leviticus 19:9–10)

> When you reap your harvest in your field and forget a sheaf in the field, you shall not go back to get it. It shall be for the sojourner, the fatherless, and the widow, that the Lord your God may bless you in all the work of your hands. When you beat your olive trees, you shall not go over them again. It shall be for the sojourner, the fatherless, and the widow. When you gather the grapes of your vineyard, you shall not strip it afterward. It shall be for the sojourner, the fatherless, and the widow. You shall remember that you were a slave in the land of Egypt; therefore I command you to do this. (Deuteronomy 24:19–22)

> At the end of every three years you shall bring out all the tithe of your produce in the same year and lay it up within your towns. And the Levite, because he has no portion or inheritance with you, and the sojourner, the fatherless, and the widow, who are within your towns, shall come and eat and be filled, that the Lord your God may bless you in all the work of your hands that you do. (Deuteronomy 14:28–29)

When harvesting by hand, lots of grain is left behind; so from a purely economic viewpoint the command not to go through the fields a second time was costly. However, rather than thinking of their own economic advantage, the farmers were required to leave the excess for the poor, the fatherless, the widow, and the aliens in the land. Widows, the fatherless, and aliens made up the great majority of the poor in Israel, as they do in every society. We should notice that there are no statements in these laws about whether the poor are "the deserving poor" (as some speak about such matters of charity). Whether a person was poor because of tragedy or because of sin and laziness is not an issue for consideration in these commandments.

The fundamental issue is to remember the undeserved kindness of God for oneself and to therefore be generous to anyone in need, for at the heart of these laws is the call to imitate the character of God and to remember his mercy in redeeming his people. Israel was never to forget its history. Twenty generations after the Exodus the people were still to base their actions on the reminder that they had been slaves in Egypt, and God had graciously delivered them. These motivations to be generous to those in need are just as applicable to Christians today. We are called to imitate God's generous character and to remember his gracious salvation. The principles of these gleaning laws still apply to every believer throughout this present age.

Of course, for the poor to be able to truly glean was dependent on the owner of the field being ready to keep the demands of the Law. We should observe carefully that these laws are not options but requirements, obligations! Just as we are commanded not to commit adultery, not to murder, not to steal, so we are commanded to obey the gleaning laws.

We can be sure that the majority of the landowners did not obey these laws, even when they were faced with people who met the requirements of the Law. Ruth meets three of the four categories of need: she is poor, she is an alien, and she is a widow. (She probably also met the fourth category of being an orphan as her father-in-law was dead, and thus she had neither a husband nor a father to provide for her once she had chosen to go with Naomi.)

When Ruth goes into the fields to glean, it is apparent that she has no idea whose field she is in, but in God's providence and because of his unseen gracious care for her, "she happened" to pick the fields of Boaz. Even though Boaz is not present, it is obvious that he has given instructions to his foreman to allow gleaning, for when Ruth makes her polite request (2:7), the foreman gladly agrees. Notice the greeting between Boaz and his harvesters: "The LORD be with you!" and their reply "The LORD bless you" (2:4). It is evident that this entire household is one of faith. The foreman is aware, of course, that it is the Moabitess who is gleaning, and we also see how aware he is of Ruth's hard work (2:7).

What is Boaz's response when he discovers that an alien is gleaning in his fields? Boaz urges Ruth to stay in his fields, knowing that some of his neighbors would not be so ready to let her glean in their fields and also acutely aware that she might even be in danger elsewhere (2:8–9). Naomi also is concerned about Ruth's vulnerability to sexual assault (2:22). Remember that this was a time of great wickedness in the nation of Israel, and many terrible things were happening (think of the raping to death of the Levite's concubine recorded in Judges 19). There must have been many men working in those fields who would gladly have taken advantage of a woman in need and without a man's protection, as was true of Ruth.

Just a few months ago on the news I heard about the widespread abuse of women and their daughters in "aid situations" around the world. Men from western aid organizations, as well as locals employed by them, regularly and systematically demand sexual favors of women and their children in return for grain and other food. Women in such settings of poverty have to accede to such demands for sex if they want to not starve themselves and if they are committed to feeding their children.

However, in Ruth's case God's merciful providence is watching over her to protect her in bringing her to the fields of this good man, Boaz. We see Boaz going way beyond the letter of the Law in his care for this widow and alien (2:9, 14–16). This is, of course, what God desires of us all—that is, that we should follow the spirit of the Law rather than the letter. We are not to be people who try to get by through either ignoring such laws or keeping them strictly to the letter and doing for those in need the minimum of what God commands. The laws simply spell out the basics—they are the floor of what should be done by us—not the reality of the spacious room of obedience to the Lord.[1] Rather, we are to ask ourselves, what is the intent of the Law? What is the principle that God desires us to observe?

God's people (in Ruth's time and today) are commanded to be generous to those less fortunate, not simply to tolerate those in need who have the courage to take advantage of such laws as the gleaning laws. This generosity, this obedience to the spirit and intent of the Law, is what we see in the life of Boaz. He urges Ruth to stay in his field, to return each day, and to keep gleaning there for her own safety. He speaks to his men to insist that they not take advantage of her or abuse her in any way. He invites her to drink with the men and to eat lunch with them. He ensures that she is given so much extra food at lunchtime that she is able to take some home to share later with Naomi for dinner that night. He commands his men to let sheaves fall so she can pick them up and thus glean plenty of grain. Boaz, as a man of true faith, is deeply moved by the account he has heard of the faith and the courageous decision of Ruth (2:11–12). Boaz acts like God in his graciousness and kindness to the less fortunate—and this is, of course, exactly what the Law requires!

At the end of the first day, because of the instructions Boaz has given his men, Ruth returns to Naomi with far more grain than a gleaner would normally have gathered and threshed and also with the excess of the roasted barley from her lunch. Naomi is deeply moved by these evidences of God's care for Ruth, for she realizes that God has providentially directed Ruth to the field of a kind and generous man (2:19–22). As she listens to Ruth's account of her day, Naomi also realizes that Boaz is a close relative.

But this is just the first day! Ruth's gleaning in Boaz's fields continues for a period of up to seven weeks, the time from the beginning of the barley harvest to the end of the wheat harvest. All through this time, Boaz makes sure that Ruth and Naomi will have enough to live on, perhaps even enough extra to sell and to store up for future months. In fact, by the end of the harvest Ruth almost certainly has gleaned sufficient grain so that she and Naomi will have enough food to eat during the coming hard times of winter. Boaz is indeed a man who is committed to observing the full intent of the Law.

THE KINSMAN-REDEEMER (*GOEL*) AND LEVIRATE MARRIAGE

To understand the next two chapters of Ruth we must familiarize ourselves with the customs in Israel of the *goel* or kinsman-redeemer and of levirate marriage. By understanding a little about these customs, we will understand the story better. The basic principle or intent at the heart of both of these customs (in fact they were not simply customs but laws) was that people not think first about their own situation or about their own rights but rather that they were required to think about others, to have a sense of responsibility for their relatives. The spirit behind these laws is one of extended family obligation. This obligation requires concern up to the level of serious self-sacrifice for one's relatives, should they find themselves in need.

Levirate marriage: The Law requires that if a man dies childless, his brother or other close relative ought to marry the widow and ought to beget children with her in order that the family name not die out (Genesis 38; Deuteronomy 25:5–10; Matthew 22:24–26). Inheritance was clearly an issue in this levirate requirement, for land belonged to a family generation after generation rather than to individuals; but in addition to this the fundamental matter is keeping the family name alive. (This issue of levirate marriage is the matter concerning which the Sadducees tried to ask Jesus a trick question about marriage in the age to come; see Matthew 22:23–33.)

Goel or the kinsman-redeemer: Land and the property on it belong to the Lord, who entrusts it to a family in perpetuity (Leviticus 25:23–28). In Israel the basis of everyone's wealth was land and the ownership of it; this is true in any agrarian society. Of fundamental importance for the people of Israel is the recognition that the land first of all belongs to God. Those who belong to God are in fact his tenants rather than absolute owners of their property and possessions.

The same is true when anyone becomes a Christian. We are to acknowledge that all that we have belongs to God, and so we are the stewards of our land, possessions, and wealth rather than the owners of it all. My father-in-law was a remarkable example of this scriptural principle (as we will see at the end of this chapter).

At the time of the settlement of Canaan the Law required that land be allotted to each family. This land was to be possessed (or tenanted) by that family's descendants in perpetuity. That is why, for example, Naboth refuses to sell his vineyard to King Ahab (see 1 Kings 21:1–3). Naboth would be disobeying God if he sold his vineyard, no matter how much profit he would make. God requires him to pass it on to his children. Given this system of tenancy, what would happen if someone lost possession of his land either through personal tragedy, misfortune such as famine, or even laziness?

In such a case the closest kinsman had the responsibility of redeeming the land for a poor relative who had sold the land in order to stay alive or who had suffered some misfortune and thus lost the family's land to a more fortunate neighbor. The kinsman-redeemer has to buy back the land. He also has the responsibility of redeeming a poor relative who might be in bond-service because of poverty (Leviticus 25:47–49). God had redeemed and bought back the people of Israel from enslavement, and so the people were required to have the same sense of obligation for each other.

Behind these laws lies the teaching that not only the land but also the Israelites themselves belonged to God, for they were redeemed by him, and they were his servants, his possession (Leviticus 25:38, 55).

Land that had been lost for whatever reason could be bought back at any time by a kinsman-redeemer. But if there was no family money forthcoming to buy back the land, or if no kinsman-redeemer would fulfill his obligation, then in the Year of Jubilee the land returned to the original family without cost. In this way the errors or mishaps of one generation did not penalize the next generation. God gave each new generation the possibility of making a living and dwelling on their own land. Think how different this is from our society, and the rest of the world! Poverty and disadvantage goes on from generation to generation.

In contrast to what we observe in our own time—the crushing burden of interest and debt that makes life so difficult for the poor—we need to recognize how very beautiful, humane, and merciful these biblical laws are. We are to reflect on their requirements and challenge ourselves as to how we should think about our responsibilities to our families and our relatives, how we should think about our money, our properties, and our businesses.

NAOMI'S PROPOSAL

This brings us to the section of the story that reads most strangely to our ears—the account of Ruth sleeping at Boaz's feet. Is Ruth behaving immorally? Is she trying to seduce Boaz? What in the world is happening here?

When Naomi sees the kindness of Boaz to Ruth, a kindness that is ongoing day after day, she realizes that Boaz might well be ready to fulfill the responsibility of being both the *levir* and the kinsman-redeemer. In order to find out whether Boaz will be willing to obey these laws, Naomi sends Ruth, dressed in her best clothes, as if she were a bride adorned for her wedding. Ruth is to lie herself down at Boaz's feet in the threshing shed where the harvesters sleep after each day's harvest. This, of course, requires trust, obedience, and courage on Ruth's part, and it also tells us something about the integrity and moral standards that Boaz lived by and that he must have communicated to his household. So Ruth goes, dressed in her wedding clothes, to lie at Boaz's feet after the evening meal has been completed and after everyone has retired for the night.

When Boaz awakes to find Ruth at his feet, she asks him to "spread the corner of your garment over me" (v. 9, NIV). She is requesting that Boaz marry her (see Ezekiel 16:8 where this expression is used to describe God as having betrothed himself to his people). Ruth is asking Boaz to fulfill the levirate law for her. She is asking him to betroth himself to her.

How does Boaz respond to Ruth? He could take advantage of

146

her and demand sexual favors of her. He could react with anger. He could refuse her request and insist that she leave. Boaz's response is neither sexual demands, nor anger, nor reluctance, but one of surprise and amazement that she has honored him in this way (3:10–15). He expresses appreciation for her kindness in not asking that a younger man be given to her but rather approaching him to ask for his hand in marriage. We see Boaz's generosity of spirit once more, as well as his faithfulness and moral purity, for he quickly agrees to do what she asks of him. He pronounces himself honored by this request from a woman of such faith and integrity. He has her remain there through the night, for safety's sake, not for any sexual advantage. He is careful to protect her, both from other men and from malicious gossip. Then he requests that she leave early in the morning before anyone sees her there, with the additional gift of a shawl full of grain.

Boaz fulfills his promise that very day. He takes his seat at the gateway to the town, where the elders of the community meet to decide on issues of law and custom. The law requires that the nearest relative fulfill the responsibilities of *levir* and *goel*, so Boaz gives the nearest kinsman the opportunity to take up the responsibility. Boaz handles this with great wisdom. By bringing up the land issue first, he makes the need for a kinsman-redeemer seem desirable.

The nearer kinsman at first accepts the offer of being the redeemer of the land (that would enhance his own estate) but then refuses when he realizes that he will also be required to marry Ruth to raise up a son for Naomi's family and for Elimelech's name. Fulfilling this second obligation would mean that his expenditure on the land would bring him no benefit, for the land would revert to any son that Ruth might bear. He is not prepared to run the risk of diminishing his own inheritance, for he would be responsible to buy the land and to support Ruth and Naomi and any children that Ruth bore to him. He is not prepared to make such self-sacrifice, even though self-sacrifice is the basis of the law of the kinsman-redeemer. It is a costly obligation, an obligation that requires mercy and kindness rather than self-interest.

Boaz, however, is glad to do what the Law requires. Boaz has none of the nearer kinsman's qualms but gladly and generously goes far beyond the legal requirement. His love fulfills the Law. This story is a wonderful demonstration of the character of God that stands behind these laws. Boaz's submission to the Law is the calling of all of us—not to do the bare minimum of what the Law asks, not to calculate the cost, not to be governed by self-interest, but to gladly fulfill the true intent of the Law—that is, to seek to imitate God.

Boaz in his self-sacrificing love is a picture to us of the loving-kindness of God himself. Boaz is also a portrait in history of what Christ would do for us as our kinsman-redeemer. In the Old Testament there are not only promises of the Messiah in words, but there are also pictures in history of what the Messiah will do when he comes into this world. In Christ God has loved us in just the way that Boaz loves Ruth and Naomi, for Christ buys us back from the desperate need and the bondage in which he finds us. Jesus is our nearest kinsman, our elder brother, who has paid the price for our redemption, so that we might belong to God and so that we might have an inheritance in his eternal kingdom. Through Christ we will inherit the earth!

THE OUTCOME

Ruth marries Boaz, and God blesses their union with a son. What is Naomi's response to this dramatic change in their fortunes? She is, of course, delighted that Ruth has found a husband, that the land of Elimelech has been redeemed, and that "a son has been born to Naomi" to inherit her husband's name and her husband's property (4:17).

The women of Bethlehem give Ruth the greatest possible praise by saying to Naomi about Ruth that she is the "daughter-in-law who loves you, who is more to you than seven sons" (v. 15). In marrying Boaz and in bearing a son, Ruth, the Moabitess, becomes the great-grandmother of David and one of the great-great-grandmothers of Jesus the Messiah. It may well be that David himself put this story in its final form for us, for the genealogy at the end of the book was clearly written in David's day, but we are not told who the author is. It could, of course, have been Naomi herself who wrote down all but these last verses, but we will have to wait to meet Naomi, Ruth, Boaz, and David in heaven to learn the answer to that question.

OBEDIENCE TO THE LAW IN THE SPIRIT OF BOAZ TODAY

I want to finish this chapter with some brief thoughts on the Christian's calling to approach God's laws with the same spirit that Boaz did. As was mentioned earlier, believers are to see the requirements of God's Law as the floor of obedience, not as the full measure of walking in God's ways. The laws give us an outline of what God desires, a minimum, not the heart and totality of righteousness. This is true of the laws about tithing, for example. The tithe represents to us that all we have is the Lord's, and so we are to see the laws about tithing as a minimum of what we ought to give. The same is true with the law against committing adultery. A woman or a man who said, "I have not committed adultery, and so I am a good wife or a good husband" would be a fool. Of course, a wife or husband should not commit adultery in deed or word or thought. But it is obvious that a good marriage requires love, service, self-sacrifice, respect, cherishing, and mutual submission. The law about adultery is a basic minimum and has within it and behind it a roomful of principles about true faithfulness in marriage.

As we have seen, Boaz understood that this is the true nature of God's Law. He looked for the spirit in the law that would fill in the room that is outlined by the obligation or prohibition of the commandment. Boaz clearly asked questions like these: What characteristic of God is behind this law? How, in this law, does the Lord require me to love my neighbor as myself?

This is our calling today, and I will include here a very personal contemporary example of someone who sought to obey the laws of God in the spirit of Boaz. My father-in-law died a few months ago at the age of ninety. At his memorial service I had the privilege of telling a story about him. "Dad," as I called him, was a fruit-grower with a small farm of about sixty acres in California's San Joaquin

Valley. When I was a seminary student in the late sixties I used to work for him each summer in the fields.

One day in the summer of 1969 I was walking back to the house for lunch through the fields, and I came across Dad kneeling in his orchards offering the firstfruits of his young peach trees to the Lord. When a peach tree is three or four years old, it will bear its first fruits—it will have four or five large beautiful peaches, some of the finest fruit the tree will ever bear. Dad was kneeling there, holding up a peach in each hand, and he was saying, "Lord, these peaches are yours. These trees are yours and all the fruit they will ever bear. This orchard is yours. My farm is yours. I am yours. Help me to serve you in all I do."

Dad loved to read the Scriptures, and he decided for himself that he wanted to put into practice some of the various offerings and services in the Old Testament Law that were required of the people of Israel. His choice was that he would regularly have this service of firstfruits just between himself and the Lord. He never told anyone about it (not even his own family)—it was a private matter between himself and the Lord. I waited until he had finished his prayer and got up from his knees—he was a bit embarrassed to find me watching and listening to what he thought was just between him and the Lord. I asked him about it, and he explained that he did this every time any of his trees started bearing their firstfruits. The Lord had taught Moses to command the people to bring the best of their firstfruits to the house of the Lord and offer them to him, so that is what he was doing. Dad's prayer showed how deeply he understood the spirit of this commandment about the offering of firstfruits.

The consequences of Dad's little ceremony were remarkable.

First, it impacted his attitude toward his employees and anyone with whom he did business. He did not ask about his bottom line when he was thinking about paying the men who worked on his farm. Rather, he asked what would be pleasing to the Lord, what was just, merciful, and fair. Just about a year before Dad's death a man who had labored on Dad's farm came by to see him and to thank him—he had worked for Dad forty or fifty years earlier. He said,

"Every summer I would come up from Mexico, and I would make a beeline for your farm. You treated us so much better than the other farmers. You never paid us the minimum wage or the going rate. You paid us far more. You often ate lunch with us. You brought us treats at break-time. You showed concern for our families. Working for you changed my whole life and the way I have raised my own sons. I should have come back to thank you before."

At the memorial service we heard testimonies of people who would say, "He paid me more than I was worth." Even when others, including relatives, took advantage of his integrity and generosity, Dad never held it against them, and he continued to treat them well, just as he treated everyone else, with the same kindness and mercy. Everyone who worked with him or who did any business with him in any setting could tell numerous stories about this aspect of his commitment to treat people with justice and mercy.

Second, when he gave, he gave generously, without thinking about how much precisely he could afford. Many years he was not a wealthy man, but he gave away more than 50 percent of his income. He gave to his church, to ministries, and to many individuals. He did not keep careful records of all his giving, though, of course, with more regular gifts he received tax-deductible receipts. When he was audited by the IRS for giving away too much of his income, they sent him a personal letter of commendation, both for the honesty and clearness of his bookkeeping and also for his extraordinary generosity. They informed him, however, that he could not give so much and claim it all as tax-deductible. He was giving over the limit! That did not cause him to give less, of course. He had no idea that there was a limit to what one could give—he kept on giving just as generously but was careful to only claim what portion of his giving was within the limits.

Third, he and Mom were extraordinarily hospitable. I will give just one example of their hospitality, though I could write many pages about it. I remember how my wife and I (we were working in the English branch of L'Abri at that time) sent a young man to stay with them. He was from Southern California, and he needed someone to take him in and to care for him, for he had no family to return to after he had become a Christian. He was a complete stranger to them, but they took him in and became like parents to him. I will never forget his breaking down at Dad's memorial service as he tried to describe to us all what this love from them had meant to him.

Fourth, all four of his children were profoundly affected by their mother and father's practice of mercy, faithfulness, integrity, and generosity, and they are all following their example in their personal lives, in their work, and in all their relationships; and all of them are also richly generous with their possessions, their homes, and their time.

SUGGESTED READINGS AND QUESTIONS

1. What do you think might be some contemporary equivalents of the gleaning laws? Obviously not all of us are farmers, but these laws apply to us whatever job we have, whatever business we own. How do you think Christians today could do something similar in caring for the poor, for widows, for orphans, and for aliens?

2. How many people are in your family or household? How many would there be if you regarded your extended family as family—e.g., brothers and sisters and their families, aunts and uncles and their families, and so on? What sense of responsibility do you have toward them? After reading this chapter do you think that you ought to have a greater sense of responsibility toward your relatives?

3. Scripture teaches us that our property belongs to God, as also does our money. What difference should such a belief make in the way you think about your home, your money, and your possessions? Would you be prepared to have some simple ceremony, similar to Dad's firstfruits service, in which you offer your possessions, your home, your workplace, your money, and your life to the Lord?

4. Scripture also teaches us that what we possess belongs to our children and to our descendants and not to us personally (in addition to our reflections from the story of Ruth and the Old Testament laws about this see the words of Paul in 2 Corinthians 12:14). What

difference might this view make in the way you save for, and pass on, an inheritance to your children?

5. What do Ruth, Naomi, Boaz, and Tamar have in common?

6. What are some of the ways in which Boaz is a picture of Christ?

7. Who are some other Old Testament believers whose lives are portraits in history of Christ's work?

8. Read 1 Samuel 1:1–2:11, 18–21, the story of Hannah, for our next chapter. In what ways do you identify with Hannah's troubles and joys?

10

HANNAH:

A Woman of Prayer

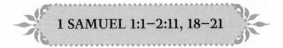

1 SAMUEL 1:1–2:11, 18–21

The book of Ruth is a story of faithfulness. It begins with the account of Ruth's faithfulness to Naomi in leaving everything that was secure and familiar for the sake of her relationship with her mother-in-law and for the sake of her commitment to the Lord. The story continues throughout the book with the record of Ruth's ongoing commitment to fulfill her oath of loyalty to Naomi. We learn also of Naomi's faithfulness to the name and memory of her dead husband Elimelech and also about Naomi's concern to fulfill her responsibilities as a mother to her young daughter-in-law. We learn of a man, Boaz, who goes far beyond the letter of the law in becoming the *levir* to Ruth and their kinsman-redeemer for Ruth and Naomi.

Overarching this history of human loving-kindness and faithfulness we discern the gracious faithfulness of the Lord as he commits himself to the keeping of his promises for those who put their trust in him. He is the one under whose wings his people can indeed take refuge. The book of Ruth is an account of how God cares for his people even when trouble and disaster bring ruin and disappointment to their lives.

The key to understanding the book of Ruth is seeing the importance of relationships at the heart of all that God teaches us in his Word. The Lord has committed himself to us, his people, and has promised that he will never leave us or forsake us but rather will always be our helper. In turn he asks us, his people, to commit ourselves to being faithful to him and to spend our days reflecting on how we might obey his commandments and so imitate his love for us. This is why Jesus could sum up our whole duty to God by teaching each of us that we are to "love the Lord your God with all your heart and with all your soul and with all your mind" (Matthew 22:37). In similar fashion he sums up our duty to one another: "You shall love your neighbor as yourself" (v. 39).

All the stories in the Bible and all the teaching of God's Word rest on this understanding of what is central in our lives. How faithful is God to us, and in return how faithful are we to him and to one another? This brings us to the history of Hannah or rather to the history of the Lord's care for Hannah and Hannah's devotion to the Lord.

THE HISTORICAL SETTING OF HANNAH'S STORY

In this chapter we turn to another story of a woman who lives in a difficult time. Like Ruth and Naomi, Hannah lives at the very end of the period of the judges, the time when "everyone did what was right in his own eyes" (Judges 21:25). So Hannah lives in the eleventh century before Christ during a time of apostasy and unbelief, a time when God's word is ignored, a time when even the public worship of God at the tabernacle in Shiloh has become debased and full of abuses.

The tabernacle—the great tent for worship made during the time of Moses—had been set up at Shiloh during the period of the conquest and settlement of the land (Joshua 18:1–10; Judges 18:31). At the time of the story of Hannah, the leader of Israel's worship of the Lord is the priest Eli. Eli, along with his two sons Hophni and Phinehas, is in charge of the care of the sanctuary and is also responsible for overseeing the worship.

This worship includes, of course, the great annual festivals when large numbers of people come together to celebrate God's goodness to them. In addition there are the daily sacrifices and services commanded in the Law and the offerings that individuals could bring to the sanctuary at any time. Despite the clear commands of God, Hophni and Phinehas live according to the spirit of their times. They lead the worship of the people by doing what is right in their own eyes rather than doing what God requires.

The text of 1 Samuel tells us that these two unfaithful priests are in the habit of stealing the choice portions of the offerings that the people make to the Lord. The equivalent today would be a pastor stealing the money that a congregation gives to the Lord Sunday by Sunday. Hophni and Phinehas also regularly become drunk (presumably on the wine from the drink offerings) and encourage drunkenness in others who come to worship at the services in the sanctuary. The equivalent today would be a pastor getting drunk during the Lord's Supper and inviting the congregation to join him in drunken celebration of the sacrament.

Hophni and Phinehas also imitate the fertility religions of the surrounding peoples by having sex with the women who serve at the gates of the holy place and in effect turning them into temple or shrine prostitutes. The equivalent today would be a pastor leading a congregation by being unfaithful to his own wife and having sex with any woman (or man or boy) he chooses, anyone who comes to him for spiritual advice or help or who is assisting him in the work of the church.

When we read of the wickedness of Hophni and Phinehas, we are shocked by their open disregard of God's commandments, by their abuse of their responsibility to lead the people in true worship, and by their violation of the sacred trust given to them by God. We respond like this because we see these priests taking sexual advantage of those whom they are supposed to be teaching, of the people before whom they are required to be modeling righteousness and fidelity.

But we too live at a time when even some of those called by God to lead his worship and his people have done instead what is right in their own eyes. For example, in the 1960s, in imitation of hippie culture, some pastors took LSD or other drugs to have "religious experiences" during the Lord's Supper and taught others to do the same. As a consequence many followed their example and teaching.

But in addition to such extreme examples of open and flagrant turning from God's Word, we live in a time when pastors have enriched themselves at the expense of the people of God by stealing the people's gifts to the Lord's work. We live in a time when pastors have been sexually unfaithful to their own wives, a time when pastors have seduced widows, women in need of help, or other women called to service in the church. We even live in a time when pastors have sexually abused young women and girls, and also young men and boys. For everyone inside and outside the church, this has been the most outrageous betrayal—this taking sexual advantage of children and young people—this abuse of children when the parents of those children believed their children were being trained in godliness and in faithfulness to the Lord by these pastors. Such behavior in churches that claim to follow Jesus brings on us the censure of the world, but it also brings the severe judgment of the Lord himself.

So it was in the days of Hophni and Phinehas. Because of their unfaithfulness to the Lord and their corruption of true worship, God would, in his time, send terrible judgment on Hophni and Phinehas and also on the nation as a whole. As is so often the situation, many others lived as these two leaders lived; many joined them in their apostasy and wickedness. But just as in the story of Ruth, the personal history we will consider tells us that some remained faithful to the Lord. Our story recounts the beginning of a new day for the nation. This new day begins with a woman named Hannah.

HANNAH'S HOME AND FAMILY

Hannah and her family live in the hill country of Ephraim—that is, in the area north and northeast of Jerusalem. Her family journeys once each year to Shiloh to celebrate one of the three great annual religious feasts of Israel. It seems probable that their annual journey to Shiloh is to observe the Feast of Tabernacles, a festival that takes place in the early fall. Shiloh is about eighteen miles north of Jerusalem, and the family has to travel about fifteen miles from their home to the tabernacle at Shiloh.

Elkanah, Hannah's husband, is almost certainly a Levite, for the list of his ancestors that is given suggests to us that he was descended from Kohath, one of the sons of Levi. We cannot be absolutely sure about this, but it is a likely proposal. In the text he is called an Ephraimite, presumably because they live in that part of the land that was given to the descendants of Joseph's son Ephraim.

HANNAH'S PERSONAL SITUATION

What do we know of Hannah? As we are introduced to Hannah, we are told quickly that her life is one of great sorrow. We are informed that her husband Elkanah loves her, but we are also told that Hannah is barren, and so, perhaps because of this barrenness, Elkanah has taken a second wife, Peninnah, to raise up children for the family.

We saw in earlier chapters, for example, in the stories of Sarah, Tamar, and Ruth, how important it was in Israel for a family to have sons. The family name and the inheritance of property passed on through the male descendants of a family. It was considered essential to have male children so that the family name might be kept alive and the possession of the land stay within the family. So it is probable that because Elkanah needs a son to preserve his name and to inherit his land, he takes a second wife to ensure this succession, even though he loves his first wife, Hannah.

The previous paragraph should not be taken as suggesting that polygamy is acceptable. The biblical text does not approve of polygamy; rather it simply recounts what took place. Just as with Sarah and Abraham, God requires Elkanah to trust him and to wait to see if God will give children to him and Hannah in his time. But, just as with Sarah and Abraham, Elkanah does not wait but takes matters into his own hands and marries a second wife. This second wife, Peninnah, unlike Hannah, is very fertile. She gives birth to many children, both boys and girls (note the expression "all her sons and daughters," 1 Samuel 1:4).

This arrangement, while it may seem useful from a purely practical point of view, inevitably produces tension and trouble in their home. Just like Hagar before her, and also like Leah (the unloved but fertile wife of Jacob), Peninnah boasts of her ability to bear children to her husband and "provokes" or mocks Hannah who is unable to conceive (vv. 6–7). Like Sarah and like Rachel (Rachel was Leah's sister and the favored wife of Jacob), Hannah is the wife more greatly loved, but she has to live with the constant taunts of her rival. There are several examples of such behavior given us in the biblical text, and it is one of the almost inevitable results of the practice of polygamy.

One of the particularly sad aspects of the story is that the tension between the two women becomes worse when the family goes to worship God in Shiloh. Peninnah's taunts and provocations reach a climax at this annual festival. Why? What is going on? The family brings a peace offering, and then each member—Elkanah, Peninnah, each of her children, and Hannah—receive a portion of the offering to eat, symbolizing the Lord's acceptance of their offering, the Lord's blessing of them, and the Lord's love for them. We need to try to imagine them sitting at the tabernacle with Elkanah handing out a portion to each one. But there is Hannah sitting by herself with no children around her receiving her personal portion, whereas Peninnah is sitting there surrounded by her sons and daughters, receiving many portions.

Even when Elkanah, to demonstrate his love for her, gives Hannah a double portion, this brings no real comfort and satisfaction to her. Peninnah uses the occasion, and the obvious difference, to triumph over Hannah, so that the public worship of God becomes an even more sorrowful time for Hannah than any other when it should have been the most joyful. Hannah's childlessness is brought home most acutely at this time, and she is inconsolable. We might speculate that Peninnah behaves so unpleasantly because she knows that Hannah is more dearly loved, but this is no excuse for her abuse of the worship of God or for her constant provocation of Hannah.

Before we condemn Peninnah too readily, we should perhaps reflect on the way public worship can indeed become a time for the raw exposure of our past sins, our failings, and even our struggles with the abnormalities of life. What should be an occasion of joy for the worshipper can readily become a time to be reminded of how one's life has been a series of disappointments. It is a frequent occurrence in a public worship service, a prayer group, or a large gathering for us to be insensitive about matters over which many people present may have broken hearts.

How easily we can talk about divorce, abortion, childlessness, financial hardship, or people being out of work and talk about these things in such a way that people who have gone through such difficulties or who are presently going through them are simply made to feel worse by the way we speak and by the way we pray. It is important to talk in public about such matters with grace and sensitivity, for then a door is opened to be able to discuss them in private and to offer the comfort of God's Word and of a caring heart.

But, acknowledging this need, we have to recognize that most public speech about these issues is insensitive and lacking in grace. Think, for example, of how many times in sermons and in public worship, marriage is spoken about in such a manner that the single person is made to feel unfulfilled and worthless. Think, for another example, of how often a single mother, whose husband has abandoned her, is publicly taught that a faithful Christian woman and a good mother should stay at home with her children and not pursue a career when such a woman has no alternative but to work to support her family.

This is particularly a problem at a time in our nation when it is important for Christians to address the moral issues that place the church under cultural pressure, such as open promiscuity, the breakdown of marriage, or the lack of respect for human life. However, it is even more important that when we address such issues, we don't make people listening who have had abortions (some of whom may be childless as a consequence) or who have gone through divorce feel worse about the tragedies of their lives. People can be made to feel as if they are being taunted, gloated over, condemned, criticized, unloved, rejected, even set outside the people of God. It is easy to do this without ever intending to be so insensitive or so mean-spirited.

We need to think very carefully about how we speak about issues that will always be represented in the lives of some in any sizable group of people. We must proclaim clearly what God's Word says about moral issues, but we must speak with the grace and mercy of Jesus Christ.

Consider, for example, the issue of homosexuality. If I ever speak about homosexual practice in public, in church, or in any other context, the test of whether I speak about it in a manner that is faithful to the gospel is if a person present who is homosexual feels free to come to me afterward and talk to me. I must speak in obedience to the biblical denunciation of homosexual practice, but I must also commend the graciousness of Christ's love so that the homosexual individual does not feel rejected, unloved, criticized, gloated over, or condemned by me.

Consider how the Gospels teach us that sinners welcomed Jesus gladly.[1] Prostitutes felt free to come to Jesus Christ—but not, of course, because he approved of prostitution. They felt free to come to him because whenever he spoke about any issue, he spoke with wonderful grace, with tenderness and gentleness, and people whose lives were caught in sin knew that they were loved and accepted by him. There are, of course, occasions when Jesus spoke very passionately in condemnation of sin, but this is usually about the sins of the teachers of the Law and the Pharisees (for a full discussion of this, see my book *Learning Evangelism from Jesus*, Crossway, 2009).

We are mistaken if we think that faithfulness to biblical righteousness means that sinners should keep far away from us, that they should feel unwelcome in our churches, in our homes, or by us personally. Rather, the opposite should be true. Our public worship and our private lives should be arenas where those whose lives are trapped in sin or whose lives are troubled by sorrow feel welcome, accepted, and encouraged. Christ welcomes the sinner, the brokenhearted, the downtrodden, and he delights in calling such people into personal fellowship with himself.

We, however, in contrast to Christ, sometimes drive people away from our churches and from ourselves. We can make people feel alienated from us and from our churches by the way we speak inappropriately about moral issues and the brokenness in the lives of people.

I regularly need to ask myself, am I being like Peninnah? Am I gloating about my comfortable situation? Am I pointing the finger at someone else? Am I making a hurting person feel distressed and downhearted in the presence of God and of God's people?

HANNAH'S PRAYER

On one such occasion, when Hannah has endured the gloating of her rival, she is even more distressed than usual. So instead of celebrating the feast with her family, she goes alone to the tabernacle where "[s]he was deeply distressed and prayed to the Lord and wept bitterly" (1:10). The honesty of the words in our text is deeply encouraging. Notice the expressions used to describe Hannah's sorrow: "wept and would not eat," "deeply distressed" ("bitterness of soul," NIV), "wept bitterly," "the affliction of your servant," "troubled in spirit," "pouring out my soul," "great anxiety and vexation" ("great anguish and grief," NIV).

Many times Scripture lets us know that it is perfectly acceptable for us to tell God what we are feeling. God desires that we be honest with him, even when our hearts are full of bitterness. He is not perturbed or critical even when we tell him of our deepest disappointments and of our hidden sorrows and anguish. He already knows what we think, and he knows the hidden hurts within our souls.

God does not reject Hannah; nor does God reject us when we pour out to him our anxieties, our frustrations, our disappointed hopes and expectations. We may even say this is a basic part of what prayer is to be—we are encouraged to bring to the Lord all the saddest and most broken places in our hearts and lives. With Hannah, it is her inability to conceive a child that brings her prayer of lamentation.

In her distress Hannah makes a vow to the Lord: "If you will . . . give to your servant a son, then I will give him to the LORD" (1:11).

Samuel, like Samson, like Jeremiah, and like Jesus, is devoted to the Lord from before his birth. In Scripture there are several examples of a parent offering a child to God long before the child is born, or in this case even before the child is conceived.

Hannah is promising the Lord two things: first, she will give her son to the service of God at the tabernacle; second, she will give her son to be a Nazirite for the whole of his life.

Nazirites, men and women, made a vow to "separate [themselves] to the LORD" (Numbers 6:2). They promised not to shave their heads for the length of their vow and not to eat or drink any fruit of the grapevine (no wine or strong alcoholic drink, no grapes, no raisins, no grape seeds). They also were to keep themselves apart from any dead body. (See Numbers 6:1–21 for the laws about the Nazirite vow; and see also the account of the promise that God made to give a son, Samson, to his childless parents [Judges 13]. Samson also was to be a Nazirite from before his birth—his mother had to refrain from eating or drinking anything from the fruit of the vine even during the days of her pregnancy.) It was up to the individual to determine the length of the vow. In Samuel's case he is offered as a Nazirite, even before his conception, for lifelong separation to the Lord.

Eli, now an elderly man no longer in full control of the tabernacle service, is nevertheless still involved in the life and worship of those who come to bring themselves and their offerings to the Lord. He sees Hannah's silent praying, and he assumes that she is drunk, like so many other worshippers at that time. Apparently because of the example of the priests, Eli's sons, many other people became drunk while they were making their offerings to the Lord.

Hannah, however, is not drunk, and when she assures Eli of this and tells him that she is pouring out her heart to God in prayer, he responds with a word of encouragement and blessing: "Go in peace, and the God of Israel grant your petition that you have made to him" (1:17). Hannah is no longer downcast as she goes away but instead takes these words as a promise from the Lord. We must assume that it is the Holy Spirit who leads her to respond with such faith to the blessing of Eli.

GOD'S ANSWER

Hannah returns home greatly comforted, for she has taken Eli's blessing as a word of hope from the Lord. Within just a few months she becomes pregnant, and Samuel is already born when the time comes for the family to return for the next fall festival. Elkanah, her husband, clearly a man of faith who desires to honor her promise, goes each year "to pay his vow" (1:21). This presumably is to be understood as his commitment to fulfill the vow that Hannah had made. After three years, the time comes when young Samuel is weaned, and so Hannah fulfills her promise and gives him to the Lord to be raised by Eli at the tabernacle. Women in many cultures breast-feed their infants for about three years before they are weaned, just as Hannah's feeding of Samuel is described in this account.

As we read her song of praise and dedication, we come to believe that Hannah gives up her son gladly, for God has answered her plea, and the burden of her shame is lifted. She takes Samuel up to the tabernacle, to Eli, to "lend him to the LORD" (1:28), and he is raised at the tent of worship. According to the biblical record, Hannah goes to see her son once each year, and each time she goes she takes him a new set of priestly clothes she has made for him. Furthermore, God takes away Hannah's sense of failure and shame and gives her, in addition to Samuel, three more sons and two daughters (2:21).

In that time, and in many other times and places, childlessness was seen as a sign of failure for a woman and as a sign of punishment from God. While it is certainly possible that God might withhold children as a punishment, we need to understand that there are many other reasons for infertility, most of which have nothing to do with the sins of an individual or with God's judgment on that person.

We have to be careful not to add to the burden and the sorrow that someone who longs for children so often bears. We also must not presume to know the mind of God as to why a particular tragedy comes on individuals or to assume that their tragedy is a result of their sin or their lack of faith. This was the view of Job's comforters, and it was the view of the Pharisees. Neither of these two groups was commended by God for their theology!

In contrast to such a theology of suffering, the Scripture encourages us to bring all our sorrows, whatever their cause, to the Lord and also to bring our joy and gladness to him when he answers our prayers. Hannah's prayer is a sorrowful lamentation. Her song, in contrast, is an outburst of happiness.

HANNAH'S SONG

As we study this beautiful song (1 Samuel 2) with care, we notice several things. It could, of course, be set to music; and, indeed, this song has been set to music many times.[2] But even if we know no music for this song, and even if we cannot sing, we can read her words aloud, for, like all poetry, Hannah's song was written to be read aloud. Only then do we begin to appreciate the rhythm, patterns, and musicality of the poem.

Hannah's song is written as *poetry*, just as with any other of the biblical Psalms and with many passages in the prophetic writings. In addition we can readily observe that her song has similar poetic patterns to the poems in the Psalter.

Notice, for example, the parallelism of verse 1, where the lines complement each other:

> *My heart exults in the LORD;*
> > *my strength is exalted in the LORD.*

In verse 2 we find a different pattern with the lines building on each other:

> *There is none holy like the LORD;*
> > *there is none besides you;*
> > *there is no rock like our God.*

In verses 4–5 we find dramatic contrast:

> *The bows of the mighty are broken,*
> > *but the feeble bind on strength.*

Those who were full have hired themselves out for bread,
    but those who were hungry have ceased to hunger.
The barren has borne seven,
    but she who has many children is forlorn.

In verse 8 we find powerful images:

He raises up the poor from the dust;
    he lifts the needy from the ash heap
to make them sit with princes
    and inherit a seat of honor.

There is also the steady rise to a climactic finish of the whole song. All of these elements are typical of the poetry of the Psalms.

In terms of the way her poem deals with her subject matter, we should observe the manner in which reflection on private experience and an answer to personal prayer becomes a framework that is used to rejoice in the triumph of God for all his people. This too is typical of Hebrew poetry. Hannah's own personal experience becomes the basis or platform from which she reflects on the way God acts within history both in judgment and in salvation. Her personal joy and her personal prayers of both sorrow and happiness become public prayers to which all the people of God can relate.

We need to think about our sorrows and our joys and about God's answers to our prayers in this same way. We should use our personal experience to write our own public prayers, songs, or testimonies, so that they become prayers, songs, and testimonies that can communicate to others what God has done for us. Many of the Psalms are like this. It is this public declaration of private experience that enables us to relate so readily to the Psalms and to use them so freely for our own prayers. Hannah, we may say, is one of the sweet singers of Israel through whom God has blessed all his people in every generation.

If we reflect on the calling of women in the church today, we need to recognize that Hannah's song was written for men to read as well as women. There is no notice at the head of the song: "For women and children only." God gifts women to teach and instruct and edify other women and also to teach and instruct and edify men. Another way to put this is that the words of women are intended by God to edify the whole people of God. The song of Hannah would not be in Scripture if that were not true.

This song of Hannah echoes the song of Miriam and Moses (Exodus 15) and, in its turn, is echoed in many Psalms and in the Song of Mary and also the Song of Zechariah (both in Luke 1). These echoes of Hannah's words by David and by other poets, poets who were writing in the generations following Hannah, and also by Mary and Zechariah in the New Testament more than a thousand years later, teach us that Hannah's song became a source of hope and encouragement for generation after generation of believers.

What are the themes of Hannah's song? They are themes that all believers recognize as their own.

• The world is full of powerful, arrogant, wealthy people who ignore God and who trust in their riches and in their strength and power; but God will cast them down and instead will raise up the poor and humble who put their trust in him.

• Those who do not have in this present time will have in the future because of the goodness and perfect justice of God.

• Those who do have now will have it taken away in the future.

This turning of the tables is also one of the major themes of Jesus' words in the Sermon on the Plain (Luke 6).

> Blessed are you who are poor, for yours is the kingdom of God.
>
> Blessed are you who are hungry now, for you shall be satisfied.
>
> Blessed are you who weep now, for you shall laugh. . . .
>
> But woe to you who are rich, for you have received your consolation.
>
> Woe to you who are full now, for you shall be hungry.
>
> Woe to you who laugh now, for you shall mourn and weep. (vv. 20–25)

These are very challenging words for those of us who live in an affluent society. I have to ask myself the urgent question, if I am one who does have wealth, plenty of food, and happiness now, where is my trust? Do I put my trust in these good gifts of God or in the Lord himself? Do I regard the good things I enjoy as his gifts that I do not merit? Or do I regard them as simply my right because of my talents, my hard work, my faith, and my righteousness?

What is particularly bizarre, in light of these biblical words about present poverty, hunger, and sorrow for so many of God's people, is the widespread and popular teaching of the "prosperity gospel." Such teaching is alien to God's Word; it is, in truth, a form of heresy.

Hannah's song is also a *prophetic* song. It is written at the end of the period of the judges, as that time is winding down to an inglorious end. Most of the leaders of the people of God have, for many generations, been disastrous leaders. Hannah looks forward to the time when the nation will become a great kingdom among the other nations. She looks for God to do something completely new for Israel. Her song looks forward to the time when there will be a king in Israel. That king will be David, who will be anointed as king by her son, Samuel. Ultimately her song looks forward to the coming of Christ himself. God will bring his anointed, his Messiah, to deliver his people. This, of course, is why Mary in particular picks up themes and phrases from the song of Hannah.

In her earlier prayer Hannah addresses God as "Lord of hosts" (1:11). This is the first time this particular title is found in a prayer in Scripture. Then in her song Hannah is looking toward a time when there will be kings with their earthly hosts, a time when there will be nations with their armies opposing the people of God, but also a time when God will reveal himself as the Lord of the heavenly hosts and the Lord of all the nations, a time when God will triumph over all earthly powers through his anointed King. God, the Heavenly Warrior, is the one in whom Hannah puts her hope. Her song is a song of victory, a song of hope, a song of confidence.

Hannah is a woman who pours out her heart to the Lord, a woman of faith who indeed trusts God to answer her prayers and her deepest longings and sorrows, a woman who is prepared to give back to the Lord what is most precious to her and to make this offering with a glad and full heart. In this way Hannah is just like Abraham. Abraham is prepared, in faith, to sacrifice his son. But God spares him from having to make that sacrifice. Hannah gives her beloved son, the son who is the fulfillment of God's promise to her, to the Lord for his service, and she does it with a glad and full heart.

In this way Hannah pictures to us God's giving his Son to us, his beloved Son. Just as with Abraham, Hannah gives her son, her only son, the son she loves, the son of the promise, to God. Just as God's own Son, Jesus, would later see the temple as his Father's house and the place where he should be doing his Father's will, so Hannah's son has his home in the sanctuary where he must be about his heavenly Father's work.

SUGGESTED READINGS AND QUESTIONS

1. As you think about the story of Hannah, with which part of it do you most identify?

2. Some of you who read this have had to struggle with the difficulty and tragedy of being childless. Has this made it difficult for you to continue to love God and to walk in his ways? What has been the most comfort to you as you have wept and prayed over this great trouble?

3. Would you find it more difficult to be childless or to give up a child that you ultimately bore after much heartache? We read, of course, that Hannah had more children (2:21), but she did not know that this would be the case when she gave Samuel up to the Lord.

4. Does the fact that Samuel was devoted to the Lord from before his birth and that he clearly was a believer devoted to God's service from his first consciousness present you with any problems? If it does present you with problems, why does it, and if you do not find this problematic, why not?

5. Scripture never teaches us that polygamy is God's design for marriage. What are some of the problems with polygamy that the text shows us and others that you might imagine?

6. Hannah's song is a wonderful example of how to thank God for his answers to our prayers as it moves from her own experience to reflect on the character of God, on the nature of God's kingdom, and on God's ultimate triumph and victory. Do you see in her song how her personal experience becomes the basis for this public reflection of faith?

7. As you look at your own life, what do you see as the clearest example you have experienced of God answering your prayers? Try to write a prayer or psalm (song) in which you praise God in the wider way that Hannah does—beginning with your own experience but using your experience to reflect on the triumph of God's broader purposes. This will be hard work, but I suggest to you that this is a good pattern for all our prayers, that we relate them to God's broader purposes so that our petitions and thanks are not simply self-centered but may encourage ourselves, our children, our friends, and anyone we teach and encourage by building their faith in the Lord.

8. Read for our next chapter the story of Abigail in 1 Samuel 25:1–42. What can we learn from this story that will be of help to us today?

11

ABIGAIL:

A Woman of Noble Character

1 SAMUEL 25:1–42

Our chapter on Hannah found us studying the beginning of the book of Samuel (now 1 and 2 Samuel), a time that was a turning point in the history of God's people. In words that are later echoed by Mary as she rejoices in the coming birth of the Christ, the Lord's anointed, Hannah praises God for his answers to her prayers in granting her a son who would be the one to anoint the coming king in Israel. Hannah is a woman of wisdom, a woman of faith, a woman of righteousness, a woman of her word who fulfills her promise to God.

How many promises to the Lord have we made that we perhaps have not kept, promises we originally made in a moment of spontaneous gratitude that later faded away to be replaced by cool calculation about what we think we can afford? For so many of us generous impulses are stifled by self-interest, folly, and greed (as with Nabal in this chapter's story), but not so in the case of Hannah. She promises her son to the Lord, and she gives her son fully to the Lord so that Samuel is raised in the tabernacle from the age of three.

As an adult Samuel becomes a great prophet and the leader of God's people during a most difficult period of Israel's history, a time when they are repeatedly subject to attacks by the Philistines from the west and by other enemies to the south and east. Samuel anoints Saul as the first king of Israel, but Saul proves himself to be unworthy of this high calling. In his anger and jealousy Saul turns against David, the man God sends to be the people's greatest help against their enemies, the Philistines. Saul drives David from his court despite David's military assistance and despite David's personal faithfulness to Saul. David, with the aid of Saul's son Jonathan, has to flee for his life and has to live as an exile and wanderer. This brings us to the immediate setting for our present chapter.

THE SETTING

The setting of Abigail's story is the period in which David is constantly on the move, hiding from Saul, fleeing for his life. Our account begins with a brief notice of the death of Samuel, who has already anointed David to be the new king in place of Saul. But David's circumstances are far from royal. He has with him about six hundred men who have fled to him (23:13), men who are distressed, in debt, or discontented—not the most promising of armies or of loyal supporters of the king, though that is what they become eventually under David's leadership.

David is in exile, and he and his men are living in the desert of Moan, in the central part of the area settled by the tribe of Judah. This is an area where the people were subject constantly to the possibility of raids from the Philistines to the west, from the Bedouin Arabs to the south, and from the Moabites and Edomites to the southeast. David, even in exile, takes his responsibility as king seriously, turning his troop of malcontents and misfits into a well-trained band of protectors for his people. Our text calls David's men "a wall" (v. 16) to the sheepherders of Nabal's household, and this was clearly what David trained them to do for all his people, wherever he and his men went.

THE MARRIED COUPLE—NABAL AND ABIGAIL

The story of Abigail and Nabal is one of those stories that remain in our minds and imaginations long after we read them. What a story! What a woman! And what a man! Perhaps many of us know men like Nabal. He is described as a very wealthy man, rather like Job, at least in this way, though not in many other of his attributes. Nabal is a man not only of wealth but also of social prominence. He is a leading figure in the Calebite family, which was rewarded with land in this fertile part of Judah. (Caleb and Joshua were the only two spies sent into the land of Canaan who were faithful and who trusted God to bring his people into the land.) But despite his position of leadership among his people, Nabal is described also as a fool, and "fool" is the meaning of his name.

What are we to make of Nabal's name? We cannot imagine that his parents named their precious son "Fool" at his birth. So what explains such a name? We know that the people of Israel loved word plays. Nabal probably meant something like "noble" or "skilled" in one of the local languages or dialects, and his parents give him this name in hope that this is the kind of man their son would be. But when he matures, if that is the appropriate word, Nabal becomes a "fool," and "fool" is the meaning of his name in Hebrew (see Psalm 14:1; 53:1). There is also a word play on the term meaning "empty wine skin"; in other words, he is a man of no worth despite his wealth and noble social position. First Samuel 25:3 also describes him as "harsh and badly behaved" ("surly and mean," NIV). "Harsh and evil" is probably an even more appropriate translation of these words. He is, in addition, we will discover, arrogant, rude, insensitive, ungenerous, and self-centered. The description of a fool in Isaiah 32:6–7 could easily be a portrait of Nabal.

> For the fool speaks folly,
>   and his heart is busy with iniquity,
> to practice ungodliness,
>   to utter error concerning the LORD,
> to leave the craving of the hungry unsatisfied,
>   and to deprive the thirsty of drink.
> As for the scoundrel—his devices are evil;
>   he plans wicked schemes
> to ruin the poor with lying words,
>   even when the plea of the needy is right.

This is Nabal, a man who ignores God, whose thinking is errant and evil, whose words are malicious lies, who hoards his wealth, who hates those who do him good, who spurns those in need of his help.

His wife, Abigail, in contrast, is introduced as beautiful and intelligent. Her name means "God, my father, rejoices." She is an example of the woman of noble character praised in Proverbs 31. Our text constantly draws a contrast between her behavior and the behavior of her fool of a husband.

DAVID'S REQUEST AND NABAL'S RESPONSE

David and his men devote their time and energy to protecting the sheepherders and the flocks of Nabal and of others who are grazing their animals in the summer pastures. David ensures that his men steal nothing from the sheepherders and that they treat these herdsmen with kindness and justice. David's men are described as "a wall" (v. 16) against bands of sheep stealers and raiding parties—a wall to guard and protect the shepherds while they are away from home with their flocks. (This area is not far from where many of the troubles are taking place today between the Palestinians and Israel.)

Our story begins at the time of shearing the sheep, a time that always finishes with a great feast in celebration of the fruitfulness and productivity of the season. David sends ten of his young men to request food and drink for his hungry troops who have spent months guarding Nabal's men and flocks. The greeting David instructs them to give to Nabal is a model of courtesy and respect. The greeting comes with a prayer for blessing on Nabal and his household: "Peace be to you, and peace be to your house, and peace be to all that you have" (v. 6). David even refers to Nabal as his father (v. 8), to underline his desire to show him honor. The request that David makes is fair and reasonable. We may set out its appropriateness in the following manner.

• The Law of God requires Nabal to share his food with the hungry at feast time. (Notice the remarkable contrast between the behavior of Boaz during the harvest and the behavior of Nabal.)

• Nabal has the added obligation to honor and reward the service done to him by David and his men. The Word of God teaches us that the "laborer is worthy of his hire,"[1] and David's men have certainly earned rich payment from Nabal.

• In addition, Nabal would most certainly know that David has been the one used by God to deliver the nation from Goliath and the Philistines (Nabal's own constant enemies, for the Philistines were the ones most likely to have harassed his workers and stolen his herds and flocks).

• Nabal probably knows that David has been anointed king by the great prophet Samuel and that David is eventually to take the place of Saul. Abigail is clearly aware of this (vv. 28–30), so her husband surely is as well. It must have been one of the major matters of discussion for everyone living in Israel at that time—especially in Judah, the part of the country where Nabal lives, for Judah is the tribe from which David comes.

How does Nabal respond to David's request, to his own obligations before God and to the Lord's commandments, and to his knowledge of David? Nabal keeps the men waiting; so we know his words are deliberate and thought out rather than angry words in the heat of a selfish moment. The response that finally comes is intended to be a terrible insult. Nabal speaks of David as a nobody, as a runaway servant who has failed to fulfill his obligations—in other words, as a thief, a vagabond, and a no-good. He says that he will give nothing from his great wealth to men of whom he knows nothing—words that he knows very well to be a lie, for in his reply he refers to David as "the son of Jesse" (v. 10), indicating that he is aware of David's family background and of his military deeds on behalf of the nation against their enemies.

When the ten young men bring back Nabal's surly and wicked response, David's anger is swiftly kindled. He, quite rightly, takes Nabal's refusal to be ungenerous and his harsh words as a total rejection of David's claim to kingship, as well as a refusal to fulfill the most basic requirements of the Law with regard to just payment, hospitality, and generosity. David's intention, receiving the insult to him as an insult to God's kingdom purposes, is to take vengeance into his own hands and to destroy Nabal and all his men. How often we all react like this—that is, we receive rudeness to us as a rejection of God's purposes, and then we seek our own vindication instead of crying out to the Lord to be our vindication and to grant us a just outcome to our troubles. We find it easy to justify our outrage as a "spiritual" response. Maybe in David's case he could have made a fairly ready and appropriate justification for his desire for revenge against Nabal, though certainly not for his plan to kill every male in the household. His response is overkill, to say the very least.

ABIGAIL AND DAVID

Abigail is made aware by a servant of the mean and churlish behavior of her husband and also of the true nature of the service that David and his men have done for her household. This servant's words in verses 14–17 make it perfectly clear that Nabal cannot be ignorant of all that David and his men have done for him. Everyone is aware of David's service to their household. Nabal's response has no justification or excuse.

Many Christians today teach that those who serve God must always be in submission to and obedient to those who are set over them. I have even read examples of preachers criticizing Abigail for not being submissive to her husband and for going against his wishes! However, we observe in this story that faithfulness does not always mean obeying those in authority over you. Here the servant goes against his master, the wife against her husband. All believers are called to do what is right in God's eyes first, regardless of what those over them believe, say, or do. (Other examples of being faithful to God first in the story of David are Jonathan and Michal, Saul's children, siding with David in disobedience to Saul, their father and king.)

The servant recognizes and states openly to Abigail that his master is "worthless" (v. 17; NIV, "wicked") and will listen to no one. Clearly some of the people in the household have tried to tell Nabal the truth about David's service to them in protecting the shepherds and the flocks. The servant implies that Nabal would not even listen to Abigail, his wife, though her intention would have been to do him good and not harm. The servant, in effect, begs Abigail to try to fix the impending disaster that is about to be brought down on the household as a consequence of her husband's wicked folly.

Abigail's reaction is immediate. "Abigail lost no time" (v. 18, NIV). We should notice the emphasis on her quick thinking and action all the way through this account. She swiftly prepares sufficient food and drink to provide David and his men a feast and sets off with this generous gift loaded on donkeys along with a retinue of servants to help her and to oversee the transportation of the food. She does all this preparation in secret and says nothing about her plans to her husband, for she knows him well enough to realize that he would prevent her from going.

God's providence brings Abigail and David together in a cleft of the mountain ravine, and what a time to meet! David, when he runs into Abigail, has just made a solemn oath to kill Nabal and his men for his lack of thanks and respect (vv. 21–22). Abigail meets David with respect and honor, and her words reveal her wisdom and faith. We need to reflect on Abigail's wisdom and to observe in her words some of wisdom's characteristics.

TEN CHARACTERISTICS OF ABIGAIL'S WISDOM

Abigail knows that "a soft answer turns away wrath" (Proverbs 15:1). She first takes the blame on herself before requesting that David hear her words (v. 24), even though she is fully aware that she is not in any way at fault.

Many women know that this is sometimes the only way to cool down a hotheaded man! Indeed, we may state as a general principle in all our personal relationships with one another that wisdom teaches us to be the first to quickly go and make our apology, confess our faults, and ask for forgiveness, even when we may not be the one who is primarily at fault. A soft answer does indeed turn away wrath.

Abigail is truthful, even when it hurts. She acknowledges the folly and wickedness of her husband, which could not be excused, and explains that she knew nothing of David's request (v. 25). There is no point in her pretending in this perilous situation that her husband is a generous or good man. She has to face the truth about him, and she has to publicly acknowledge his wickedness and folly to save his life. Truth is better than a house full of the dead!

There are times for us all when the truth about people, even family members, is more important than loyalty to them. We all perhaps have friends who have had to live for many years in marriages that are miserable. We need to ask whether it might be more helpful to speak to them about their "harsh and badly behaved" husbands (v. 3) rather than just watching their sad situation and silently sympathizing. Burdens that no one will talk about are harder to bear. It is not wise to leave people to suffer in silence. On this occasion straight talk about her husband's evil behavior is a necessity.

Abigail appeals to the providence of God that has brought her and David together so David will not shed the innocent blood of God's people. "The LORD has restrained you from bloodguilt" (v. 26). Abigail knows that all timely meetings that bring good to us are not random events but rather are evidence of God's gracious dealings in our lives.

We can all look back at moments in our own histories when we can see God's hand at work in timing particularly significant meetings and events. Abigail must have prayed that God would bring her to David in time to prevent a massacre.

Abigail declares that God must be allowed to take his vengeance on the wicked rather than David taking vindication into his own hands (v. 26). This is a principle that Scripture teaches us repeatedly. "Vengeance is mine, I will repay, says the Lord" (Romans 12:19; Proverbs 20:22). Many of us have been in situations when we have longed to take vengeance on someone who has mistreated us. Sometimes it is indeed right for us to seek justice and to figure out how to bring that about; but we are to seek justice through God's appointed means. We are all mistreated many times in life, and in such cases the only right response is to take our troubles to the Lord and ask him to vindicate us and deal with the difficult person. God asks us to leave it to him to bring justice into many of the situations we face.

Abigail is honest in the face of God's righteousness. She accepts that her husband deserves the judgment of God (v. 25). This is one of the most difficult things for any of us to do; it is a bitter pill to swallow—to have to acknowledge that one's own husband or father, wife or mother, son or daughter, or some other loved member of one's family deserves the judgment of God.

Abigail is generous (v. 27). She offers to David a present for his men as thanks for their service and as a gift of hospitality. She is not giving a bribe to David, for God condemns any kind of bribery and perversion of justice; rather she is offering an appropriate gift. Abigail fulfills the requirements of God's Law, and not minimally but generously. It is feast time, and she gladly shares the bounty of God's blessing on her household.

That is God's calling for all of us—we are to give gladly and to give generously to those who need our help and to those who have been kind and faithful in the way they serve us. My own mother and father were very poor, but they were extraordinarily hospitable and generous. At feast times, such as Christmas, Easter, and Harvest, they would send us around our village with baskets of food for families who had even less than we did. God asks all of us to be like this, especially at festival times, to remember his generous love to us and to share his good gifts with anyone who is in need.[2]

Abigail is a woman of humility. She asks for David's forgiveness and prays for God's blessing on David (v. 28).

How hard it is to ask others for forgiveness and to bless them, especially when we think we are in the right. Abigail has done nothing wrong herself. She is just married to the wrong man! But she humbly begs forgiveness for herself and her household. For many women there will be times when a woman has to ask forgiveness on behalf of the men in her household. A man, too, sometimes has to ask forgiveness for the behavior of his wife.

Abigail sees where God's hand is at work in her moment of history. She recognizes and acknowledges that David is the Lord's anointed king (v. 30), and we should see her words as a prophecy of the future of David's line. Abigail discerns the work of God among his people. She is a woman of wisdom who can read "the signs of the times" (see Matthew 16:3).

This should be our prayer for ourselves—that we become people of wisdom who can read the times so that we can see where the Lord is at work in our moment of history.

Abigail is full of faith. She knows that God cares for the righteous in this life. Her words "the life of my lord shall be bound in the bundle of the living in the care of the LORD your God" (v. 29) are beautiful words to describe those who belong to the Lord. Abigail knows also that this protection of God will endure forever for those who love God, in contrast to the wicked whose souls God "shall sling out as from the hollow of a sling." Abigail is a woman of faith who belongs to the Lord.

The words "the bundle of life" (KJV) were some of Francis Schaeffer's favorite words from the Scriptures; he would often pray about "those who are bound together in a bundle of life with us" in the work of L'Abri Fellowship that he and Edith founded and in the International Presbyterian Church in which he served as a pastor.

Abigail is a woman of wise counsel. She is prepared to give David strong and courageous advice. She tells him that when the Lord has fulfilled his promises to make David king (she is clearly a believer who had paid heed to the words of the prophet Samuel), he will not have on his conscience the guilt of shedding innocent blood or of avenging himself (vv. 30–31). God will grant David success; David does not need to try to bring his success about by his own rash actions.

There are many times when a wife needs to give her husband this counsel—"Let the Lord resolve your problem. He can do a much better job than you." I need to point out here the folly of those who teach that it is never appropriate for a woman to give strong advice and counsel to her husband or to any other man because to do so would be to usurp her position as one in submission. Women are made in the image of God. Women, as human persons, are able to develop wisdom and understanding, and men need to be willing to listen to women as their equals before God. Abigail's preparedness to give strong and courageous advice to the man who she knows will someday be her king is a beautiful example of the way God has indeed made us as equals. She also gives us a wonderful example of how to give counsel to an angry man in a manner that is gracious and respectful.

David's reply is a song of praise to the Lord (vv. 32–35). He has the humility and sense to listen to this wise woman of God. His song expresses his words of gratitude and blessing for her, and pardon and peace for her household. David sang to the Lord to praise him and to honor Abigail. This is a calling we all have—to praise God for the wise people he brings into our lives who help us to love the Lord and to walk in his ways. As a husband it is my calling to thank the Lord for my wise, courageous, faithful, and beautiful wife. She is a true Abigail. *Thank you, Lord!*

THE OUTCOME—THE END OF THE STORY

On her return from her mission of mercy, her mission to save the life of Nabal and the lives of all the other men of her household, Abigail finds Nabal indulging in a great feast, "like the feast of a king"! She wisely refrains from saying anything until the following morning when he is no longer drunk. When he learns how close he was to death he is paralyzed by a stroke, and ten days after his stroke he dies. Nabal's death is declared to be God's just judgment on him for his wickedness and folly (vv. 36–39a).

David sees Nabal's death as the fulfillment of God's vengeance on a wicked man who had disdained and dishonored the Lord's anointed. We should notice the parallels between the life of Nabal and the life of Saul in terms of their treatment of David. We should also observe the consequences of their mistreatment of David—God brings his just judgment on those who do not recognize this man who is God's chosen king, God's friend, a man after God's own heart.

The reward for David and Abigail is marriage (vv. 39b–42). Two godly people (and two handsome people) are brought together by the Lord. For David this marriage is also a union that brings him political advantage. Abigail is from a prominent Calebite family. In marrying Abigail, David becomes allied to a woman of stature socially. The capital of the Calebite territory is Hebron, eight miles to the north, and it is in Hebron, after Saul's death, that David is formally anointed king over the house of Judah (2 Samuel 2:2–4). Abigail loses a wicked and foolish husband and in his place receives the future king in marriage.

Abigail is a woman of beauty, humility, wisdom, courage, and faith. She saves the lives of her household. She keeps David free from the guilt of shedding innocent blood and becomes the wife of the future king.

Some might see her actions as political—she chooses the right side in the struggle for the kingship (whereas the foolish Nabal chooses the wrong side). But there is more than political pragmatism in this story. Abigail's words show a deep understanding of the Word of God and of his Law—they show the wisdom of a heart instructed by faith.

SUGGESTED READINGS AND QUESTIONS

1. As you reflect on this story, do you find Abigail's words about her husband a betrayal, an example of dishonor, or an expression of inappropriate disrespect? If you have been taught to think this way and are still struggling with whether her behavior is appropriate, why do you imagine that in the text there is no hint of criticism of her words about Nabal? Notice at the very least, if you still find what she said problematic, that her words and actions saved the lives of many people, including Nabal (though very temporarily in his case!).

2. Her preparedness to go against her husband teaches us that human authority is never absolute (as does the example of the servant). In what other biblical examples do we see people going against human authority?

3. Scripture teaches us that only God's authority is absolute. What do you see to be the limits of human authority according to Scripture?

4. When in your life has it been necessary to go against someone in authority over you in order that you might do what is wise, just, and right before God?

5. What do you see as Abigail's most admirable characteristics? Make a list. In what ways would you like to be more like Abigail?

6. In what ways do you think that Abigail shows herself to be like the noble woman of Proverbs 31?

7. Is self-vindication ever appropriate? When is it right to wait for the Lord to vindicate our cause, to wait for him to take vengeance on those we perceive to be our enemies?

8. What is the appropriate way for us to seek justice within this world when we are wronged by someone? When is it right for us to seek justice in this way in addition to asking the Lord to intervene?

9. Read for our next chapter the story of Tamar in 2 Samuel 13. (If you want to read another terrible story of violation as well, read Genesis 34 also, the story of Dinah.) What are your reactions to the account of Amnon's sin against Tamar, and to Absalom's response to Amnon's sin? What is God teaching us in this account?

12

TAMAR:
A Woman of Tragedy

2 SAMUEL 13:1–39

Our last chapter brought us to a juncture in David's life when he had been anointed by Samuel as king but had not yet been crowned. In addition to his not being able to formally ascend the throne, David was not yet popularly recognized as king. He was living on the move with his band of men, in perpetual flight from Saul, and yet even during this difficult time he was trying to fulfill his responsibility to protect his people from their enemies. David was already seeking to serve God by defending the people of Israel, people who would one day be his subjects.

The heroine of our previous study was Abigail, a woman of faith, a woman of wisdom, a woman of beauty, and also a woman of tremendous courage as she confronted David. Abigail saved the lives of her household through her quick action; she kept David free from the guilt of shedding innocent blood; and she made such an impression on the future king that she later became his wife.

We are right to see her actions as political—she chose the right side in the struggle for the kingship, whereas the foolish Nabal chose the wrong side. She had clearly been listening to the prophet Samuel. But there was far more than political motivation involved in her choice. Abigail's words to David reveal a deep understanding of the Law of God, and they also reveal the wisdom of a heart of faith.

At the end of our study we saw David and Abigail married, and David later crowned as the King of the Israelites in Abigail's Calebite city of Hebron. In marrying Abigail, he had allied himself with a powerful family from that part of the southern kingdom of Judah. We now move on to a later stage in the life of David and his family.

THE HISTORICAL SETTING

The events recounted in this present chapter are set more than twenty years later than David's encounter with Abigail. Saul has been long dead. David is now reigning as the undisputed king, and his kingdom is expanding far beyond its borders under Saul. With the blessing of God David fights and wins battle after battle against the enemies of Israel. For the first time we see God fulfilling his promise, a promise made many centuries earlier, that he would give the whole of the land of Palestine to his people.

This issue of the proper size of Israel's territory is, of course, an interesting question in its own right. It is certainly true that God promised Israel a geographical area that extends far into present-day Lebanon and Syria as well as including the Palestinian territories. But does that mean that Israel at every point in the history of the nation has the right to dispossess those living on the land and to claim that the land properly belongs to the people of Israel because the Lord promised it to them? The answer to this question is certainly no, for it is quite clear in Scripture that the possession of the land promised by God is conditional on Israel having true faith in the Lord and living in obedience to his commandments. Possession of the land is a gift of God, not an inalienable right for the nation of Israel. This is true for all people, of course, in any nation anywhere in the world. We are God's tenants on this earth with no absolute right of ownership. At the present time only a tiny minority of the population of Israel has true biblical faith, the great majority of the people being thoroughly secular in their outlook. In fact, Israel is one of the most secular countries in the world at the present time. It vies with France for that dubious honor.

But in the time of David's kingship we see the kingdom of Israel growing, for God gives David victory on every side. This territorial expansion continues through the reign of David and then into the reign of Solomon, his son. It is during Solomon's lifetime that the kingdom reaches its furthest extent as a result of the favor and protection of God.

However, despite the favor of God upon David and despite the deep reality of David's faith in God and his love for God, we are constantly shown another side of David. He is presented to us in the biblical text as a man of weakness and sin, and it is basic to our understanding of David's relationship with God, and of our own relationship with God, that we recognize this reality of David's and our own moral flaws.

All of us find David's psalms tremendously encouraging and comforting. We recognize in David a kindred spirit. In the Psalms we see the portrait of someone who dearly loves the Lord, someone who knows God's blessing, someone who repeatedly struggles with sin and unbelief, someone who experiences the chastening and painful discipline of his heavenly Father, and yet someone who is forgiven by God's redeeming love over and over again. When we read David's psalms, we see into the heart of a true believer—a believer just like ourselves, one who is in constant need of the grace and mercy of God.

There are no plaster saints in the Bible. There are no ideal believers with perfect, unflawed faces and lives. There are no sentimental heroes and heroines, men and women who make us feel ill when we read about them because we know that the story is a lie, a story about unreal people, people with whom we will never be able to identify.

Preachers and teachers of the Bible often make the mistake of presenting only those parts of the lives of the heroes and heroines of the faith that show their strengths and goodness. They seem to ignore those parts of their lives that show their weaknesses and sin. Consequently such Bible lessons can be very discouraging, for we hear about people with whom we have little in common.

The Scripture itself, however, never glosses over the failures of

God's people. Rather, right alongside the stories of faith, righteousness, courage, and faithfulness, we read episodes of weak faith and impoverished obedience, for Scripture presents these stories with complete openness. Think of some of the examples we have already studied in this book—for example, Abraham, Sarah, and Tamar (Judah's daughter-in-law).

As we read the life of David, we learn very quickly that David had failures that were apparent in every part of his life. Despite this, David is presented to us as a friend of God, "a man after [God's] own heart" (1 Samuel 13:14), for the grace of God to a sinner like you and me, and like David, is at the heart of David's story. Just as God can say that he is proud to be called the God of David or Eve or Sarah or Abraham, so it is with you and with me.[1] This is possible because the whole story of the Bible is a story of God's unmerited love for deeply sinful individuals.

In imitation of this candid presentation of the sinfulness of the heroes and heroines of the faith that we find in Scripture, Christians should be always ready to acknowledge the failings of God's people, so that the theme of God's grace and faithfulness becomes the central theme in the stories that we tell. This is to be true if we are speaking about the failures and weaknesses of God's people in the past of our own nations and our own church's heritage and also to be true when we acknowledge the failures and weaknesses of God's people in the present. This is even more so when we turn to ourselves. Our calling, when we reflect on our own personal lives, is for "judgment to begin at the household of God" (1 Peter 4:17) rather than imagining that we are to devote ourselves to criticizing the unbelievers around us.

Second Samuel 13 is an illustration of this principle of openness about sin among God's people. The section of Scripture that comes immediately before the story we are considering in this study is an example of this openness of Scripture. Second Samuel 11 gives the account of David's devious plan to commit adultery with Bathsheba and his carrying out that plan. It tells of David's purposeful and callous abandonment of a godly man, Uriah, to the enemy so that Uriah is left without military support and is quickly killed. And the next chapter contains the words of judgment brought from God to David by the prophet Nathan: "Now therefore the sword shall never depart from your house, because you have despised me and have taken the wife of Uriah the Hittite to be your wife" (12:10). The story that we are about to reflect on is one sad part of the fulfillment of that prophecy.

THE CONTEXT OF OUR STORY

In the account of his adultery with Bathsheba, David shows himself to be a man who is undisciplined in the area of his sexuality. He copies the kings of the nations around him by multiplying wives, a sign to them of political strength, warrior virility, kingly power, and stature (2 Samuel 3:1–5; 5:13–16). At that time, one of the marks of a great king was that he had many wives. Some of these royal marriages were primarily political alliances. For example, in David's case Ahinoam, the mother of Absalom and Tamar, is herself the daughter of a king, the king of Geshur, a small nation beyond Gilead to the northeast, between Israel and Syria. We saw how David's marriage with Abigail also had a political element to it.

This, of course, is not to excuse polygamy. Rather we learn by this example how readily believers in Israel were influenced by the customs and lifestyle of the peoples around them. It was not just the king who copied the behavior of other kings. The people desired a king who was like the kings of the other nations, for they thought this was the way to become a great nation. So, as God had foretold, they were governed by kings who took their land to expand their property, took their horses and sons to strengthen their armies, took their money to give themselves a pleasant life, and took their daughters to increase the number of their wives and concubines. The people of Israel got the kind of king they desired when they insisted on being like the other nations.

The text of Scripture teaches us how this imitation of the polygamous practice of the neighboring nations works its destructive consequences out in the lives of God's people. We have seen this already in the story of Sarah and in the story of Hannah. We will see some of those consequences in this chapter as well. Polygamy is not what God intended for the human race, and whenever it is practiced, it has disastrous results. This is true with what we might call traditional polygamy, when a man has several wives at once as did David, or with the serial polygamy practiced in our own time when a man has several wives (or women to whom he is not married) one after another.

David is presented to us as a father who is himself a sinner in his sexuality. Indeed, he is a father who commits grievous wrongs, particularly in his affair with Bathsheba. What kind of an example of sexual chastity and fidelity could he be to his sons? We also learn that David fathers sons by different wives. Each of these wives is, of course, jealous of the others and is, quite understandably, ambitious for her son's place in the royal dynasty.

The sons appear to have been raised by their mothers with little fatherly input from David. David is presented to us as indulgent toward his sons and as a father who fails to discipline them when discipline is needed. In this way David is rather like Eli at an earlier stage in Israel's history, for he also is a man who completely fails to exercise appropriate discipline over his sons (1 Samuel 3:13).

One of the further extensions of the destructive nature of polygamy is that the sons themselves will each be ambitious to succeed his father on the throne. Amnon is the eldest son, the heir to David's throne; he is the crown prince. Absalom is the second in line to the throne, a half-brother to Amnon and full brother to Tamar. Absalom is also presented to us as a man who has a strong personality. He is a more powerful individual than his elder brother. These personality differences and political ambitions are part of the background to the story.

THE RAPE OF TAMAR

The story of the rape is told swiftly, powerfully, and dramatically. The Hebrew words are clear and precise. Nothing is wasted. This is a dramatic account. To read it is like watching a well-made and shocking movie unfolding before our eyes (one many Christians might try to have banned). We have all seen or read accounts of such wicked behavior. There is, of course, not much that is new under the sun. Tamar is described as beautiful, but she is also presented as modest and chaste (vv. 1–2). Amnon is prevented from getting his way with her by her virtue, not simply by the fact of her separate living quarters. He can see no way of getting what he wants—sex with his half-sister.

Amnon becomes sick with lust for Tamar. He mistakes his lust for love, as men so often do (and sometimes women), but Amnon's passion is totally sensual, as the rest of the story makes absolutely clear. Amnon becomes so wretched, one of the marks of self-indulgent passion rather than of genuine love, that others observe his state. In particular his cousin Jonadab, a man who is shrewd but without any moral character whatsoever, notices that Amnon looks sick. To love another truly, in a self-sacrificing way, does not make people sick like this. While genuine love can bring deep passion, even passion that makes one faint, it is also true that genuine love desires the good of the other person even more than the satisfaction of sexual desire.

Jonadab asks what is making Amnon sick. We should notice just how shrewd Jonadab is. He would do well in politics today! He knows that Amnon is first in line for the throne, so he is eager to demonstrate his loyalty to Amnon, his concern for him, and his willingness to help him. Perhaps in his mind's eye Jonadab sees himself as the right-hand man to the future king. He asks, "Why are you so haggard morning after morning?" His question implies that it is inappropriate for a king's son to have such unsatisfied needs. Amnon falls into the trap and tells Jonadab of his illicit passion for Tamar. We should notice, too, how Amnon disguises to himself the sin of his passion by distancing himself from Tamar a little. She is not "my sister" but "my brother Absalom's sister" (v. 4).

Jonadab's response to Amnon's confession of his lust for his sister is to devise a clever plan. Amnon is to pretend to be truly ill and is to stay in bed, so that his father will come and visit him. Jonadab knows that David is an indulgent father and will grant anything Amnon asks as a favor for a sick son. This is the heir to the throne, so of course David will come to check on him. David duly comes and accedes to the request that Amnon's sister Tamar be sent for and that she be asked to prepare the sick man a favorite meal.

This account tells us how removed David is from understanding his own sons. If a shrewd observer can see the real problem of Amnon, as Jonadab does, a good father should know his son well enough to see through this ruse to the unsatisfied and uncontrolled passion that lies behind it. At the very least David should be asking penetrating questions such as "Why Tamar?" or "Why won't a meal made by your mother suffice?"

In obedience to her father, Tamar arrives. Amnon is probably reclining on a bed in the next room in a position from which he can watch her. She, with love and care for her brother, prepares the dish he requests. This all takes time, probably a couple of hours, for she kneads and bakes bread for him. Up to this point Tamar is never alone with Amnon. Servants are present. Once the food is prepared and is brought to him (perhaps by a servant), he pretends to be too sick to eat and orders the servants to leave a poor sick man alone. Then he begs Tamar to come and feed it to him herself.

When they are alone, he immediately grabs her to force her into his bed to have sex with him. Her words to him are remarkable, for they demonstrate faith, wisdom, and righteousness.

Tamar reveals herself to be a woman of faith and virtue. She appeals to Amnon as her brother that he should not do something so wicked. Such behavior, she argues, is not in any way tolerated by the Law that God has given to his people Israel. The Canaanites may do such things, she implies, but not us, not the people of God (v. 12). This is her first appeal.

Tamar then appeals to Amnon's sense of honor and to the respect that he ought to have for her as his sister and as a woman. She tells him that he is about to ruin her life. He is going to be king, but she will become a woman disgraced, unmarriageable, with no possibility of a future life, no possibility of a home of her own, no possibility of a family of her own. This wicked act will ruin her life completely (v. 13a).

She then appeals to his conscience and to his need, at the very least to be practical and to consider his own future. She asks him to reflect on how he will be perceived by the people. She warns him that he will be regarded as a "wicked fool" (NIV) by the people of Israel (like Nabal). How will he ever be accepted as a worthy king by the people if he can stoop so low and if he can be so wicked as to rape his own sister? (v. 13b)

Finally, seeing that he is not listening and that he will insist on having his way, *she begs him to ask the king for her hand in marriage* (v. 13c). Even though it is against the Law to marry a half-sister (Leviticus 18:9, 11), she knows there is precedent (Abraham had married his half-sister Sarah before the giving of the Law by Moses). She also knows that David is indulgent. She recognizes that marriage to Amnon would be better for them both than total disgrace.

We must assume that she hoped, too, that this suggestion might give her time to get away and give him time to think it all over at a less heated moment, to think about the lawlessness, the public disgrace, and the ruin of his own future and of her life that his sinful action would bring.

AMNON'S RESPONSE

Sadly, all her pleas have absolutely no impact on him at all. Amnon ignores her wisdom and her evident reluctance and distress, and he violently rapes her (v. 14). Now the text takes a remarkable turn. We are told that immediately after he has finished raping her, he hates her; his hatred for her is even stronger than his earlier passionate longing (v. 15). We should not be surprised by his immediate revulsion. It demonstrates the total absence of genuine love for her; instead of abiding love, honor, and respect, there is simply sexual passion and nothing more.

We see this sequence of reaction whenever rape is followed by further violence and even by murder—the man who rapes has no love, respect, or care for the woman. After his lust is satisfied, she is just an object to be discarded. We see this same pattern in incest, when sexual passion is followed by the rejection and despising of the child. A father who molests his child often treats the child abominably at other times, hating her and blaming her. We see the same pattern in wife abuse, where there is both rapacious sexual demand and often, at the same time or shortly afterward, violent physical mistreatment of the wife. We are all aware of this kind of practical reality. If Amnon is a man with any conscience at all, we can be sure that his revulsion is compounded by guilt and self-loathing.

AFTER THE RAPE

Tamar is again presented as a woman of extraordinary strength of character when we listen to what she has to say to her brother, even in the immediate aftermath of being so horribly abused by him.

She begs Amnon not to cast her out. She still hopes she can prevail upon his sense of honor and his sense of the need for both of them to avoid public dishonor and disgrace. She begs him to let her stay and to request that they be married, to save both her name and his (v. 16). We can be sure that she had no desire to marry him, but that would have been less shameful than the prospect that awaited them otherwise.

Amnon ignores her distress completely. He summons a servant (thus making the affair public) and has him drive "this woman" away and bolt the door against her (v. 17). He no longer calls her his sister. He demonstrates himself to be a man with no compassion, no sense, no justice, and no honor. He is a self-indulgent, thoroughly heartless, and cruel man. Imagine the gossip that would have spread about him from the servants!

Tamar, driven out, tears her virgin's robe, covers her head with ashes, and leaves, lamenting her destroyed life. She has become a public spectacle of a woman whose life is ruined.

THE CONSEQUENCES

David is furious, but anger is no substitute for action. The Law requires the death penalty for Amnon (Leviticus 20:17), but what is David to do? David had himself sinned grievously with Bathsheba; so it is hard for him to act now without publicly condemning his own sins. In addition he has been an overly indulgent father in the past, so how is he suddenly to change? He also loves Amnon, and Amnon is his eldest son. So David does nothing to discipline or even rebuke his son—he is merely angry.

A Woman of Tragedy

Absalom, however, has other plans. His words to Tamar show little
sympathy for her plight (v. 20). They are, to say the least, somewhat
superficial, not at all the right words to try to comfort her broken
heart and give some solace to her ruined life. But in his heart he
plans revenge. Absalom now has a double motive for getting rid
of Amnon as he silently nurses his hatred for two years, during
which time he speaks not a word to Amnon. The first motive is that
Absalom wants revenge for his sister Tamar's disgrace. His second
motive is power for himself: he now has a reason to kill his main
rival to the throne.

Our story tells us how he accomplished this. When open passions seem to have died down and Tamar's disgrace is not so much
in the forefront, Absalom has Amnon and the rest of David's sons
invited to a feast at the time of the sheepshearing. Once more we
see David's lack of knowledge of his own sons, and we see his lack
of fatherly oversight. Once Amnon is somewhat drunk, Absalom
has his servants kill Amnon during the feast. Absalom is presented
to us as a man filled with vengeful thoughts, ambitious schemes,
bitterness, and above all inordinate self-love. Absalom's ambition
and self-love will lead, in due course, to armed rebellion against
David his father and will lead ultimately to his own death.

We see Nathan's prophecy coming true in David's own lifetime. David
lives to see his sins working themselves out in the lives of his children and in his own life. This raises a difficult problem: do these
painful events of David's later years mean that God simply judges
and abandons David?

We are told with crystal clarity, both in the book of Samuel and
also in the Psalms, that God forgives David's sin. In the same way,
God forgives our sins, but this does not mean that the consequences
of our sins will disappear in this life. There are two different issues
here. One is the forgiveness and mercy of God; the other is the consequences of sin. David is indeed fully forgiven, made completely
righteous, and saved to the uttermost. But David has to live with
the consequences of his adultery with Bathsheba, with the consequences of his polygamous marriages, with the consequences of his
indulgence toward his sons. He is forgiven for these sins, but he

has to endure the results of his lack of self-discipline, and he has to endure the results of his failure to discipline his sons.

Our histories are significant. Our choices and actions, and our failures to act, have real results in the histories of our lives and in the lives of others. God forgives David completely. God forgives us completely. You and I will meet David one day, and he will be a man totally forgiven, just as you and I will be totally forgiven by Christ. However, David had to live with the shocking and distressing results of his choices—in his own life and in his daughter's life—and it is the same with us.

We want to know what happens to Tamar. *She is the only character in this account who comes out of this terrible story with her virtue, her strength of character, and her wisdom intact.* But even though she is presented to us as a woman of faith, modesty, and dignity, her story is also one of absolute desolation in this life. This sad reality is true for many around us today. This story of a ruined life shows the reality of a broken world. There are people like Tamar whose stories are thoroughly miserable, people whose lives are made desolate by the sins of others. That is how the text sums up her life: "a desolate woman" (v. 20).

There are tears in some of our lives for which there will be no resolution until the coming of the kingdom of God; there is mourning for which there is no end here; there is pain for which there is no true respite now. And that is why the book of Revelation expresses God's Word to us as it does in 21:2–5.

> And I saw the holy city, new Jerusalem, coming down out of heaven from God, prepared as a bride adorned for her husband. And I heard a loud voice from the throne saying, "Behold, the dwelling place of God is with man. He will dwell with them, and they will be his people, and God himself will be with them as their God. He will wipe away every tear from their eyes, and death shall be no more, neither shall there be mourning, nor crying, nor pain anymore, for the former things have passed away." And he who was seated on the throne said, "Behold, I am making all things new." Also he said, "Write this down, for these words are trustworthy and true."

This is Tamar—a woman of virtue and dignity—a woman whose tears would not be wiped away until she stood in the presence of Christ; Tamar, a woman of virtue and dignity, yet a woman with a life of absolute desolation and disgrace; Tamar, a woman who will be loved and honored forever in the kingdom of God; Tamar, a woman whom we will meet with her head held high and with her modesty, her wisdom, and her righteousness secure for eternity.

SUGGESTED READINGS AND QUESTIONS

1. Do you personally know women who have had to suffer the kind of indignity and shame that Tamar endured?

2. What lessons can you take from this story to be of any help to a woman who might face or who has faced the violence of a man like Amnon?

3. Are there any words or deeds of comfort that you think you would be able to provide for a woman who has been raped or abused?

4. Do you think there are other kinds of sorrow that are as inconsolable as the particular kind of sorrow that Tamar experienced?

5. Do you struggle with accepting the idea that God forgave David for such serious sins?

6. Do you understand the difference between the forgiveness of sins—for example, David being forgiven his adultery or his polygamy—and David having to live with the consequences of those sins in this life?

7. Are there sins in your life for which you know have been forgiven but you recognize that you still have to live with the consequences of what you have done in the past, consequences that affect not only you but also others, including perhaps your children?

8. Are there questions, doubts, and struggles that you have because of tragedies like Tamar's?

13

TAMAR'S QUESTION:
A Meditation on Tragedy

2 CORINTHIANS 1:3-5

O ur recounting of the story of Tamar brings into every sensitive heart and inquiring mind a troubling question. It is the question that is most frequently asked of us by unbelievers and also by fellow believers. It is a question with which we find the psalmist wrestling and also the prophet Jeremiah.[1]

The question is this, and after this past chapter it is perhaps appropriate to call it Tamar's question: how can we believe in a good God given the brokenness of this world, given the terrible reality of the sorrow we meet in people's lives? Whenever I speak publicly about the abuse of women, it is my estimation that about 10 percent of the women present come afterward to talk to me (or to someone else who is responsible for the conference or particular ministry setting) about the violence, either physical or emotional, that they have suffered. Some recount how they have had to endure such abuse not just once in their lives but repeatedly—from fathers, stepfathers, boyfriends, husbands, brothers, uncles, or others who are part of their immediate or extended family. In the news media when we hear about rape, most often a woman is raped by a stranger; but in daily life it is far more common for rape or other physical, sexual, or emotional abuse to take place in the context of the home, just as with Tamar.

This proportion of 10 percent is, of course, my approximation, not the result of careful research, though if one looks at the scientific research on this issue it may well be that 10 percent is in fact on the low side.[2] However, this personal experience is like a window into the dark interiors of homes, a window that reveals the reality of widespread suffering.

The common existence of such misery and sorrow also reminds us how necessary it is for the church to address issues of abuse in an open, clear, loving, and compassionate way so that women will be free to talk about it without expecting rejection or ridicule and without the fear of being misunderstood or ignored. The first time I preached on the subject of Tamar's rape, women in their seventies and eighties who had never before spoken to anyone about the abuse they had endured, some of them sixty or seventy years earlier, felt free for the first time in their lives to talk about their suffering, shed tears, and seek help. Openness and the freedom to begin to talk about such deep hurts make possible the beginning of healing for the wounded heart. Openly dealing with such issues also enables men who have been abusers to begin to open up about their terrible secrets and to seek support to help them stop such shocking treatment of a wife, sister, or daughter.

If pastors and others in teaching and leadership positions do not speak about such pain and abuse openly, it is probable that victims will never come forward to express their hurt, because they do not sense the freedom to be able to make known what has taken place in their lives. I have discussed this issue with pastors who say that no one in their churches has ever been raped or abused or violently treated. But if I ask whether they have ever made it clear that they are aware of such problems and that they have a heart of compassion for those so wounded, the reply is invariably that they have never addressed such a subject. Until these dark places are brought into the light there can be very little healing or solace.

What kind of answers can we give when people share the pain of terrible suffering and tragedy? Here are a few suggestions from the Scriptures, given with the hope that they will be of some assistance to those who seek to offer comfort to the victims of such tragedies as that endured by Tamar.

God himself is not the author of such evil acts as Amnon's rape of Tamar. Rather, the Scripture teaches us that God hates every abominable act, such as the rape of one's sister.

Indeed God hates all wicked behavior, first, because it is a negation of his own holy character; second, because it is a violation of our human calling to live as those designed to reflect his image and righteousness; and third, because it is a denial, a distortion, a perversion of all that is good that God has made. God does not cause men to rape their sisters, nor does God tempt his human creatures with evil. God's sovereignty must not be understood to mean that God is behind such evil acts and that he is in any sense their cause. Hear what Scripture says about such a wicked slander on the character of God:

> Let no one say when he is tempted, "I am being tempted by God," for God cannot be tempted with evil, and he himself tempts no one. But each person is tempted when he is lured and enticed by his own desire. Then desire when it has conceived gives birth to sin, and sin when it is fully grown brings forth death. (James 1:13–15)

Evil arises within the human heart, a heart led astray by itself, without any urging from God. It is, in fact, evil to accuse God of being the one who is the author of rape, abuse, brutality, and violence to women. To charge the Lord God with responsibility for such acts is blasphemy.

We have to see that for us to acknowledge that this is a fallen and broken world, an abnormal world rather than a normal world, is a comforting truth.

Most religions and philosophies in this world regard life as it is now as normal. Things are now the way they have always been, it is claimed. Nothing ever really changes or has changed at any point in the past; nor will there be any real change in the future, except perhaps for the death of all things with the end of our solar system.

Christianity does not agree with this understanding of the world. The Bible teaches us that this is an abnormal world, a world that is twisted and confused and gone awry from the way God made it to be. This world of violence and suffering is *not* the way that life has to be—it is not a necessity of creation. This world of violence and suffering is not the way it was meant to be by God. This means that we can look at evil in its wicked face, call it by its name, and resist it.

As a consequence we do not have to pretend that such behavior as the rape of Tamar is good from some perspective, that if we turn it to the light in just the right way we will be able to say, "Now I see it! When we look carefully enough, we see that the violence Tamar suffers actually works out for the best. This rape is a spiritual lesson, intended for Tamar's long-term benefit."

We are to say no such thing. Rather we are to say that rape is inherently evil. There is nothing good, no matter how we look at it, about such an act of violence and wickedness toward a man's sister or his wife or his daughter. This is a comforting truth. I do not have to look at examples of human wickedness and pretend that they are somehow good.

God not only hates evil behavior, he also has compassion on the one who is broken in spirit, the brokenhearted.

God who is "the Father of mercies and God of all comfort" (2 Corinthians 1:3) is full of tenderness toward those who are subject to violation, such as the victims of rape. God longs to bring his healing hand into the life of every Tamar in this world. He desires to

> *comfort all who mourn;*
> *to grant to those who mourn in Zion—*
> *to give them a beautiful headdress instead of ashes,*
> *the oil of gladness instead of mourning,*
> *the garment of praise instead of a faint spirit. (Isaiah 61:2–3)*

The very heart of the Christian gospel is that Christ came into the world to heal the bruised reed and the broken spirit, for he is humble and gentle in heart.

This is how the prophet Isaiah pictures the coming of the

Messiah (Isaiah 42:3). Christ is tender and kind to those who are crushed by the tragedies of life, for he is the revelation of the compassionate heart of God, the God who reveals himself as having a particular care for widows, orphans, aliens, and the poor (which is why we are given a whole book in Scripture about Naomi and Ruth). The Lord describes himself, through Moses, in these words: "He executes justice for the fatherless and the widow, and loves the sojourner, giving him food and clothing" (Deuteronomy 10:18). The apostle James applies this characteristic of God to us, his people: "Religion that is pure and undefiled before God, the Father, is this: to visit orphans and widows in their affliction" (James 1:27).

So it should not surprise us when we read through the Gospels and see Christ, all through his ministry, delighting in reaching out to women and men with damaged lives. One of the repeated themes of the Gospels is: "Jesus, filled with compassion, reached out to heal." When we see Christ responding to the wounded person, we are seeing into the heart of God. This is still the delight of Jesus Christ, for he is the same yesterday, today, and forever. He cares for, and he asks those who trust in him to care for, the Tamars of this world.

One day Christ will return to wipe away every tear from eyes that can never quite overcome their weeping in this present dark time.

This wiping away of our tears will take place for each individual either when we die or when Jesus comes again, if that comes first. We all recognize that some wounds are so deep that while there may be partial healing in this life and a measure of comfort, yet our tears will never be fully wiped away in this life.

But the time is coming when our tears will be gone and our sorrow will turn to joy. How can we be sure that such a day is coming? Christ's resurrection is the pledge to us of his absolutely sure promise that he will make all things new. He has been raised from the dead to destroy all the works of the evil one, to set everything right. This old order of things, this time in which there is rape, brutality, violence, and abuse, will pass away forever.

In the meantime, *Christ does indeed come to us to comfort and encourage us by his Spirit and brings us the hope of a better world to come.*

Jesus promised that even though he was leaving his disciples, he would not leave them (or us) as orphans. Rather, he sends the Comforter, the Holy Spirit, to be our friend and helper, to apply the love and hope of the gospel to our hearts. The Spirit is the firstfruits and the guarantee of the better world that is coming, a future in which there will be no more death, no more mourning, no more crying, no more pain. We live in hope, poured into our hearts by the Spirit, that the very real troubles of this present time will be overwhelmed by an eternal glory that will far outweigh them all.

In the meantime, *the Lord calls us to comfort one another with the comfort we have received from him.*

He calls us to weep when we see someone weeping. He calls us to come alongside and be a friend to the one who is hurting. Of course, there are times when he calls us to bring to the wounded words of understanding and encouragement. But there are also times when we are called to bring only ourselves without any words.

Christ calls us to be present to help and to serve in some practical way, to follow the example he set when he washed his disciples' feet. Whenever we see someone suffering deeply, we need to ask ourselves the question, how may I help this individual who is hurting? What can I do to ease the burden that weighs this person down? And we need to pray for the discernment of the Spirit to answer the questions appropriately. We also need to learn to be comfortable with having nothing to say, because sometimes the words we utter may be sincere attempts to heal wounds, but we end up "heal[ing] the wound . . . lightly, saying, 'Peace, peace,' when there is no peace" (Jeremiah 6:14).

Paul, writing about his own experience of losing hope, tells us that he was so utterly, unbearably crushed that he despaired of life itself; in his heart he felt the sentence of death (2 Corinthians 1:8–9). He adds later, "God, who comforts the downcast, comforted us by the coming of Titus" (2 Corinthians 7:6).

These very strong words of Paul about his own suffering are an encouragement to us. They teach us that God is pleased when we express our sense of complete desolation to him. They teach us that it is not unspiritual to tell the Lord, or to tell one another, that we are so overwhelmed with the burdens of life that we are in utter despair. There will be many times in the lives of the Tamars of this world when a person so wounded will be in overwhelming misery, and we need to let people know that it is right and proper and, yes, truly godly and spiritual to feel like this and to share such sorrows honestly. Of course, these words also teach us that we are to be eager to be God's means of comfort to the wounded, whether with words or without them. This is the gospel of Christ.

SUGGESTED READINGS AND QUESTIONS

1. In your church has there been open teaching about subjects such as rape, incest, domestic violence, and other forms of abuse?

2. Do you recognize that there are times when it is better not to try to bring words of comfort because anything you say may merely be adding insult to injury?

3. What are some of the practical things you might choose to do to be a comfort by your presence and by your acts of kindness to a person who has just been bereaved or who has experienced rape or some other form of personal violation or violence?

4. As you reflect on the points made in this past chapter about the comfort of Christian truth in the face of suffering, which points of truth are most helpful to you at the present time?

5. Do you find it encouraging that the Scriptures are so honest about the deep pain of God's people, and have you found that this gives you the freedom to express your own sorrows to the Lord without feeling guilty or unspiritual about the anguish you try to express?

6. Read for our next chapter the entire book of Esther.

14

ESTHER:
Such a Time as This

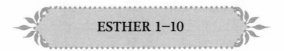

ESTHER 1–10

In several of our chapters we have studied the lives of women who lived in difficult times. This was true of Rahab who in a time of war forsook her people to identify with the Israelite spies and to cast her lot with the people of God. This was true of Deborah, a woman of great courage, a military and political leader in a time when Israel was subject to oppression by ruthless enemies. This was true of Ruth who lived in a time of widespread apostasy and refusal to obey God's commandments. Yet Ruth gladly chose to follow her mother-in-law, to leave her own people and tie herself to the one true God regardless of the consequences. This was true of Hannah who also lived in a time of widespread lawlessness but who herself was a woman devoted to the Lord.

We see in the stories of these women how God is always at work, reaching into the history of his people. God raises up women such as Rahab, Deborah, Ruth, or Hannah to meet his people's needs, to deliver them in times of trouble, or to be an example to them of fidelity, righteousness, and self-sacrifice.

These stories teach us that ultimately no enemy will come against God's people that will be victorious. The enemy may be the Devil himself. The enemy may be a nation bent on destroying the people of God. The enemy may be the faithlessness of Israel to the Lord. The enemy may be deep disobedience to God's commandments by the very nation that has promised to devote itself to walking in his ways. In such terrible times the personal happiness of those who love the Lord may be ruined in this life. This was true for the prophet Jeremiah, and it was certainly true for Tamar. But it is also true that God will never forsake his people. Rather, he commits himself to them, promising to be their God both in this life and forever.

For our reflections in this present chapter we turn to another time of trouble in the lives of God's people, the time of Esther. We move several hundred years forward to the early part of the fifth century before Christ. We will begin with a brief look at the historical moment in which Esther was living. She was a Jew in exile. Already more than two hundred years have passed since the time that the northern kingdom of Samaria (Israel) was destroyed by the Assyrians, its people taken captive and many of them transported to the far reaches of the Assyrian Empire. About a hundred years before the time of Esther the same fate has happened to the southern kingdom of Judah, this time at the hands of the Babylonian Empire.

So the historical setting of the book of Esther is that a great many of the people of both Israel and Judah are living far away from the land of Palestine. Both those scattered and those still in Palestine are subject to the domination of the great power of their day, the kingdom of Medo-Persia.

BACKGROUND AND HISTORY

Ahasuerus (Xerxes) was the ruler of the Medo-Persian Empire from 486–465 B.C., and it is during his reign that the story of Esther takes place. The book of Esther begins by setting down the extent of the kingdom of Ahasuerus. His empire stretches, as the text tells us, from Ethiopia to India (1:1). "Ethiopia" or "Cush" (NIV) is the name frequently used in the Bible to describe southern Egypt and northern Ethiopia on the east side of northern Africa. Ethiopia is the farthest to the southwest that the Persian kingdom extended. Ahasuerus' empire also included part of present-day Libya along the northern coast of Africa. Cyrene (known to us from the New Testament) is part of this area.[1]

If we use the contemporary names of countries, we can get some sense of the vast extent of the kingdom of Ahasuerus. In addition to its reaching into Africa, the Persian Empire also included all of present-day Turkey and swept westward into Greece and Bulgaria and northwestward up across Romania and into what is now the Ukraine. To its south it ruled over part of Saudi Arabia as well as Israel, Jordan, Syria, and Iraq. Northward from Turkey and Iraq it reached to Georgia, Armenia, Azerbaijan, and even into southern Russia. To the northeast the Persian armies had pushed the kingdom so far that it extended into Turkmenistan, Uzbekistan, Kazakhstan, and Tadzhikistan. Further east it reached across Afghanistan and Pakistan and into India.

This, then, was an enormous empire and, indeed, one of the greatest kingdoms the world has ever seen. At the center of this kingdom was Persia, present-day Iran. This is one of the powerful empires that we read about in the prophecies of the book of Daniel. The Medo-Persians had conquered the Babylonians and would eventually be conquered by the Greeks. (Some of the most famous battles in history took place between the Greeks and the Persians.)

As we meet people from Iran today (many have emigrated to the United States, Canada, Western Europe, and South America because of the political upheaval in Iran over the past three decades), it is important to remember the greatness of their past. Iranian people have a tremendous pride in their history, while most of us who come from America today have very little sense of history, and in particular almost no knowledge of the history of other parts of the world. Consequently we often have little understanding of the pride that other peoples have in their former glory. We take the glory of our own history as obvious, but we all need to learn to show respect for the glory of other people's histories.

In the time of the story of Esther, the kingdom of Medo-Persia is at its greatest extent and power. This sense of almost universal dominion comes through in the book repeatedly as we read of the laws that Ahasuerus passes. Ahasuerus has an easy sense of self-confidence. He thinks of himself as having universal dominion. He heads the superpower of that time. He knows he rules a vast empire; he knows he has supreme authority over this vast empire and over many of the peoples of the world. He assumes that others will think exactly as he does, for his command is the law.

Who wrote this book? We cannot give any confident answer to this question, for the author's identity is unknown to us. Because of the language used in the text (many words of Persian origin) and the authenticity that this lends to the account, it seems that the book was written shortly after the events it describes. Perhaps Esther herself wrote her story down for us. We will have to wait until we see her and then we can learn the answer to this and many other questions we may have.

Besides the impression of great power, the story also stresses the glory, splendor, and fabulous wealth of Persia. The book begins with Ahasuerus sending an invitation to all the rulers of the many provinces of his empire to come and be entertained by him in the capital city of Susa (which was also known as Elim). He entertains them for a hundred and eighty days, displaying the wealth and glory of his kingdom, and then ends the time with a banquet that lasts for seven days.

As in any great nation, the corridors of power in the Persian court are full of intrigue as courtiers struggle for status, and schemers vie for influence with the king. There are also the usual attempts to discredit others by lies, half-truths, and vicious scheming. This is not too different from what we see from time to time in Washington, London, Paris, Brasilia, or any other seat of government in this world. The use and abuse of power is a constant reality in political affairs. We even read in Esther of an assassination attempt on the life of the king (2:21–23), an attempt of which the Jew Mordecai becomes aware. He, in turn, informs Esther so that she can warn the king.

GOD'S PEOPLE

We read that this was a time of very serious danger for the Jewish people. As at every other period of their history, they have their enemies, here represented by and focused in the person of Haman, the most important official in Ahasuerus' court (the contemporary equivalent of a premier or prime minister). Haman is the leader of the attempt to discredit and ultimately to destroy the Jewish people, and he has carefully developed a scheme to accomplish this.

Against Haman stand two individuals—Mordecai, a stubborn and courageous Jew, and his cousin and adopted daughter Esther (and, there is of course a third and far more important, person—the unseen God). Mordecai and Esther are descended from Jews who were taken captive when Nebuchadnezzar, ruler of the Babylonian Empire, attacked and defeated Judah. This victory for the Babylonians and the accompanying exile took place during the reign of Jehoiachin in Judah (597 B.C.).

The ancestors of Mordecai and Esther would have been taken into captivity just over a hundred years before our present story begins. Others of Israeli descent had been in this part of the world already for well over two hundred years, for the northern tribes of Israel had been deported into this same area by the Assyrians. So there had been two dispersions of the Hebrews across this vast empire.

We will refer to these scattered remnants of both the northern kingdom of Israel and the southern kingdom of Judah by the name Jews as that is the name given to them in the text. At this particular time in history the Jews are not subject to continual persecution in the Persian Empire because of their worship of the Lord God of Israel. The religion of Persia at the time of Esther is Zoroastrianism, and among the great religions of the world this has been one of the more tolerant religions. Consequently, within the Medo-Persian Empire there is respect for diverse religious beliefs. The immediate setting for the story of Esther is an attempt by Haman to reverse this policy of religious toleration because of his personal hatred of the Jews and because of his desire to profit by stealing their wealth.

As we reflect on the events recorded in the book of Esther, it is important to remember that God does his work in particular moments of history, in actual times and places, not in ideal situations, for ideal situations never exist in this fallen world. In this story we read about real kingdoms and real people, and we read of many shocking things that are set down for us as a true account of what took place.

The book of Esther is not a Pollyanna tale in which, once the heroine of the story appears on the scene, nothing seriously objectionable or genuinely wicked takes place. Instead of such an unreal pretense we find ourselves caught up in a plainly told account of political intrigue and evil. We read how an enormously powerful and utterly ruthless ruler appointed officials, how he chose hundreds of women to fill his harem based on their beauty, how he selected his queens and cast them aside, how he made laws, how he gave some life and others death, and how he ruled with extraordinary authority over his vast and diverse empire. All this is simply reported in a matter-of-fact way.

Our text makes very little comment on the moral virtues or failings of this pattern of life or on the way that Ahasuerus ruled the Persian Empire. We may want to raise our voices in protest: "What appalling treatment of women! What cavalier disregard for the value of human life! Why is there no condemnation of such behavior?" But we need to remember that this brief historical account does not need to address these issues, for the book of Esther is written after almost all the rest of the Old Testament books. Scripture has already taught God's people what righteous and just rule is, what marriage ought to be like, and how wives are to be treated by their husbands. Many biblical texts address such issues. This is not one of them!

So rather than reading this book as a story of righteous rule or as an account of a happy and godly marriage, we are to read it to discern how God cares for his people in times of trouble. At this particular time, perhaps because of the enmity toward the Jews by men like Haman, not even God's name can be publicly mentioned, and we presume this is the reason why God is never referred to in the ten chapters of Esther.

At such a time, when it is dangerous for God's people even to utter God's name, his people discover the good news that his loving care for his people is not dependent upon believers shouting his name abroad. God is at work ruling history for those who love and serve him, even when they have to keep their faith hidden. He is the true ruler of this world and its kingdoms, though at first sight and on the surface it may seem that emperors have total control over the lives of nations and peoples and the individuals under their authority.

So we read the book of Esther to see the working out in history of the reign of the invisible yet almighty God. We also read this book to learn how God's people are to fulfill their obligations to him and to their fellow believers even in times of great danger to themselves.

This book teaches us that believers can serve God in the most difficult situations by being faithful to God and to each other. Christians today can be very naive when they say, "I couldn't possibly work in this government" or "There is no way a believer can work in this business." We make such statements because we think there is just too much unrighteousness in the world, so we have to retreat from it.

But if we are tempted to think this way, consider the examples that Scripture gives us. Ahab is wicked and weak, and Jezebel is wicked and utterly ruthless; yet Obadiah works for them as their right-hand man and faithfully serves the Lord as he does his work. Or we read about Daniel serving Nebuchadnezzar, a brutal tyrant who thinks of himself as having divine majesty and authority. In this study we read about Esther having to be faithful to God and to her people by becoming one of a vast number of concubines and then a favored member of a ruthless and self-centered emperor's harem and finally the queen of this great kingdom and the bride of its ruler.

The Scriptures are completely realistic about the difficulties we believers face as we live out our faith in a broken and sinful world, about the trials that come when we work and serve in a society that does not honor God. But Christians are never told to opt out, as if it is too hard for us to live in the world. The Bible teaches us that God's people can serve him and each other faithfully, even in times of great wickedness. Of course, there are particular challenges facing a believer in such a setting, as indeed there were many challenges facing Esther.

THE WOMAN ESTHER

The first thing we are told about Esther is that God has given her the gift of extraordinary physical beauty. Because of this gift she is raised up to a position that enables her to enter into the palace and to influence the counsels of the king. Most of us are not physically beautiful in this life, and we may presume that this is a consequence of the Fall. Indeed, in this sad world some suffer from some miserable deformity or physical disability and desperately need the comfort and hope that only the gospel can bring, for one day all these sorrows will be set right. They and the rest of us, whose lack of physical beauty makes us long to be different, are called to focus on the inner beauty of a quiet and gentle spirit.[2] Whatever our physical appearance now, one day we will all be beautiful when our bodies are made new. We will, each of us, be so glorious in appearance that, humanly speaking, others might be tempted to worship us.

But in Esther's case God gave Esther beauty in this life, that she might use this gift to his glory. The great athlete and missionary Eric Liddell said, "When I run, I feel God's pleasure."[3] In the same way the woman or man who has great physical beauty should see this gift as glorifying to God. Beauty can, of course, become an idol. Indeed, we only have to watch television or read accounts of the stars to encounter many examples of women and men for whom their beauty or good looks is a snare and a temptation to self-worship. However, like any other gift of God, great beauty does not have to be an idol, and it clearly is not an idol for Esther.

We must assume that Esther agrees to try out for a position as one of the king's concubines, as there seems to have been a kind of Miss Medo-Persia contest that great numbers of beautiful girls from all over the kingdom entered. Of course, unlike the Miss America or Miss World contests, the winner of Miss Medo-Persia does not simply win a monetary prize, a trip abroad, a college scholarship, or a year in the spotlight. When Esther is noticed as a great beauty, she is taken into the royal household under the care of the chief

eunuch. Harems such as the harem of Ahasuerus always had cas-
trated males in charge of the women. Once in the harem, Esther is
given special treatment for a year to enhance her beauty. Of course,
once Esther puts herself forward as a candidate for this beauty
contest she has no choice in the matter. To refuse to submit to the
beauty treatments might well have meant death for her and, at the
least, total public disgrace and humiliation.

When she is ready to "serve" the king, he finds her particularly
pleasing, and then, from among the great number of her fellow
concubines, she is chosen to be the queen. While this may seem
to be a great honor, being queen to such a man is not exactly an
enviable or secure position. The previous queen, Vashti, infuriated
the king when she refused to display her beauty before him while
he and his fellow revelers were thoroughly inebriated at the end of
his great feast and seven-day drinking party. As a consequence of
this disrespect for the king, Queen Vashti was summarily removed
from her royal throne. We are not told what else happened to her.
We are merely informed that the former queen's lack of respect for
the king led to her downfall and that Esther replaced her.

In addition to the gift of beauty, Esther also has the virtue of
respect for and obedience to her adoptive father Mordecai and a
humble willingness to be submissive to the king. Esther was an
orphan whom Mordecai had taken in and raised as his own child.
In return she shows him honor, submission, and obedience, both
through all the years of her youth and when she moves into the
royal household.

What is remarkable about Esther is this continued respect for
Mordecai even when obedience to him becomes more difficult for
her. Once in the king's favor, it would have been an obvious temptation to hope that she would escape from the troubles of the Jews if
she simply remained silent and didn't draw attention to herself by
speaking up on their behalf. But instead of thinking only of herself
and of her newfound status with its wealth and power, Esther continues to listen to her adoptive father and to obey his counsel.

We live in a time when being submissive and obedient is hardly
considered a virtue, whether it involves honor, submission, and

obedience in the home to our parents or in society to our presidents, governors, judges, senators, or congressional representatives or in some other setting to anyone in authority. However, the Scripture commands us to show such honor, submission, and obedience to all who are in authority over us.[4] We assume that only those who deserve our honor should receive it from us, but the New Testament Scriptures are referring to the Roman emperors when commanding believers to respect the one in authority. There is no question that the rule of Claudius and Nero, the Roman emperors at the time when Paul and Peter wrote their letters, were far worse than present or recent examples of political leadership in most of our countries.

Esther is an example of one who gladly obeys God's command to respect and obey both her parent and her ruler, though her ruler is Ahasuerus. She honors not only the office of King Ahasuerus but also the man who holds the office, despite his obvious idolatry and sin. She continues to honor him even when her people, the Jews, are in great danger because of the intrigues of their enemies. Esther is respectful to the king even at this time of trouble, and her respect is clearly not pretense. We see her submitting to him with grace and dignity rather than simply judging him because of his weaknesses and failures—though she is evidently acutely aware of these weaknesses and failures, for she knows how volatile and ruthless a man he is.

ESTHER'S TEST

What is the greatest test of Esther's respectful and submissive character? That test comes when Haman and the other enemies of the Jews have laid their plot with great care, and Mordecai appeals to Esther to intervene on behalf of her people. The key phrase in the book of Esther is, "who knows whether you have not come to the kingdom for such a time as this?" When Mordecai sends this message back to Esther, telling her that she is the one raised up by God for this time of trouble (4:12–14), she listens to him and obeys.

Esther is also a woman of remarkable patience and wisdom. She is prepared to plan her strategy of deliverance for her people with care. She is willing to wait for the right moment to make her plea to the king rather than responding the first time the king offers to do whatever she desires. Then when the time is right, she brings out her request. The king has so committed himself that when Esther finally does ask for a favor, he has very little alternative but to act upon her wishes. We need to learn from her example, waiting and praying for wisdom before we act.

Though the text does not say it explicitly, we should also see Esther as a woman of faith. We read that she and her maids devote themselves to three days of fasting (and, therefore, of prayer, 4:16). She trusts God when she must be full of fear for her own life as well as for the life of her fellow Jews. If we try to put ourselves in her situation, we can imagine that she is sleepless, anxious, and terrified. Like Abraham and Ruth, Esther is a believer who puts her trust in the Lord in an extraordinary situation. She knows that she is in constant danger of being swept aside with just a word from the king. She is at the mercy of his slightest whim, for he is a man whose anger is easily kindled and whose word, once uttered, is unalterable law.

Esther's faith enables her to be a woman of courage and of true loyalty to her people. It would, of course, be easy for her to forget her origin, now that she is in a position of honor. Yet she does not forget her fellow Jews and their plight. Instead she is prepared to identify herself with God's people and to risk rejection and death rather than to think only of herself.

If we want to try to recapture the pressure she is under, we should remember that a license to kill has been issued to all the enemies of the Jews. There is also a license to plunder the property of any Jew, and we may be sure that this law must have swelled the numbers of their enemies.

In France, Austria, and Germany during the time of the Holocaust, people denounced the Jews in the hope that they might profit from the confiscation of their property, for some were eager to take personal advantage of the laws against the Jews, even in situations when they were long-time neighbors. Human beings are so self-centered and greedy for gain that it takes great strength of character and moral virtue to refuse to take advantage of those who are discriminated against, especially when we have the opportunity to profit. The conscience is very easily silenced in such settings.

THE TURNING POINT

In Esther's case we find her coming out and identifying herself as a Jew before there are any laws to protect her. She prepares with great care, winning the king's favor and arousing his interest in what she wishes to say to him, but waiting and waiting for just the right moment. First she invites both the king and Haman to a feast, then does this again, and then finally she says to Ahasuerus, "If I have found favor in your sight, O king, and if it please the king, let my life be granted me for my wish, and my people for my request. For we have been sold, I and my people, to be destroyed, to be killed, and to be annihilated" (7:3–4).

Later, waiting once more for the appropriate time, when Ahasuerus holds out the golden scepter to her, granting her the privilege of speaking to him, she is even more explicit:

> "If it please the king, and if I have found favor in his sight, and if the thing seems right before the king, and I am pleasing in his eyes, let an order be written to revoke the letters devised by Haman the Agagite, the son of Hammedatha, which he wrote to destroy the Jews who are in all the provinces of the king. For how can I bear to see the calamity that is coming to my people? Or how can I bear to see the destruction of my kindred?" (8:4–6)

Esther reveals herself to be a woman of deep loyalty to her people, even though this involves great danger to herself. It is clear as we read this story that Haman is not the only enemy of the people of God. Her public exposure of her own Jewish identity puts her at great risk, but it is the turning point in the book. She takes her step with eyes that are fully open: "If I perish, I perish" (4:16).

Her stand of faith and courage is indeed the turning point, for God uses Esther to deliver his people from destruction. Esther then shows herself to be a woman who honors God for the victory that he brings. She does not ask for praise or glory for herself but rather she calls all of the Jews to celebrate a religious feast to give glory and thanks to God (9:20, 29–32). The Feast of Purim is sometimes called Esther's Decree and has been celebrated by the Jews ever since her day. The decree for that first Purim feast goes out across the vast Persian Empire and is a day for joy, honoring God, and giving gifts to the poor.

This inclusion of "gifts to the poor" (v. 22) is an aspect of that religious festival that believers need to think about today because this has been largely forgotten. A hundred years ago right across the western world one of the central parts of the celebration of Christmas was the giving of gifts to the poor. This element of charity in the celebration of Christmas was observed out of obedience to the Scriptures, for charity is commanded of God's people at every one of the great annual feasts.

Whenever the people of God stop their regular cycle of work to rejoice in God's goodness and generosity, they are required by his law to remember those who need their mercy and kindness.[5] In the Old Testament, every celebration, every feast, was a time to include the widow and the orphan, the poor and the alien. They were to be included so they too could rejoice in the kindness of the Lord.

For us today, Christmas, in particular, is the time when we give thanks to God for his giving his Son to us to meet our greatest need. Because of this, Christians in the past made a special effort to give gifts to those in need at Christmastime. This aspect of Christmas has largely been forgotten, for most of us see Christmas as a time to receive gifts ourselves and to give gifts to our immediate family, regardless of need. But perhaps we should begin to work at rebuilding this element of biblical feasting back into our celebration of Christmas, Easter, and Thanksgiving. We need to ask ourselves, are we celebrating God's goodness or have we turned celebrations, including Christian festivals, into times to celebrate the pursuit of happiness for the individual and for the family?

GOD'S DELIVERANCE

The heart of this story is the wonderful providence of God. He prepares Esther for "such a time as this" (4:14). The Lord is the one who gives the king a restless night and who puts on his heart the desire to read "the book of memorable deeds" (6:1–2). It is God who leads Ahasuerus to discover that it was Mordecai who had saved him from a plot to assassinate him and that Mordecai had not been honored or rewarded for this act of loyalty. It is God who leads Haman into imagining that he is going to be honored and into devising an extravagant public display of honor for himself but then discovering that he has to lead this extravagant public display to the honor of Mordecai, the very man he hates and whom he plans to destroy. It is God who turns the tables on Haman and who brings about a great increase in the fortune of the Jewish people.

God, not Haman, is the one who is sovereign over the casting of "lots" (see 9:24), the *pur*, the word from which the name of the Feast of Purim comes (v. 26). The meaning of Purim is that God is in control over what seem to us to be chance events, such as the casting of lots. This is the heart of the story of Esther. Men cast the lot, but God has determined the outcome. Haman casts the lot against God's people, but God rules against him, turning Haman's plans for a day of destruction of the Jews into the day of their deliverance.

This story is full of irony as it celebrates the way that God can turn the plans of the wicked against themselves, so that they initiate their own downfall. Everything is turned upside-down in the book of Esther. Haman devises a tribute to his own glory, but it is Mordecai who is honored. Haman wants to see Mordecai's career ruined and to see him put to death, but Haman finds himself helping honor Mordecai. Haman boasts that he is the only person invited to the queen's banquet along with the king, but it is at the banquet that his wickedness is exposed. Haman decides to throw himself on the mercy of Esther, but the king thinks he is molesting the queen. Haman erects a very tall gallows for the public hanging of Mordecai's body, so everyone will be able to see Mordecai's final humiliation; but it is Haman and his sons whose bodies are publicly displayed on those gallows. God's enemies figure out a brilliant plan to seize the wealth of the Jews, but instead they end up losing their own property to those they wanted to despoil.

Ahasuerus is the all-powerful king, making unalterable decrees from the throne of the Medo-Persian Empire, but all through the story we see that there is actually another King on the throne, overruling the affairs of this great empire and of the whole world, even though this other King's name is never mentioned anywhere in the book of Esther. That book is about the almighty King, the Lord God of heaven and earth. Because of his kingship, arbitrary and wicked decrees are turned into instruments of deliverance. God turns everything on its head.

This irony is at the heart of biblical revelation. Whatever plans God's enemies may have, those plans are turned against them. We see this irony supremely in the death of Jesus, for on the cross the schemes of God's greatest enemy, Satan, are turned against him to bring about his defeat. The second Psalm celebrates this irony:

> *The kings of the earth set themselves,*
> *and the rulers take counsel together,*
> *against the LORD and against his Anointed, saying,*
> *"Let us burst their bonds apart*
> *and cast away their cords from us."*
> *He who sits in the heavens laughs;*
> *the Lord holds them in derision.*
> *Then he will speak to them in his wrath,*
> *and terrify them in his fury, saying,*
> *"As for me, I have set my King*
> *on Zion, my holy hill." (vv. 2–6)*

No matter how the rulers of this world scheme, no matter how Satan, the one who stands behind all wicked plans in this world, rages against the Lord, God will bring about his purposes of salvation. He will deliver those he loves. This is the story of the gospel of Christ. This is also the story of the book of Esther. This great irony of human history is the theme of Esther's story.

Another message in the book of Esther is related to this theme of God's saving purposes: even in times of great trouble and persecution, God's kingdom grows. The enemies of God's people plan to decimate them. But the outcome of the casting of the dice is that instead of reducing or destroying the people of God, the *pur*, the lot, brings people from all the nations in the empire to their number and to the worship of the one true God (8:17). Many people are joined to the people of God as a result of this attempt to rid the world of them. Again, this is the theme of the gospel itself. Jesus said that his death would bring life to others. Out of apparent defeat and in the face of death, God gives the gift of eternal life to people from every nation.

This beautiful irony is repeated over and over in history, and it is true in our own time. I remember an Iranian (a Persian) speaking in our seminary chapel a couple of years ago. He was himself a converted Moslem. He said to us all, "The greatest prophet for the kingdom of God in the history of Iran is the Ayatollah Khomeini." This seems like an absurd statement at first hearing, for everyone knows that Khomeini was the leader of the Fundamentalist Islamic Revolution in Iran. However, this young Persian went on to say, "When Khomeini came to power there were thirty thousand Christians in Iran. Today there are more than three hundred and fifty thousand." His point was that great numbers of thoughtful Moslems were so appalled by the excesses of the Islamic Fundamentalism that Khomeini introduced that they became open to the Christian gospel. The enemies of Christ, in our day or in Esther's day, have their plans turned upside-down by the Lord. He will build his kingdom.

SUMMING UP

Esther's story is a story of courage, wisdom, and faith. Esther is an example to us of how we may serve God even in the darkest times and in the most difficult circumstances. God's people may find themselves surrounded by unbelievers and even by great wickedness and cruelty. They may find themselves called to serve men who are not only powerful but are also brutal and tyrannical. They may have to serve men like Ahasuerus whose word was absolute law over his great empire.

But despite such an unpropitious and troubling place of service, it is possible to honor God in one's words and actions. Esther responds to her seemingly impossible situation with practical wisdom, courage, and above all trust in the Lord who rules history for his followers. In the face of what seems to be insurmountable odds God brings about a remarkable deliverance for his people. He so turns the tables that there is a great increase in the number of those who worship him as the one true God.

The Lord we worship is the Lord of history. He delights in using the faith and obedience of his children to work out his purposes in this world. He is the same yesterday in Esther's day, today in our day, and tomorrow in the day of our children and our children's children.

SUGGESTED READINGS AND QUESTIONS

1. What would you have found most difficult about the life that Esther was asked to live—entering the contest for Miss Medo-Persia, spending a whole year enduring beauty treatments, living as a member of Ahasuerus' harem, or enduring the constant danger of being queen in a palace so full of intrigue? Or is there some other problem of her life that you identify as the most challenging?

2. Do you think that Esther was compromising her testimony by being prepared to be a member of the king's harem? If you answer yes to this question, do you have any alternative proposals for her and for delivering the Jews from widespread slaughter?

3. What do you admire most about Esther?

4. What situations today do you think might be comparable to the kind of pressures that Esther had to live under—situations where a Christian woman might find herself living in a place where faithfulness required her to stay with and to honor a man who was clearly doing wrong? Or perhaps situations where a Christian man might find himself in a place where, like Obadiah or Daniel, he is required to serve someone who is thoroughly wicked and ruthless.

5. Do you have problems with the account of the destruction of many of the enemies of the Jews at the end of this story? Is their destruction necessary? Why are they destroyed, and, if you con-

clude that their destruction is necessary, what does this teach us about the judgment of God?

6. Which of the ironies of this story do you find most interesting or even surprising? In addition to those mentioned in the chapter, you might wish to add others. Do you think that God has a sense of humor? (Read chapter 6 of the book of Esther again.)

7. Are there "feasts" in your own life or in the life of your family that have at their heart the remembrance and celebration of the particular love of God for you? If you do not have any such feast, what "feast" could you add into the schedule of your year so that you will regularly and specifically praise God for what he has done in your life? What could be your "Esther's Decree"?

8. Read for our next chapter the account of the woman of noble character in Proverbs 31:10–31.

15

THE WOMAN OF NOBLE CHARACTER

In our last chapter's reflections we found ourselves in the court of the king of a vast and powerful empire. There in the midst of palace intrigue and struggles for power we watched God raise up a young girl to be the deliverer of his people. Esther's story is one of courage, wisdom, and faith. She is an example to us of how we may serve God even in the darkest times and in the most difficult circumstances.

As God's people we almost always find ourselves surrounded by non-Christians, for Christ has called us to live in this world of unbelief, idolatry, and sin. We all long to be with the Lord, to see him face-to-face, to have our own struggles with our self-centered and sinful ways over, to live in peace and security, to see everyone we know loving the Lord. But this is not our situation in this age. So rather than fighting against this reality, rather than resenting it, rather than trying to create an evangelical ghetto for ourselves and our children, we are to obey Christ gladly. We are to follow him into the world, and there we are to love unbelievers as he did; we are to serve them as he did. He commands us to live in the world as imitators of him.[1]

In Esther's case this calling into the world meant that she was required to become one of the wives of a man who was not only an unbeliever but also a man with the capability and the power to make ruthless decisions, decisions that would impact the lives of vast numbers of people. Most of us never have to live in quite such a difficult or such an influential setting!

We learn from the story of Esther that it is possible to honor God in one's words and actions, no matter how tough the situation into which God calls us. Esther responds to her impossible place with practical wisdom and with trust in the Lord. God honors her faith in him, for he is always faithful to his people, even though his people's faith is never perfect and his people's obedience is always far from ideal.

The woman we meet in this chapter has a more usual place of service. She is married to a fellow believer, someone who also delights in serving the Lord. However, the woman of Proverbs 31 has no name, and so we cannot make the usual introduction to her life and times. While she is obviously set in a particular historical context, we do not need to focus, as we typically do, on the place and moment of history in which she lives.

Proverbs 31 is not about a particular individual as is true in the other passages of Scripture that we have studied. We might say that this "wife of noble character" (v. 10, NIV), this woman of "strength" (vv. 17, 25), is a model, a composite, of all the virtues and noble characteristics of the women whose lives we have considered in earlier chapters. We can see in her the dignity of Tamar when raped by her brother, the wisdom of Abigail, the faithfulness of Hannah, the fear of God that motivated Esther's heart, the moral strength of Deborah, the courage of Rahab, the devotion of Ruth, the faith of Naomi, the perseverance of Sarah; and we could add a quality from the life of each of the other women whose stories are set down in God's Word. The woman of noble character brings all these things together in one person.

Another way for us to look at the woman of Proverbs 31 is to see that she is an exemplar to us of what it means to be the image of God; in her we see a woman who shows the first face of Eve. She is a woman as she should be, a woman as God made her to be. We will consider her life by selecting some of the ways in which she is a portrait of the likeness of God.

She is a woman who is fully given to the relationships in which God has set her. It seems appropriate to say that her commitment to her relationships is at the heart of this woman's life. She loves her husband. She loves her children. She loves those who share her household and who serve in it. She loves people in need who come into her life.

We might ask, "Who is God?" or as one of my little grandsons put it on the way home from church one Sunday, "What is God's body made of?" The answer to the question "Who is God? is "God is love" or, to my grandson's question, "God is made of love." At the heart of the Godhead there is a deep commitment to relationships within the Trinity. There at the heart and beginning of all things is the love with which the Father, the Son, and the Spirit have loved each other through all eternity.

If we turn from God's life to our own, we can ask at the most basic level, what does it mean to be human? or, what are humans made of? and, what are humans made for? The answer to these questions is that we are created to love; we are made for relationships. God has made us for love. He has made us to show love for him and to live a life of love that is expressed in service for others.

The woman of noble character loves in just this way. Love is her life. Her life is lived for the well-being of others. This means, too, that her life is deeply fulfilling to her, as well as being a constant blessing to everyone around her.

I must admit here that I wondered whether to write first about the noble woman's life of love, for to speak about this is challenging to us at the beginning of the twenty-first century. This emphasis on relationships, on living for others, is seen as the great gender trap, the means by which women have been enslaved into service of the family and to domesticity in their homes. It is important to admit that sometimes women are treated as servants, or even as slaves, by their husbands and by their cultures, and we need, as Christians, to protest such treatment and work to present a different model of family life in which there is mutual obligation, mutual service, and mutual self-sacrificing love.

So we must acknowledge that there is, in this critique of traditional gender roles, an appropriate protest against the mistreatment of women. However, we need to see that this is not the most foundational issue in the discussion. We live in societies where there is also a serious error in the understanding of what it means to be human. Our culture makes the mistake of believing that fulfillment comes to us when we live to love and serve ourselves. It does not. Fulfillment comes about only through loving and serving other people. This is true for women, and it is true for men. This is the way God is, and this is the way he has designed us to be.

The two great commandments are that we are to love God and to love our neighbor as ourselves. These commandments are simply a description of what it means to be human. God has created us to be in his image, and this means that we are to live our lives loving him and loving one another. There can be no truly human life without such a life of love, and there can be no deep fulfillment unless we live such a life of love. The woman of Proverbs 31 is a model to us of this life of love.

What will it mean to me if I begin to take her model with utmost seriousness in my own life? I intend this question both for women and for men! I can begin by asking myself which individuals live in the circles of relationship in which God has set me— wives and husbands, daughters and sons, mothers and fathers, sisters and brothers, grandchildren and grandparents, aunts and uncles, nieces and nephews, cousins and members of my extended families and households, people at work and school, friends and neighbors, those in need whom God brings into my life.

So, first, I am to identify the individuals to whom God binds me. Then I am to ask myself, how does God require me to love each of these people? What is my responsibility to serve and to care for each one of them? This is quite clearly how the woman of Proverbs 31 is living. I need to ask myself, what difference would it make in my life if I began to live in imitation of her rather than living with my own comfort, my own fulfillment, and my own financial security as my primary goals?

At the very beginning of this book we looked at the face of Eve at creation. There we saw that the second foundational aspect of the image of God, brought out by the Genesis text, is that she and Adam were created to have dominion over the earth. *The woman of strength described in Proverbs 31 is a woman who exercises dominion over this world.* She is a true daughter of Eve, a queen of this earth. We read of her buying and selling land, planting vineyards, providing food for her household, earning income for her family, being involved in business decisions out in society as well as running a cottage industry at home. She is a woman who joyfully applies herself to whatever tasks she can to benefit her family, those dependent on her, and anyone else she can help.

This woman is a hard worker, for work is what dominion is about. Dominion is imaging God: God worked in creation; God works in upholding the world and caring for it; God works to save people and to build the kingdom of his Son. The Lord calls us to give ourselves to work in imitation of him. He demands of us that we apply ourselves to the tasks at hand. The woman of noble character is busy, tending the particular "garden" in which her Lord has placed her.

We might say that there are five aspects to a biblical understanding of work that are fundamental to our daily lives.

• *When we work, we work to the glory of God.* This is true wherever we work, whether our work is at home or out in society. God has created us to work, to labor, to exercise dominion; and as we work, whatever the particular task, we work to the glory of God simply because we reflect his nature and his character when we work. The Lord himself delights in the way the woman of noble character brings praise and honor to him in all she does.

• *We do our work to be a blessing to those around us.* We read in Genesis that God looks at what he has made, and he sees that it is good. Everyone in this world looks every day at what God has made, and we find that what he made is good, for life itself and everything we have comes from him. He is the One who brings the seasons, day and night, rain and sunshine. He is the One who makes the earth fruitful and who enables our work to be productive. In the same way people look at the work of the noble woman, and they declare her work good. Her work is a blessing and a benefit to other people. Her children and her husband call her "blessed" (v. 28), and her works are praised in the city gates.

• *Our work, our exercise of dominion, is intended to bring satisfaction to our own hearts and lives as we use and develop the gifts that God has given us.* As we use our hands, our minds, and our imaginations to do our daily tasks, work becomes fulfilling to us, for God has designed us to find pleasure and joy in what we do. We find satisfaction in a job well done, just as God himself delights in his work of creating, upholding, and caring for the world. The noble woman gives herself to her work, rejoicing in the sense of dignity and strength of character that is made evident in all that she does.

• *Our work extends our rule over creation.* God created this earth for us to imitate his sovereign reign as we exercise dominion here. "The heavens are the LORD's heavens, but the earth he has given to the children of man" (Psalm 115:16). Some of us are farmers, gardeners, foresters, environmental biologists, working directly to "tend the garden" of this world; but all of us are engaged in the task of dominion, whether we are working in our homes, with books or computers, in building or mining. Whatever our task, we are ruling this world and demonstrating that we are made in the image of our Creator. We are his stewards and are answerable to him for all our work. One day he will ask each one of us, "How did you exercise rule over the part of my world that I put under your care?" The noble woman is a good steward, exercising dominion in a way that brings praise to God, respect to her husband, and honor to herself.

• *Because we live in a fallen world, there is an additional factor in our exercise of dominion.* Now our work is intended to limit the effects of the fallen world, to hold back the curse, and to seek to restrain sin's damage and trouble in our lives and in the lives of those we love. Some of us may be doctors or nurses, counselors and social workers, directly limiting the problems of this fallen world, bringing healing and hope to the wounded, comfort to the sorrowing, help to the struggling. But all of us are called to work in such a way that we help to overcome the consequences of the Fall in this world. The woman of noble character laughs at the days to come. She is prepared for the trouble that may be ahead, whether that trouble is predictable, like the annual winter snow and cold, or whether it is unpredictable, like the unfolding events of today or tomorrow.

Those five aspects of our understanding of our work are all drawn from Genesis 1–3, and each of them is fulfilled in the life of the woman of Proverbs 31. She is an earthly portrait of God, the heavenly artisan. In her daily life, here in this world, all that she does reflects the nature of God.

The woman of noble character is a woman who knows God, who lives to honor God in each moment of her life. She is a woman devoted to righteousness and justice. To be in the image of God means to be moral, righteous, and just, as God himself is moral, righteous, and just. We are all called to be renewed in righteousness and holiness in the image of our Creator and to pursue justice so that we might reflect his character.

Proverbs 31 reveals a woman like this. When her husband thinks of her, he sees the moral beauty of her character. She is a woman who fears and honors God and who desires to be like him, reflecting his righteousness in her life. Just as she is eager to imitate God, so her children find in her a source of inspiration for their own lives: "I want to be like Mother. I want to emulate her virtue." There is no greater compliment we can receive on this earth than for someone to desire to be like us. My wife is such a woman. She is an inspiration and a model to me, to our three sons, to our three daughters-in-law, and to our grandchildren (seven so far). They admire her enormously and think of her as a person they long to be like.

The woman of noble character is a woman whose life makes a difference to everyone around her. She is a history-maker. God, the sovereign Lord of all history, has created us to be significant. Our choices matter, for in everything we do we are making marks in history, writing the future onto the page that God sets before us. God rules over the whole history of the universe, and we imitate him as we use our time wisely. Every moment of our lives, to use an image of Francis Schaeffer, we are making ripples, like the ripples made on a pool when stones are thrown into it, and these ripples will go on forever.

Each choice we make, the way we spend our time today and tomorrow—our choices and our use of time—will affect the lives of other people for good or for ill, both now and for eternity. This is the nature of our human significance. The woman of noble character knows that God has called her to use her time wisely, to make the most of every opportunity that God has given her. She is committed to redeem the time because the days to come may well be evil (cf. Ephesians 5:16). She knows that God rules all things well, and so her desire is to seek to live her life in such a way that there will be a difference because she has lived. She is committed to being a blessing to other people's lives. One day she will hear the voice of the Lord say, "Well done, good and faithful servant! You have used your time, gifts, and abilities well. You wrote a good story with your life." We each need to ask ourselves, what difference is my life making to other people? Are the ripples I am making ripples for good or for ill? What story am I writing with my life?

The woman of noble character wants to think thoughts that are like God's thoughts. She is anxious to have her mind renewed by her understanding of what is faithful, true, and good. She meditates in her heart and mind on what is pleasing to the Lord. She is a woman who is committed to fearing God, eager to know his Word, desirous that her mind be shaped by what she sees in the mirror of his commandments, and then devoted to putting into practice her knowledge of the truth. Are we like her? Are we women and men who are being transformed into the likeness of God by the renewing of our minds?

We worship a God who speaks and communicates, and he has given us the wonderful gift of language. How are we going to use that gift of words, of language, of communication? *The woman of noble character is one whose mouth speaks words of wisdom and grace.*

The apostle James teaches us that wise and kind words coming out of the mouth reveal what is in the heart—just as the water, pure or brackish, reveals the nature of the spring from which it gushes. James also charges us with the inappropriateness of using our mouths to praise God and yet using the same mouth to curse people who are made in God's image.

The woman of noble character is one whose words demonstrate a pure and consistent heart. Out of her mouth come praise for God and blessing for those made in his likeness. Her words are words of wisdom, grace, respect, and gentleness. Do my words reveal such a consistency of heart?

This woman of noble character is "an excellent wife" (v. 10). This wife is presented here as fully her husband's equal. She is his complement and his helpmate. She honors her husband gladly, and in return he has full confidence in her. These are wonderful words to describe the mutual respect, honor, and appreciation that ought to exist in every marriage. We need to ask, if we are married, if this is how others see our marriage—as a marriage of equals, a marriage in which there is mutual honor, respect, love, and service?

How do we express our confidence in our husband or wife? Does my spouse know that I honor her or him? Let me suggest a creative way. When one is celebrating an anniversary—let's say a tenth or twenty-fifth or thirty-fifth—collect blank cards for each year of marriage. If you have been married a long time, it might take several months to find high-quality cards from gift shops, museum shops, garden shops, art shops, anywhere you can find beautiful blank cards. On each one of the cards write a quotation either from God's Word or somewhere else, a quotation that sets forth something you believe about your spouse, something that expresses your confidence in her or in him, something that is true, something from various favorite writers. Collect those quotations, write one down on each card, and then make a personal comment about each one, applying the quotation to your spouse. Your spouse will treasure such a present. This is just a suggestion, of course, but, the point is, we all need to be intentional and to work at ways in which we can express our delight in each other and show to the other the honor with which we regard him or her.

The husband of the woman of noble character is able to have full confidence in his wife. He is a man who can leave his home knowing his partner can be fully trusted, for she has eyes for no other man. He is a man who can be sure that wherever he goes he will hear his wife well spoken of, for her reputation, her character, and her good deeds are known throughout the community. Her glory reflects on him. He is respected in the city because of the loveliness of his wife's reputation.

Proverbs 31 brings out one final characteristic of the woman of noble character, and we did not mention this characteristic in our study of the first face of Eve because it arises from the fallen nature of our world. *This woman is a woman of mercy and grace to those in need.* She is the kind of woman who if she were alive in the time of Tamar, daughter of King David, would be her friend and her comforter; she would be Tamar's close companion, ready to serve in any practical way and eager to wipe away some of Tamar's tears.

For each one of us living in this abnormal world, a fundamental part of being in the image of God is showing God's mercy and grace, his compassion for the wounded. He calls us to have, just as he does, an openness of heart and life to those who are in trouble and sorrow. We are to be a comfort to those who are hurting, sharing the comfort with which God has comforted us (2 Corinthians 1:3–4). This is the nature of God himself, who loves not only within his immediate family, the family of the Trinity, but also loves those who are weeping because of the brokenness of their lives. This, of course, is the gospel of Christ—God so loved this sad world that he sent his Son to bring "healing in [his] wings" (Malachi 4:2).

The woman of noble character reflects this aspect of God's character. She loves deeply enough to love beyond her own family. Her heart is full of the kindness of Jesus Christ. She "opens her hand to the poor and reaches out her hands to the needy" (v. 20). Just as Christ reached out and touched the sick and sorrowing, so she reaches out her hands, touches people, and shares her life and love with them.

CONCLUDING THOUGHTS

In the woman of noble character we are presented with a model, an example for our imitation. Her image is not set before us to discourage us, for this kind of life is not beyond the reach of any one of us who sees her portrait. Her life is not beyond our emulation or imitation, for God has indeed created us in his likeness. "He has crowned [us] with glory and honor" (Psalm 8:5). He has created us to love, to be significant, to have dominion, to reflect his moral character, to think his thoughts after him, to show mercy. This is truly how he has made us.

In addition God has also given us his Word to direct us in these paths of love, justice, mercy, and righteousness. We have the privilege of being able to read the desires of his heart for our lives.

We can read them in his commandments, in the record of his acts of love and mercy in history, in the accounts of women and men who have loved and served him. He calls us to delight in his Word, to treasure the way of life he has shown us there, and to commit ourselves to walking in that way.

Beyond all else he has loved us himself, in his Son's redeeming work, so that our hearts, as well as knowing his forgiveness for our failures, might be also filled with his grace and mercy to empower us to live in imitation of him.

We have the written record of this love of Christ so that we may treasure the knowledge of such love; but Christ has also poured his love into our hearts and has come to dwell in us by his Spirit, so that we might have the strength to take up the tasks that each day brings and so do all we do to the glory of God and to the benefit of others.

The Lord is indeed at work in us. So for us to seek to model our lives on the life of this woman of noble character is not something out of reach or absurdly unrealistic.

But you may ask, what about our constant sins and failures to measure up to such a high standard? Of course we sin, and of course we fail. Not one of us can say, I am fully like the woman of noble character.

However, we should know by our experience and we should know from the encouragement of the Scriptures that any tiny, faltering steps we make in the direction of being like the woman of noble character will bring blessing to others—to our families, friends, and neighbors—and will bring life and fulfillment to ourselves. Any little movement we make to walk in the way of these characteristics of being like God will surely bring blessing—this is his promise.

God delights to honor us when we seek to offer our lives to him by attempting to stumble in his footsteps. He does not wait for perfection in our lives before he shows his pleasure in us or before he makes our lives a benefit to others. God understands our weaknesses. God delights in us. God is not ashamed to be called our God. Despite our failure, despite our brokenness, despite our sin,

God reacts with absolute delight when we make any movements toward seeking to walk in his image, when we cry out to him in some poor way, *Lord, make me just a little like your Son.* How can God delight in such an imperfect person as me or you? Christ has died for us. Christ has been perfect for us. Christ is glad to help us by his Spirit. Christ is eager for us to walk in his way. Christ loves us.

Therefore we can say, as Proverbs 4:18 does indeed say, "The path of the righteous is like the light of dawn, which shines brighter and brighter until full day." All of us, at present, are living in partial darkness, but we are also living in partial light. We see the light beginning to shine in the lives of those around us and in our own lives as God does his work in us. But any light is true light, even if it just a weak glimmer of dawn; and any tiny faltering light holds the promise of the full day to come. We may aim at the characteristics of the woman of noble character, and as we follow that aim we will find blessing in our lives and will bring blessing to the lives of those around us.

SUGGESTED READINGS AND QUESTIONS

1. As you think about the woman of noble character, which of her characteristics do you most admire?

2. Which of her characteristics do you see most clearly in yourself—not perfectly lived out but the faint outline of some of these characteristics already being formed in you?

3. Which aspects of her character do you feel are least present in your life—not that any of them will be absent altogether, but which of them do you find the most difficult to bring into the beginnings of daily realization in your life?

4. As you think about the work you do day by day, where do you see your work expressing the five aspects of work set out in this chapter?

5. In what ways do you see yourself expressing the love of God? Where are you involved in loving those within your family, both in your own household and in your extended family? Try to make

a list of those whom you serve regularly in some way, no matter how small.

6. Are there ways in which you are expressing the redemptive grace of God to anyone outside your own immediate household or extended family? How are you seeking to imitate the mercy of Christ by reaching out to touch the needy? We need to look for more of an answer here than charitable giving, though that, of course, is good; what God desires is some level of personal involvement in the lives of those in trouble, some extending of our hands.

7. Has this study depressed you, or has it encouraged you to see that to be a woman (or man) of noble character is not an unrealizable ideal but rather is a pattern of life toward which you are asked to make some stumbling steps? Do you know that such steps, no matter how small, will bring blessing to yourself and to others and will also bring the delight of the Lord?

8. Read for our next chapter the account of Mary in Luke 1:26–56. As we begin to think about Mary and about the annunciation to her by the angel and about the birth of Jesus, try to put yourself in her place as she lived through these events. For men reading this, try to put yourself in the place of Joseph as he waited for the birth of Mary's child, conceived by the Holy Spirit. What would have been difficult and what joyful for Mary (or for Joseph) as they reflected on the words of the angel to each of them (for Joseph, see Matthew 1:18–25)? What would have been some of the challenges facing Mary (or Joseph) through the months of pregnancy and expectation?

16

MARY:

The Handmaid of the Lord

> ### LUKE 1:26–56; 2:1–7;
> ### MATTHEW 1:18–25

In the last chapter of our studies of Old Testament women of God we thought about the woman of noble character of Proverbs 31. We saw that she is presented to us as a model of what women (and men) are meant to be. She is a portrait of what it means for a woman to live out the image of God in her daily life. She is a woman who shows the first and the third face of Eve, Eve as God's likeness at creation and Eve as the bearer of redemption into the world of sin and suffering. In our reflections we saw that the woman of Proverbs 31 had eight characteristics that reveal to us our human calling.

• She is a woman who loves and who gives herself to relationships that will reveal God's love to the watching world.
• She is a woman who exercises dominion over the earth, who works hard to hold back the consequences of the Fall.
• She is a woman who lives to honor God in her whole life, a woman of virtue and righteousness, praised by all, a woman who is a moral inspiration to her children.
• She is a woman who is a history-maker, using her time wisely to make a difference in this world because she has passed her days living to impact others for eternity.

241

• She is a woman committed to thinking God's thoughts after him and then living by the divinely inspired knowledge that she has gained.

• She is a woman who speaks words of wisdom and grace and whose tongue brings peace.

• She is a wife who is faithful in her marriage and who is honored by her husband and family.

• She is a woman of compassion for anyone in trouble, displaying God's mercy in a needy world.

Here is a woman who fulfills what it means to be God's image-bearer, a model indeed of godliness and righteousness. But as we saw at the end of our last chapter, this is not a portrait intended to intimidate or discourage us. Rather we are to see that any steps we take toward being like this woman, faltering though they be, will bring blessing to ourselves and to others. God delights to honor those who seek to offer their lives to him in this kind of service. He does not wait until we are perfect before he shows his pleasure in us or makes our lives a gift to others.

We turn for our first New Testament study to the person of Mary, the mother of Jesus, a woman who most certainly is a shining example in her life of the pattern set out for us in Proverbs 31. But the story of Mary takes us back far beyond the time of the writing of the book of Proverbs, back to the beginning, back to God's promise to Eve in Genesis 3:15. Mary is the one whom God chooses to honor by asking her to bear the Seed of Eve. Mary's story is the fulfillment of that first great promise.

Matthew tells us Mary's story in a brief account. Luke, however, gives us much more detail. Luke informs his readers at the beginning of his Gospel that he had spoken to the eyewitnesses of the history that he is about to tell.

It is evident from what Luke describes to us that he must have been given the account he records in Luke 1–2 by Mary herself. She is the only one who could have told him much of what he presents to us. In fact Luke tells us, "Mary treasured up all these things, pondering them in her heart" (2:19). Of course she did!

The events that took place in Mary's life are demonstrations of the powerful activity of God. In Mary, God is bringing to fulfillment all the promises of the Old Testament about the coming of the Messiah into this world. All Christian believers, and even many non-Christians, are familiar with at least the outlines of the story of the birth of Jesus. But we need to set out its main features to see the important matters that Luke and Matthew draw to our attention.

THE ANNUNCIATION

The angel Gabriel, described as one who "stand[s] in the presence of God" (1:19), comes to Mary in her home at Nazareth, a small town in Galilee. Mary is already betrothed to Joseph. To help our understanding, we need to know that in those times betrothal was regarded as much more serious and binding than engagement is to most of us today. The equivalent of a divorce was needed to break a betrothal (Matthew 1:19). However, the betrothed couple did not move in together or start sleeping together until after the marriage, and Luke draws our attention to this fact of Mary's virgin status until the marriage takes place.

We need to take note of how different this is from the times in which we live, times in which it is commonplace for both non-Christians and committed Christians to start sleeping together before any marriage ceremony occurs, often even before engagement. Many in the media tell us that young people's hormones are so powerful that of course teenagers will start becoming involved sexually—it is only natural that they will. It is unreasonable to expect a young person to remain chaste, it is said. Christians and many other people of sense ought to know that this is nonsense. It is perfectly possible and also liberating for young people themselves and for those with whom they are tempted to have sex—teens, twenty somethings, and single people of any age—to exercise restraint and self-discipline with regard to their sexuality.[1]

Gabriel greets Mary with words that express God's desire to be gracious to her and honor her. His words "O favored one" draw attention not primarily to Mary's righteousness but to the grace and favor of God toward her. Mary is overwhelmed by these words and afraid. Why is her reaction one of fear? Whenever we read, in Scripture, of anyone being visited by an angel, we observe that his or her response is one of agitation and fear (see Luke 1:12 for Zechariah's reaction). Compare this presentation of angels by God's Word with the rather anemic angels that we encounter in popular culture today. No one would fear television show angels! But Mary is afraid when Gabriel comes to her. Gabriel calms her fears and tells her that she is to bear a child and then gives her some information about who this child will be. He says:

• Her child will be given the name Jesus (Luke 1:31), a name that has the meaning "He will save" or "Savior." Her son will grow up to become one who, like Joshua (the Hebrew form of the name Jesus), will be the deliverer or savior of his people.

• This child will not only be great, but he will be "the Son of the Most High" (v. 32). What does this title signify? Does it designate Christ as the divine Son, the eternal second person of the Trinity? That is not an easy question, and if there were not the additional words from Gabriel (see below on v. 35) we would have to say, first, that "the Son of the Most High" would refer to the promises made to David that he and his descendants would be called God's Son (see 2 Samuel 7:11–13; Psalm 89:19-37). However, because of what Gabriel adds later, we are almost certainly right to see in "the Son of the Most High" both a reference to Jesus as one in David's line and also as the one who is uniquely the Son of God, the eternal Son.

• He will be the Son of David; (v. 32) that is, he will be the promised Messiah descended from the line of David. He will reign as everlasting king on the throne of David, fulfilling the hopes and aspirations of God's people, Israel.

• He will "reign over the house of Jacob" (v. 33); that is, he will be the one to satisfy all the promises made to the patriarchs Abraham, Isaac, and Jacob. This is another way of saying that Mary's son will be the seed of Abraham, the one who will bring blessing to all the nations of the world and not only to Israel.

• His kingdom will be everlasting (v. 33). These words too point to the deity of Christ, as well as to the emphatic statement that he is to be the Messiah, the one whose eternal reign was pictured in the brief reigns of every previous king who sat on David's throne. He will be the one to establish the kingdom of God, and he will be the one who will overcome Satan, the tempter and usurper, and who will deliver the human race from the Devil's power.

We can only imagine the thoughts that flood through Mary's mind and heart as she hears these astonishing words. In Mary's moment of history, the land of Palestine is one small territory within the vast empire that Rome has conquered. The Israelites are longing for deliverance from Roman imperial rule and for the establishment of a truly free nation once more. Mary must have thought of this hope of deliverance from Rome, as did everyone else in her day when they thought about the coming of the Messiah. We can picture her in the days to come—reading and reflecting on the Old Testament promises of the Messiah, full of wonder at the kindness of God to her.

She probably understands only a little of what it means that her child is to be "the Son of the Most High." As she is a fallen and fallible person just like us, her mind must also be full of doubts. Mary is still a virgin and wonders, therefore, how she can possibly conceive this promised child; so she expresses this concern to Gabriel. In response to Mary's question, Gabriel tells her more about the manner in which conception will take place.

• The Holy Spirit will in his power enable her to conceive this child. Her son will not be conceived through the ordinary means of human sexual intercourse.

• The child will be holy because he will indeed be God's Son. Unlike all other human persons, this child will not be "sinful at birth, sinful from the time [his] mother conceived [him]" (Psalm 51:5, NIV). Instead God's Son will be born without a sinful nature.

• As an encouragement to believe this amazing declaration, Gabriel reminds Mary of how her cousin Elizabeth has conceived in her old age. Mary knows that Elizabeth's womb is well past the possibility of child-bearing, and yet she has conceived. God is able to bring about what is impossible for men and women to accomplish.

Mary responds to this encouragement with faith and obedient trust. She is ready to be the Lord's handmaid, to offer herself to him as his servant. We must assume that her conception takes place immediately or very shortly thereafter through the power of the Spirit. She leaves Nazareth and takes the eighty- to a hundred-mile journey south to stay for the first three months of her pregnancy with Elizabeth, who lives in the rural hill country of Judea.

THE VISIT TO ELIZABETH

As soon as Mary greets Elizabeth, Elizabeth's baby leaps for joy in her womb, sensing and delighting in the presence of the Christ-child. John, the infant son of Elizabeth and Zechariah, is at this time about six months old in the womb. This account should encourage us as we care for, pray for, and then later teach our own children the truth of the gospel. God is able to regenerate children even while they are still in the womb. All of us know many believers who, just like John the Baptist, can remember no time in their life when they did not believe in Christ and when they did not love God. Just as the Holy Spirit is already at work in her unborn son, so the Holy Spirit is at work in Elizabeth's heart. The Spirit reveals to Elizabeth that Mary is pregnant with the promised Messiah, and so, filled with the Spirit, she utters her famous words.

Elizabeth declares that Mary is "blessed" (v. 42); that is, God has delighted to show his love and grace to her. Mary is "blessed . . . among women"; that is, God has singled her out for particular favor and honor. It is true, of course, that all believers are blessed by God's favor and are honored by him. However, no other woman in the history of the human race has experienced the honor of being asked to be the bearer of the Messiah, to carry the Son of God in her womb, to give birth to him, and to care for him as an infant. And, of course, no man could fulfill such a calling! Just as Eve is "the mother of all living" (Genesis 3:20), so Mary is the mother of the Christ-child. All childbearing (and therefore every woman) is touched with the grace of God's blessing because of this womanly solidarity with Eve and with Mary.

The child within her, "the fruit of [her] womb," is also one who is "blessed" by God (v. 42), one to whom God delights to show his love and favor. Jesus is the one who is blessed above all others, the one blessed without measure by the fullness of the presence of the Holy Spirit.

Elizabeth recognizes that she herself is honored by the presence of the one who will bear "my Lord" (v. 43). Elizabeth understands (to some degree) that the child in Mary's womb is divine, the Son of God, the Lord himself. Even the baby in her own womb has sensed the presence of the Lord God. In this case, of course, John the Baptist is full of the Spirit even in his mother's womb, but in fact all babies in the womb have far more response to external stimuli than most people have ever imagined. In the past few years we have learned much more about the development of little children in the womb. For example, a baby in the womb responds to familiar voices (the voices of the mother and father that the baby hears every day), responds to the language that the parents speak, responds to music, and prefers some kinds of music to others.

Elizabeth blesses Mary for her response of faith to God's word given to her by the angel Gabriel. The response of faith is always the first obedience that God requires from us, whatever our situation and whatever our particular calling. In the Bible Mary is the primary female example of the obedience of faith, just as Abraham is the primary male example. It is important to acknowledge this without hesitation, just as we do not think twice about calling Abraham the exemplar of faith or referring to him as the father of the faithful.

At this point of their meeting Mary is inspired by the Spirit to speak out her great song, the *Magnificat*, and then she stays with Elizabeth for three months before returning to Nazareth to face her family, her friends, and her betrothed, Joseph. What discussions these two women must have had during those three months! In God's providence and timing they are able to comfort and encourage each other during this happy and challenging period of their lives. And, we may be sure, they reflected together on the words of the angel, on the power of God at work in both of their lives, and on the Old Testament promises of the Messiah and how they would be fulfilled through the child that Mary is carrying. One day we can ask them about those months together and about their conversations. For us the most amazing miracle is that through these "ordinary" means of conception and pregnancy, the Master of the universe and of our souls came into this world.

As we read the *Magnificat*, we note many similarities between

Hannah's hymn of praise and Mary's prayer. There are also allusions to the book of Ruth, to God's power demonstrated at the Exodus, to the Messianic promises in Isaiah, to the covenant made with Abraham, and to the blessings promised to David. Mary's song is rich with Old Testament themes and prophecies. It has a poetic form similar to the Psalms, with its parallelism and its contrasts, with its exalted language and its rhythmic patterns. Because it is great poetry and because it also has such marvelous content, Christians have sung Mary's song from the earliest years of the church until today, and it has been set to music by many great composers.[2]

THEMES OF THE *MAGNIFICAT*

Mary gives all the glory to God, her Savior and her Lord. He is the Mighty One who has brought about all the great things that are taking place in and around her life. In contrast to her declaration of the glory of God, Mary acknowledges her own status to be one of lowliness and humble service.

Mary declares that all future generations will acknowledge how greatly blessed by God she is. She will be called "blessed" (v. 48) because of the great things God has done for her and in her. God is the Holy One who works his mighty deeds in the history of his people, and now the Lord is doing his greatest work—the greatest work of all history—through her life.

Mary compares what God is doing in bringing the Christ-child into the world to God's power at work in bringing his people out of Egypt into the Promised Land. She recognizes that the Exodus was God's greatest work of salvation up to this point in time; now he is doing a similar great work, indeed an even greater work of salvation, in bringing his Son into the world.

The coming of her son, the Messiah, will bring about a new world order in which the proud and the powerful will be brought down, the humble in heart (like Mary herself) will be exalted, the hungry will be filled with good things, the rich will be sent away empty. The gospel holds out to us this hope of the transformation of society through the reign of Christ. Because he is God, Christ sees the secrets of human hearts rather than looking on the external circumstances of people's lives. He also sees the reality of faith and humility in hearts, and he will bring blessing to those who have this faith and humility. He sees the arrogance of the powerful and wealthy too, and he will bring judgment on them.

"BLESSED" MARY

In our text the angel Gabriel honors Mary. He greets her as one who is a "favored one" (v. 28). She is declared "blessed" twice by her cousin Elizabeth (vv. 42, 45), and Elizabeth says these words because she is filled with the Holy Spirit. Elizabeth recognizes that she is honored by Mary's visit to her. Mary herself, inspired by the Holy Spirit, declares that all future generations of believers will call her "blessed" (v. 48). These are the clear, inerrant, and authoritative words of Scripture.

When did you last, or did you ever, call Mary "blessed"? Why are we to think and speak of Mary as "blessed"?

Mary has a unique place in salvation history. No other woman, no other person, holds her place. Her position in history is one of being specially honored by God. She is chosen by God to be the one to conceive and bear Jesus Christ, our Savior. As Mary says, "he who is mighty has done great things for me" (v. 49). God magnified her, and so she gladly and humbly magnifies God.

Let all Christians gladly acknowledge Mary's special place in God's work of redemption. We happily acknowledge Abraham's part—that he is the father of the faithful, that we are Abraham's children, that God honored him by calling him and choosing him to be the one through whom blessing would come to the human race. Let us honor Mary and call her "blessed" for the place she holds in God's purposes for our salvation. Mary was from the time of her conception of Jesus, she is now, and she always will be, as Elizabeth says, "the mother of my Lord" (v. 43).

Mary is held before us as an example of faith. "Blessed is she who believed that there would be a fulfillment of what was spoken to her from the Lord" (v. 45). Mary is the primary model for us of humble obedience, willing submission, and glad trust in the word of God that came to her through Gabriel.

Let us gladly honor Mary by seeing her as a primary model of the obedience of faith.

In reading this song of praise we are being taught by Mary, for Mary's song, the Magnificat, *is part of the Word of God.* We are being taught, all of us, all of God's people, by the words of a woman. We should note that her words are a thoughtful meditation on Scripture and an exposition of Old Testament texts. As we saw earlier, there are allusions to Hannah's song, to passages from the book of Ruth, to God's power manifest in the Exodus, to the Messianic promises in the book of Isaiah, to the covenant made with Abraham and his descendants, and to the blessings promised to David. Mary shows a deep knowledge of the Old Testament's central themes and prophecies.

Mary is clearly a student of Scripture, one taught by God and by his Word, and she is now teaching us. As we noted earlier, the form of her song is similar to the poetic patterns of the Psalms with its parallelism and contrasts, with its exalted language and rhythmical patterns. Christians have been taught by Mary's words and have used them to praise God from the first century until today. Because the *Magnificat* has been set to music by many composers, from the time of the early church up until today, it is sung every Sunday in tens of thousands of churches all over the world.

We have no hesitation in praising God for David as a man after God's own heart, as the sweet singer of Israel, as the one whose songs regularly lead our worship. Let us thank God for Mary also, for she too is one whose song teaches us, whose song enriches our lives, whose song helps us worship—indeed, her song often leads our worship.

We should not fail to call Mary "blessed" because some of us may fear or dislike certain aspects of Roman Catholic theology and practice. We should not fail to call Mary "blessed" because she is a woman. Instead, let us gladly acknowledge that the Lord himself teaches us to call Mary "blessed" and that in learning to honor Mary we are taught to honor all women.

The apostle Paul teaches us that "there is no male and female . . . in Christ Jesus" (Galatians 3:28); that is, in Christ there is spiritual equality. Men and women are joint-heirs of the grace of life (cf. 1 Peter 3:7). As men and women we are equal partners in the spiritual blessings that come to all who are Abraham and Sarah's descendants and heirs and to all who share Abraham and Sarah's faith in the son of Mary. As men and women we are those on whom Christ has poured out his Spirit, so that, like Mary, we may pray for each other as royal priests, and we may prophesy for each other's comfort, encouragement, and edification (cf. 1 Corinthians 14:3).

I have urged us to honor Mary for her unique place in salvation history. I have encouraged us to call Mary "blessed" and to do so gladly. I have challenged us all to acknowledge Mary as our teacher and as an example of faith to admire and imitate.

However, it is necessary for us to look at the way Mary is sometimes presented to us and to ask, is such a view of Mary truly faithful to Scripture? To answer this question we will think about a very popular honoring of Mary that goes far beyond these wonderful words that we have studied in Luke's Gospel.

MARY IN ROMAN CATHOLIC TRADITION

A famous painting by El Greco (*The Burial of the Count of Orgaz*) represents the view of Mary held by the Counter-Reformation Catholic Church.[3] In this painting Mary is depicted as the Queen of Heaven. She is the one toward whom those on earth direct their prayers. She is the one to whom the spirit of the man, whose body is being buried below, appeals in heaven, asking her to intercede with Christ on his behalf. She is the one to whom all the patriarchs, apostles, and saints of the church are looking, to see what her response will be to this man's prayers and to the prayers of those on earth. Peter is waiting for her verdict, the keys to heaven at his side. Christ is watching the scene, listening to his mother. She has the place of prominence in the painting.

We need to ask whether this is an appropriate representation of Mary. Is this what it means that all generations are to call Mary "blessed"? Does the Scripture speak about Mary in the way this painting presents her? Is she given this exalted place of being the Queen of Heaven? Are we to direct our prayers to her so that she will intercede with Christ on our behalf? I think it is necessary to answer these questions, no!

Mary's blessedness is great, but her blessedness is not qualitatively different from the blessedness that all believers enjoy. God blesses us all in many marvelous ways, for he has redeemed Mary and he has redeemed us through the blood of his Son, shed on the cross for the forgiveness of her sins and of our sins. Mary's blessedness, just like yours or mine (see the Beatitudes), is a result of the love, favor, kindness, grace, and power of God. Her blessedness is not something inherent in her, as if Mary were morally flawless in her life here on earth.

Mary herself acknowledges this need of God's mercy and forgiveness, her need of salvation. In her song Mary delights in calling God "my Savior" (v. 47). She is morally flawless now, in heaven, but so are the spirits of all those who have died and gone to be with the Lord. Just like the spirit of every other believer who has died, Mary's spirit has been made perfect by God (cf. Hebrews 12:23).

Mary's blessedness is not a consequence of exalted status in heaven as its queen. Her blessedness does not mean that Christ will listen to her prayers more favorably than he would listen to yours or mine. To say this is not to denigrate Mary—we say this simply because God has promised to hear everyone who comes to him with faith in his Son, Jesus Christ. Consider these wonderful words from Hebrews 4:14–16:

> Since then we have a great high priest who has passed through the heavens, Jesus, the Son of God, let us hold fast our confession. For we do not have a high priest who is unable to sympathize with our weaknesses, but one who in every respect has been tempted as we are, yet without sin. Let us then with confidence draw near to the throne of grace, that we may receive mercy and find grace to help in time of need.

There is only one Savior, there is only one Mediator, there is only one priest in heaven, and that is Jesus. He is eager to hear our prayers, and he does not need his mother's urging to listen to us. Rather, he invites us to come to him at any time, to come to him with the confidence that he understands all our struggles and weaknesses and that he will always listen to us and will answer us in love.

The exalted view of Mary, expressed in the El Greco painting and in much popular devotion, is not the view of herself that she expresses in her song. Such an overly exalted view of Mary dishonors Christ, for God's Word teaches us explicitly that Christ is the only mediator between any human person and God: "There is one God, and there is one mediator between God and men, the man Christ Jesus [himself human], who gave himself as a ransom for all" (1 Timothy 2:5–6).

In reaction to such overexaltation of Mary we are not to ignore her, nor are we to downplay her response of humility and faith to the angel's words. She is indeed presented to us as one we should honor, just as Elizabeth honored Mary when Mary visited her. Mary is the one through whom the promise to Eve, the promise to Abraham and Sarah, the promise to Ruth, the promise to David came—the one through whom all these promises came to fulfillment in her bringing Jesus into the world. When we honor her, Mary points us toward honoring the Lord, her son, but the one who is also God's Son and Mary's own Savior from sin and death.

SUGGESTED READINGS AND QUESTIONS

1. How do you respond to the teaching of Scripture that John the Baptist was rejoicing in the presence of the newly conceived infant Jesus when both of these babies were still within their mothers' wombs?

2. What do you think this rejoicing of the pre-born John means for the way we are to think about our own children when they are still within the womb?

3. Why do you think so many people in our society ignore what we know about the development of babies within the womb?

4. The biblical text honors Mary because she declares herself willing to be the Lord's servant. What do you think this meant for Mary, both in her initial yielding to God's will and all through her pregnancy and through the time of her caring for her infant son?

5. You, too, are to declare yourself willing to be the Lord's servant. What do you think this means for you? In what specific ways do you see yourself as the Lord's servant now?

6. How have you thought of Mary? Have you been influenced by the teaching that honors Mary as the Queen of Heaven, as the Mother of God, as Co-mediatrix (co-mediator) with Christ?

7. Have you, in reaction to the exaltation of Mary, tended to ignore her and therefore found that you have been reluctant to say anything positive about her?

8. In what ways do you think it is appropriate to honor Mary, without intruding on the exclusive nature of Christ's work and therefore dishonoring him?

9. Read for our next chapter the accounts of the birth of Jesus and of his childhood (Luke 2:1–52; Matthew 1:18–2:23). What do we learn about Mary from these accounts?

17

MARY:

Queen of Heaven or the Mother of Jesus?

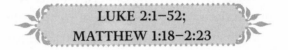

**LUKE 2:1–52;
MATTHEW 1:18–2:23**

I n the first of our chapters on Mary we considered the announcement by the angel Gabriel to Mary that the Messiah would be conceived in her womb. We reflected also on Mary's visit to her cousin Elizabeth who was then several months pregnant with John the Baptist. We looked carefully at the response of the two women to the miracle of which they were privileged to be a part—the miracle of their being involved so fully in events that are the focal point of all human history. For this is indeed the significance of the birth of Christ—it is the turning point, the fulcrum, of all that takes place between the Fall and the end of this age. In her song, the *Magnificat*, it is clear that Mary is aware that God is bringing salvation into this world as he, by his power, enables her to conceive and to bear this child who is God's Messiah.

Toward the end of our first study on Mary we considered the question, what should it mean to us that we are to call Mary "blessed"? Throughout the period of the Middle Ages, Mary gradually became more exalted in popular devotion. Wherever the Reformation spread, it rejected the medieval church's teaching about this elevated status of Mary. The Reformers spoke out against such a view of Mary, for they understood that it undermines the uniqueness of Christ and that it is disobedient to the biblical demand that we recognize Christ as the only Redeemer and as the only Mediator and Advocate between all human persons and God.

The Counter-Reformation, beginning in the 1560s in reaction to the Reformation, solidified in a new and formal way Roman Catholic doctrine about Mary. We referred earlier to a painting by El Greco as an illustration of this Counter-Reformation view of Mary. In the painting the Roman Catholic Church's formal teaching about Mary is set out plainly. Mary is the Queen of Heaven, the one interceding on behalf of sinners with her Son, Jesus, the King of Glory. We see Jesus paying close attention to her prayers of intercession for the soul of a man who had died. Everyone on earth and in heaven is giving their attention to Mary. The focus of attention is on Mary rather than on the person of Christ.

It is important for us to reflect further on this issue. But why is this matter of such importance? Since the time of the sixteenth-century Counter-Reformation, Mary's status has become ever more exalted in the devotion of some sections, though certainly not all, of the Roman Catholic Church. This has been particularly true in the past two centuries. During this period there have been claims of many appearances of Mary to various individuals and to groups of people. Here is a list of such visions that the Roman Catholic Church has recognized or formally acknowledged as being genuine appearances of Mary.

- At the chapel of St. Vincent, Paris, in 1830
- At a grotto near Lourdes, France, in 1858 (Lourdes is a place of pilgrimage where millions of people go each year to pray to Mary for healing)
- At Pontmain, France, in 1871
- At Knock, Ireland, in 1879 (this is another shrine that millions of people visit every year)
- At Fatima, Portugal, in 1917 (another popular place of visitation)
- At Beauraing, Belgium, in 1932 and 1933
- At Banneux, Belgium, in 1933

• At Amsterdam, the Netherlands, where a woman named Ida Pearl-man claimed many appearances in 1945–1959
• At Kibeho, Rwanda, Africa, in 1981–1989 (again many supposed appearances)
• At Medjugorje, Bosnia-Herzegovina, from 1981 to the present.

Each one of these sites attracts great numbers of pilgrims. At the last mentioned site in Bosnia, every year tens of millions of people visit the shrine erected there. People journey to this place in the hope of either seeing Mary or at least with the intention of offering devotion to her at the shrine built in her honor.

Along with the building of shrines and chapels that have multiplied because of the increased "appearances" of Mary, there has been a steady increase of popular devotion to Mary. At each of these sites and in each of these appearances, Mary is said to call herself by some particular name. She then requests that people offer their devotion to her by this name—as "the Immaculate Conception" (Lourdes), confirming the words of a doctrine that the Pope had declared to be true and faithful; "Our Lady of Hope" (Pontmain); the "Immaculate Heart" (Fatima); "the Virgin of the Golden Heart" (Beauraing); "the Virgin of the Poor" (Banneux); "the Lady of All Nations" (Amsterdam); "the Mother of the World" (Kibeho); "the Queen of Peace" (Medjugorje).

In one of these visions Mary is reported to have told the one who saw her to petition the Pope on behalf of what she called "the Last Dogma in Marian History" (Marian History is the history of devotion to Mary). Mary is said to have asked that she be given the titles "Co-Redemptrix" (co-redeemer with Christ), "Mediatrix" (mediator), and "Advocate." The late Pope John Paul II on several occasions used each of these titles to refer to Mary.[1]

It is crystal-clear as we read the New Testament (and also the Old Testament) that each of these three titles is explicitly reserved for Christ. There is only one Redeemer, Christ, who has shed his blood for us (Job 19:25; Romans 3:24; 1 Corinthians 1:30; Ephesians 1:7; Colossians 1:14; Hebrews 9:12; these are just a few of the passages of Scripture addressing this issue of the absolute uniqueness of the redeeming work of Christ).

The apostles teach us that there is only one mediator between the human race and God, the man Christ Jesus (1 Timothy 2:5; Hebrews 9:15; 12:24; again many more references could be set down here that insist on the exclusive nature of Christ's mediating role).

There is only one human advocate, and that is Christ himself (1 John 2:1), who is both human and divine. The third person of the Trinity, the Holy Spirit, is also, of course, an advocate. But there is only one who intercedes at the Father's right hand for us, and that is Jesus (again many passages in the Bible support the final and full efficacy of Christ's intercessory work for us as our only High Priest).

These texts and many others teach us to regard with the utmost doubt and suspicion these supposed requests by Mary to be given the titles of "Co-Redeemer," "Mediatrix," and "Advocate." It is not possible or right to simply respond to such claims and to the devotion they engender by saying that this is a harmless matter or that it is simply a matter of personal conviction that should be ignored. We read regularly in the newspapers that frequent petitions are sent to the Pope signed by millions of Roman Catholics asking that he declare infallibly that Mary be given these titles.

During this same period of about a hundred and fifty years two Popes made dogmatic declarations about Mary. The Pope in office gives public teaching almost every day. However, from time to time, not frequently but on very rare occasions, the Pope makes statements that are declared to be dogma that must be believed by all the faithful. Such dogma is regarded as infallible, like Scripture itself. This means that these dogmatic declarations are claimed to be absolutely true and therefore are to be believed by all the Roman Catholic faithful and by all Christian believers if they wish to be regarded as faithful by the Roman Catholic Church. Because the Roman Catholic Church claims to be the one true Church and consequently God's only true representative on earth, it also demands that all Christian believers accept these dogmatic declarations about Mary if they wish to be regarded by God himself as faithful believers.

The first of these dogmatic statements regarding Mary was given in 1854 when Mary was declared infallibly by the Pope to have been "immaculately conceived." The meaning of this expression is that when her mother conceived her, Mary was preserved from the taint of original sin. In other words, this dogma claims that Mary was conceived and then born into this world without original sin, the sin that is part of our inheritance as descendants of Adam and Eve. The Scripture declares, in contrast, that every descendant of Eve and Adam is born into this world bearing the sinful image of our first parents, and this includes Mary. The only exception to this rule is Jesus himself, for he was conceived in Mary's womb by the power of the Spirit while Mary was yet a virgin.

The second of these dogmatic statements came in 1950 when the Pope declared the "bodily assumption" of Mary. This doctrine claimed that Mary had been "assumed," that is, taken up body and soul into heaven. Her body had no opportunity to decay but rather was taken immediately into glory.

It needs to be said that both of these doctrines have absolutely no foundation in Scripture. With a little research one can trace the development of these doctrines quite readily if one has a basic knowledge of the history of the church from the early medieval period and onward.

The statement on the Assumption of Mary was the last infallible dogma to be declared by the Pope. We have to respond to such Roman Catholic claims about Mary with care and with respect, but we have to be prepared to say that such claims have an element of idolatry. This teaching is far removed from the account that Scripture gives us, and especially far from Mary's own sense of herself as a servant who gives all glory to God (that is the heart of her song) rather than one who asks for glory and titles for herself. In the scriptural accounts of her life Mary is never presented as asking for worship or as demanding heavenly titles.

From this sobering reflection on a particular aspect of the theology and devotion of some Roman Catholics (though certainly not all), we turn to the birth narratives in the Gospels of Luke and of Matthew and to the accounts of Jesus' early childhood and growing up.

From Matthew we learn of Joseph's initial concern at Mary's pregnancy. We hear that as a righteous man, he has no desire to cause Mary public dishonor but instead plans a quiet divorce. However, an angel appears to Joseph and assures him that he can trust Mary, for the child she bears in her womb is not the result of infidelity on her part. Rather, the Spirit of God has conceived the child within her. Joseph responds to this astonishing revelation with faith. He believes and obeys the words of the angel and takes Mary into his home until it is time for the child to be born. Another way we can put this is to say that Joseph marries Mary early, so there will be no gossip about her as her pregnancy continues and as it begins to be publicly obvious that she is with child.

In Luke's Gospel we are given a fuller account of the birth than we are by Matthew. We learn that Joseph and Mary have to travel, late in the pregnancy, to Bethlehem, some seventy to eighty miles south of Nazareth. Bethlehem is Joseph's hometown and the birthplace of David (hence it is called "the city of David," Luke 2:4). Joseph, as a descendant of David, returns to Bethlehem to be taxed under a new census being taken at the insistence of the Roman authorities.

In the kind providence of God, Mary is away from the gossip of her neighborhood when her baby is born, so no one can speculate about the date of the child's conception in relation to the date of her marriage. Yet, despite this merciful distance from Nazareth, the circumstances of the birth of her son are not those that any of us would choose! Who would want to bear their firstborn far away from home and family? What woman would elect to have her child in a strange place after a long journey because of a census required by a foreign occupying power? Who would like to experience labor and birth in a shelter shared by animals and then have to put the newborn baby in a feeding place for cattle? Yet this is the account we read of the coming into this world of its Creator. This does not seem the most auspicious beginning to the life of the King of angels!

Arriving in Bethlehem, there is no room for them at the inn because of so many people arriving for the census; so they make their temporary home in an animal shelter. I use the word *shelter* rather than *stable* because we are not told in the biblical record what kind of place the shelter was. A quite early tradition (second century) places the birth of Jesus in a cave. Caves were often used as stabling places for animals, and one such stabling cave has in fact been discovered under the Church of the Nativity in Bethlehem.

Although we cannot be certain whether the place of Jesus' birth was a stable or a cave, for Luke does not tell us, we do know for sure that it was a place for stabling animals, for Mary puts the newborn child, wrapped fairly tightly in strips of cloth, in a manger or feeding trough for cattle and donkeys.

This is a remarkable part of the history of Christ's birth. What must Mary's thoughts have been at this time, after the amazing words of Gabriel to her? The Lord of Heaven, the Son of God, has to be laid to rest in a manger! There is no palace, or even a pleasant and comfortable home, for the Messiah to be born in and set down to sleep. This disjunction between the circumstances of his birth and what they had been told of his person by the angels must have caused some doubts and struggles in the minds of both Mary and Joseph. They must both have wondered if they had imagined the revelations given to them about their child's origin and significance.

Encouragement comes for Mary and Joseph's faith in the form of the visit of the shepherds arriving to worship the newborn child. Of course, shepherds are not who we might expect to see attending the birth of a king. But they come, this rather lowly group of people, recounting the appearance to them of an angel. This angel surrounded by the blazing glory of God has declared to them the birth of the Christ, the Savior, the Lord.

They report that the angel has also told them that the sign of the truth of this declaration would be that they would find the baby from heaven laid to rest in a manger. (The very early tradition of the second-century church, referred to above, says that this particular cave in Bethlehem was in fact the cave that these shepherds used. Whether that is true or not, we don't know. As with so many of the questions we might like to ask, we will have to wait until we meet the shepherds or Mary or Joseph or even the Lord himself. Then we will be able to ask to our heart's content.)

After the shepherds come and discover the baby lying in the manger and find that everything that the angel has said is true, the shepherds make their announcement to Mary and Joseph. They tell them of the vast choir of heavenly beings that appeared with the angel and of this choir praising God for the peace and favor that will come to the human race because of the birth of the child they have come to worship.

Mary treasures all that the shepherds say in her heart. We may assume that she is eager to remember what she has heard and also that she is desirous of reflecting on the true meaning of these remarkable events.

We can be fairly sure that it is Mary's committing these events to memory that serves many years later to help Luke in the composition of his Gospel. She is the one who must have given these details to Luke so they could be written down. At the time she must have simply wanted to treasure these memories just as any mother treasures the memories of the birth of a child. Mary has the additional motivation in storing these events in her heart so that she may later understand more fully the significance of all that is occurring.

All through the Gospel accounts we read how slow people are, including the apostles, to understand fully just what it means that Jesus is the Messiah. Even though they are with him day after day, listening to his teaching—both the things he teaches publicly and those he says to them in private—they still struggle to understand who Jesus truly is. They do not come to a full understanding until after his resurrection. Through the years of his ministry they wrestle with doubts and unbelief, with uncertainty and questions. Later in the Gospel narratives we see that the same is clearly true of Mary and Joseph and of Jesus' brothers and sisters, the other children who are born to Mary and Joseph after Jesus.[2] Mary, like everyone else, spent her life learning the full truth about her son.

Mary and Joseph, in obedience to the angel, agree that their son is to be named Jesus. The social custom was that parents would choose a family name for the child, but Mary and Joseph obey the angel, just as Elizabeth and Zechariah named their son John in obedience to the angel's command. The naming takes place on the day of Jesus' circumcision. Circumcision is performed on the eighth day of a boy's life.

Why is Jesus circumcised? Circumcision was a requirement of the Law for every male born in Israel. The meaning of circumcision was putting one's trust in God rather than in oneself, and this trust in God for one's life and salvation was symbolized by the cutting away of the flesh. Circumcision was a sign of the cutting away of the body of sin, the cutting away of self-reliance. In this way the meaning of circumcision and baptism are very similar. Both signs look away from oneself to God. Both express trust in him rather than in oneself. Both signs picture the need for sin and the self to be put away (the one by cutting, the other by washing). Both circumcision and baptism are God's seal of his love marked on the body of the one who belongs to him.

But understanding the meaning of circumcision simply makes us ask more insistently, why does the infant Jesus need to be circumcised? We ask this question because we know that Jesus lived a sinless life. However, from the very beginning of his life, Jesus identified himself with sinners as well as with the lowly and humble (his birth in an animal shelter; the visit of shepherds; an ordinary couple as his parents). His mission in this world was to save sinners, and so he identifies himself with you and with me and with the whole sinful human race. The rite of circumcision is part of this identification with the sinners he came to save.

CLEANSING AND DEDICATION

Following this account of Jesus' circumcision, Luke's record of events tells us of the journey up to Jerusalem. What was their journey for? Parents rarely take a tiny baby any distance so soon after his birth without some strong reason. Mary and Joseph travel to Jerusalem on the fortieth day after Jesus' birth, and their journey is an indication of their faith. They take the child up to the temple in Jerusalem to offer him to the Lord, just as Samuel had been dedicated to God at the house of worship. Two things are taking place in this visit to the temple.

The first of these is that according to the Law, because of the flow of blood associated with birth, Mary is ritually unclean before God until the fortieth day, at which time she has to go up to the temple to offer a sacrifice for her own cleansing from impurity and sin (Leviticus 12:1–8).

The parents' poverty is shown by the fact that they cannot afford to offer a lamb, the usual sacrifice in this situation, but rather have to offer two pigeons or two turtledoves, one for a burnt offering (the rededication of oneself to God), the other for a sin offering. Joseph and Mary present the least expensive, smallest sacrifice allowed by the Law—"a pair of turtledoves, or two young pigeons" (Luke 2:24).

What loving parents would give such a little sacrifice as they publicly present their firstborn son to God in his temple unless they are completely unable to afford something more? What do these details about the difficult circumstances of Jesus' birth and early days (the poverty of Mary and Joseph; the concern about illegitimacy; the closeness of scandal; the birth far from home in an animal shelter) teach us?

They point us to the paradox at the heart of Jesus' life and ministry. He is the Lord of the heavens, worshipped by angels—yet he is born as a frail human baby. He is the King of all kings—yet he takes his first breath among farm animals. He is rich beyond any splendor that can be imagined—yet he is poor. He is the Son of God—yet he is a servant. This is the mystery at the heart of the Incarnation, a mystery that will fill our hearts and minds with wonder and praise for all eternity.

At the same time as making their offering for Mary's cleansing, Mary and Joseph accomplish their second purpose in journeying to Jerusalem: they offer Jesus, their firstborn son, to the Lord. In recounting this offering Luke quotes a passage that comes from Exodus 13:2, 12, 15. The offering of the firstborn to God was an element of the original celebration of the Passover.

In fact, we learn from the biblical account that the dedication of the firstborn was changed shortly after the Exodus, the time at which God instituted the Passover along with the requirement for each family to offer their firstborn, as the firstborn of each Egyptian family was slain by the Angel of Death. Not long after the first Passover, the offering of the firstborn was replaced by the offering of the Levites to God as a substitute for them. But when this substitution takes place, the parents pay five shekels for the substitution each time a first son is born.

Mary and Joseph, however, like Hannah, go to offer their son to God's service at the temple, dedicating their son to the service of God just as Samuel had been dedicated to God. This offering is an expression of their faith in God and of their confidence that the child is indeed the one that the angel had said he would be.

There at the temple Mary and Joseph receive further confirmation about the true nature of their son. First there is Simeon, a devout man who is waiting for the coming of the Messiah, "the consolation of Israel" (Luke 2:25; see Isaiah 40:1–2). The Spirit of God reveals to Simeon that he should go to the temple and that this little child, just forty days old, is indeed the Messiah.

Inspired by the Spirit, Simeon utters his famous words, sung ever since by believers as the *Nunc Dimmittis.* He reveals that the Christ-child will not only save and comfort his people Israel but will also be the Savior of "all peoples" (v. 31), the Light of the world. The mention of "all peoples" appears to be news for the parents, and they are astonished by Simeon's words (if they had reflected with care on the Old Testament prophecies, they would have eventually realized there would be this international aspect to their son's ministry). In addition, Simeon turns to the parents, who are marveling at these words, and gives them some troubling information. Simeon's hard words are for Mary in particular.

Her child, Jesus, will be the stone on which people will stumble and fall into judgment when they reject him or do not believe in him or he will be the rock in which they put their trust and so are built up into life (cf. Isaiah 8:14). Each person's eternal destiny will be determined by his or her response to this little child. He is the cornerstone of all history; he is the fulcrum on which eternity is balanced.

This passage from Isaiah is a Scripture to which Jesus would refer many times during the years of his public ministry. This determinative significance of Jesus, means, of course, that he will always be a source of controversy and division as well as a source of eternal life and blessing. Later on Jesus himself would say that he came not to bring peace but a sword (Matthew 10:34).

Simeon also warns Mary that her son will be criticized and condemned by many and that her own heart will be pierced as with a sword. Here Simeon predicts the rejection of Jesus and his death and the anguish that this will bring to Mary. (There is a wonderful painting by Rembrandt of this scene.) No mother wants to hear of her child's death when she is so full of joy over his birth!

In addition to Simeon another person is present at the temple on the day Jesus is taken there. This other person is Anna, an elderly woman (either eighty-four or more probably 105), who is waiting for the coming of the Christ. The Spirit of God reveals to her that the long-awaited Christ is there in the temple. She too comes forward, thanking God for Christ's presence and also proclaiming his coming to all those who are looking for God's redemption through the fulfillment of his promise to send the Messiah.

Anna, of course, is another example of a woman who declares to others the good news of God's salvation, and it is clear that she speaks to everyone—to women and to men—for she, like Simeon, is filled with the Holy Spirit, who enables her to communicate to all the people the good news about Jesus.

JESUS, THE BOY AT THE TEMPLE

Our final scene for our reflections in this chapter takes place twelve years later. Jesus has been living in Nazareth, his parents' permanent home, and all through these years he has given himself to loving them and to living in submission to them. He has been steadily growing in stature and in wisdom and in favor with all who know him, both those around him on earth and also his ever-present and ever watchful heavenly Father (Luke 2:52).

Each year, as the Law requires (Exodus 23:15; Deuteronomy 16:1–8), Jesus' parents take him up to Jerusalem at the Feast of the

Passover. This is a time when, for a week every year, there are great family reunions as Jerusalem is filled with a far larger population than usual because of all the people who are coming up for the celebration of the Feast. Many of the families stay in tents around the city if they have no relatives in Jerusalem to offer them hospitality. So this annual event is a season of feasting and rejoicing, a time for worship, and also a time for reacquainting oneself with distant relatives and friends.

At the age of twelve Jesus demonstrates to his parents that he is indeed the Son of God and that his true home is the temple in Jerusalem, the place where he must serve his heavenly Father and where he will begin his life's work of teaching the people. It is only after a whole day on the journey home that Mary and Joseph miss the boy. They assume that he is visiting with friends or relatives, spending time together as they travel among the crowds back north to Nazareth (about seventy to eighty miles). However, they do not find him with his friends and relatives, and so they make their way back to Jerusalem.

On their anxious return to Jerusalem they search for three days until they find the boy at the temple (they should, perhaps, have gone there first to look for him). There in the temple Jesus is causing astonishment among the teachers of the Law both by the wisdom of his questions and by the depth of understanding revealed in his answers. Jesus has obviously been studying hard at his local school, taking his lessons very seriously, and he already has a deep knowledge of the Scriptures. (Each community had its own synagogue school to teach reading and to study the Scriptures.)

This knowledge of the Scriptures is not innate in him, nor does it simply come to him without the exertion of effort. Rather, just like any other child, Jesus has to learn all that he knows, for he is fully human and so must grow physically and spiritually as all other children do.

This realization of his true humanity and what being fully human means for Jesus is always a challenge for our minds to grasp. How can the One who is Very God have to grow in wisdom? we want to ask. There is, of course, an element of mystery in our understanding of how Jesus experienced being both human and divine, an element of mystery that I doubt we can ever move beyond, not only in this life but also in the life to come. However, we should note that this element of mystery is actually present in many of the most important aspects of our knowledge.[3]

Mary is, quite naturally, troubled by the anxious search for her son; so she asks why he has treated her and Joseph in this way. Jesus replies that they should have known that he would be in his Father's house, serving him there. They have known since before his birth that his true calling is to serve the heavenly Father; so they should not have been surprised by discovering him teaching in the temple.

What is the point of this story? Jesus is teaching Mary and Joseph that they have to be prepared to let him go, that they need to recognize that their authority over him is only temporary, and that his calling is to give his life to the ministry for which his true Father sent him into the world. Coming to such a realization must have been difficult for Mary and Joseph, just as it is difficult for all of us who are parents to recognize that God is the true Father and Lord of all of our children and that we are to submit to his purposes for their lives.

When baptizing children as children of God's covenant promises, I always ask the parents of the child, "Do you realize that this child belongs to God rather than to you? If God should call this child to serve him in a distant place, far from you, do you promise that you will not stand in your child's way but will rather encourage your child to seek the Father's will?" I also ask, "If this child should die before you do, will you promise not to complain against God that he has taken the child back to be with his/her true Father?" We all need to understand that all of our children belong to God before they belong to us—he is the true parent of each one of our children.[4] We are to fulfill the calling of teaching our children that they belong first of all to their heavenly Father. I am not suggesting that our children are in exactly the same position as the child Jesus. Of course, he was unique as the only Son of the Father. Rather, my point is that all parents face a challenge similar to that of Mary and

Joseph, for we all have to recognize God's primary authority over our children.

Mary and Joseph struggle to understand and to accept Jesus' behavior and his words, and once more we read that Mary keeps these events in her heart to ponder on their true meaning (v. 51). Jesus is eager for his parents to acknowledge that his first desire must be to serve his heavenly Father, for this is the first and greatest commandment to which to give his life—indeed, this is the first and greatest commandment for each one of us to follow. In Jesus' case, loving God first will mean separation from his parents. On this occasion, however, Jesus returns with them, ready to live in submission to them for the rest of his youth. But they would need to remember this lesson about his life's work in all the years to come.

We see Mary having to relearn this lesson at a later date (Mark 3:31–35), on an occasion when she and her other sons try to call Jesus away from his ministry. Mary and the brothers of Jesus are disturbed by what people are saying about Jesus. Some are declaring that Jesus is crazy; others are saying that he has an evil spirit. And so Mary and his brothers arrive to try to take him back home with them.

Their request that he should go home with them comes to Jesus as he is teaching. However, he dismisses their request by telling those listening that all who do his will are his mother, his brothers, and his sisters. These words are clearly intended as a rebuke to his mother and to his siblings. Their first calling is to do the will of God, not to seek to control Jesus' life. Again this is a difficult challenge for each one of us to hear and to obey.

No doubt Jesus' rebuke on this occasion is a difficult word for Mary to hear. Mary has to be ready to let Jesus go, both in his life and then later at his death. Yet even at his death we see Jesus still committed to her, still tender to her in his concern for her (John 19:25–27), when, on the cross, he asks his beloved disciple John to care for Mary as if she were his own mother.

In each of these scenes we see Mary growing in her faith in God, and we see her growing in understanding and in accepting God's purposes for her son. Yet the biblical text also requires us to see Mary as one who struggles to understand the true nature of Jesus as the Son of God. Steadily and with some confusion along the way, Mary has to come to terms with Jesus' calling to be the Messiah whom God had promised, his mission to be the revealer of truth to all peoples, his destiny to be the one who will bring rejection on himself because of his clear teaching about his uniqueness as the only Son of God, his central purpose to be the one who will die as a sacrificial lamb for the sins of all nations.

Quite understandably, we see Mary finding it difficult to let Jesus go, wrestling with allowing him to fulfill his heavenly Father's calling. In these texts Mary is presented to us as an ordinary woman. Mary is just like every other woman and mother in this world; and like every other mother she has to learn to let her son grow up and go out into the world in pursuit of his life's goal. This means that Mary is one to whose life every other woman can relate.

But these reflections on Mary's struggles to come to terms with the true nature and calling of her son also remind us of the inappropriateness of regarding her as exalted above her humanity in status. Nowhere in Scripture is Mary presented to us as one who desires to be followed and addressed in devotion as the Queen of Heaven or with any other grandiloquent title.

Nowhere in Scripture do we see Mary presented as one without sin or as one who has a far greater righteousness or much more extensive wisdom than other women or men. She is certainly a wonderful example to us, as Abraham is an example for us all; and she is a heroine of the faith, just as Ruth and Rahab are heroines of the faith.

We are indeed to honor Mary, and we are to recognize joyfully the blessed position she occupies in salvation history. By God's sovereign choice Mary always will hold her unique position as the mother of Jesus. All Christians are to call her "blessed" (Luke 1:41, 48) because of this. All of us are to see her as a model of faith and as a shining example of humble submission to the Lord. In this sense Mary is the mother of the faithful just as Abraham is the father of the faithful. However, our honor for Mary is to extend no further than these glad acknowledgments of her unique place and calling in the history of our redemption through Christ.

SUGGESTED READINGS AND QUESTIONS

1. Can you imagine yourself giving birth to a child in the circumstances in which Mary had to give birth to Jesus or being a father like Joseph, who had to endure seeing his wife give birth in an animal shelter?

2. What do you think would have been the most difficult things for Mary (or for Joseph) at the time of Jesus' birth, and which do you think would have been the most precious memories that she (or Joseph) would never forget?

3. For those of you reading this who have given birth to a child (or have fathered one), what, for you, are the most difficult memories and what are the most precious?

4. Are there ways in which you identify with Mary's situation (or with Joseph's)? For those of you reading this who do not have children, what do you imagine would be the ways in which you might identify with Mary (or with Joseph)?

5. Are you attracted to the teaching that Mary is the Queen of Heaven or that she should be titled Advocate, Mediatrix, and Co-Redeemer? If you are attracted to this teaching and the devotion to Mary that it engenders, what biblical support would you cite to defend your views?

6. The first scene at the temple (the time of dedication and cleansing) teaches us much. For example, we learn that Mary needed a sacrifice to be offered for her sin, that she was prepared to dedicate her child to the Lord, that she was understanding more all the time about who he truly was, that God was revealing to other believers the nature of his destiny. What do you think would have been the most important thing that Mary and Joseph learned at that time of the dedication of their son?

7. Why do you think that Jesus had to teach Mary and Joseph a lesson in a way that was so difficult and so anxiety-causing for them when he remained behind at the temple for several days without notifying them when he was only twelve years old?

8. For those of you who are mothers or fathers, what do you find most difficult about letting your children grow up and leave home to take up their own calling in life? For those of you who are not mothers or fathers, what were the stresses in your home at the time you began to mature and to pursue your own vision for your life? What did your parents find difficult about that time?

9. Read for our next chapter John 4:4–42. What do we learn about Jesus' treatment of women from this passage? Why, for example, is the Samaritan woman so surprised by Jesus' words to her? Why are the disciples so surprised when they return and find him talking to the woman at the well?

18

THE WOMAN OF SAMARIA
BELOVED OUTCAST

JOHN 4:4–42

In our two studies of Mary we discovered Mary to be a woman who was gentle and humble in spirit. She understood her place in history; she submitted with faith and with grace to the role that God called her to play as the mother of the one who was to be the Messiah, the one who is both truly human and also the divine Son of God. Yet we see Mary as a faithful believer who drew attention to what God was doing in history rather than to her own role. In the stories that are recounted for us in the pages of the New Testament, we never find Mary seeking titles for herself. Nor do we discover her desiring a place of exaltation alongside her Son. Nor do we hear her asking people to pray to her because of her unique relationship with Christ. Mary does not present herself and the New Testament does not present her as Co-Redemptrix, Mediatrix, or Advocate.

Yet we all know people personally who address their prayers to Mary, people who think of her as their advocate with the Son, our Lord Jesus Christ, people who regularly pray, "Blessed Mary, Mother of God, pray for us now, and at the hour of our death." St. Louis, the city in which I live, has a large number of Roman Catholics, its two major population groups being, first, German, and, second, Irish in their national origin; and today there is a rapidly increasing Hispanic population, many of whom, like the Germans and the Irish, have Catholic convictions. The reality of knowing many Roman Catholics raises a question for us: how are we to relate to those who have a confused theology when it comes to the uniqueness and complete sufficiency of the redeeming, mediating, and advocating work of Christ?

This leads us to a broader question: how are we to relate to anyone whose theology we believe to be mistaken or confused in any area of God's truth? One common answer is that often we allow barriers to exist between ourselves and other people whose theology, beliefs, and practices are different from our own, whether those beliefs and practices arise within other Christian traditions or whether they are completely outside the Christian church.

The barriers we raise might come from pride in ourselves and in our own convictions or from hostility to others and their beliefs. They might be barriers of condemnation because of what others think or because of their manner of life. Such barriers may lead to personal separation from other people, both for us and for our children. Believers in Christ can all too readily desire a kind of cultural isolation. "We are to be separate," we say, and so we have nothing to do with these others, whoever they may be, and so we never allow the gospel of grace to penetrate through the barriers we raise because we are intent on keeping ourselves and our children "pure" and "apart" from anyone whose theology and life is not exactly like our own.

But is this how we ought to think and live? To answer this question we will look at the occasion when Jesus met the Samaritan woman in John 4 and reflect on the way he related to her. As we reflect on Jesus' encounter with the woman at the well, we can perhaps learn something about tearing down barriers that confront us and instead beginning to build bridges into the lives of other people out of obedience to Christ.

JESUS' INTENTIONAL LIFE

Our text in John's Gospel describes a brief meeting that Jesus has with the Samaritan woman, but this conversation leads to a two-day stay in the village of Sychar, and as a consequence of his time there, many more of the villagers come to believe in Jesus. We might ask the question, does this meeting with the woman come about by chance? Does she just happen to be at the well when Jesus stops there to rest from his journey?

We saw in our last chapter that from his earliest years Jesus was committed to being about his Father's work. Later Jesus teaches explicitly that everything he does, everything he says, and even the words he speaks are all in obedience to his Father's will (John 12:49; 14:31). This means that Jesus does not go anywhere by chance. His whole life is a series of divine appointments. So it should be no surprise that in describing Jesus' sojourn in Samaria, John opens his account with the words, "And he *had to* pass through Samaria" (John 4:4).

Why does Jesus *have* to go through Samaria? In Jesus' day Jewish people usually did not go through Samaria unless they were in a hurry, and if they were in haste, then they "had to pass through Samaria." But Jesus is clearly not in a hurry, for we read in verse 40 that he stays two days in Sychar.

There were three routes by which a Jew could travel north from Judea to Galilee. First, one could journey inland along the Jordan River to the east; second, one could go by the coast road along the Mediterranean to the west; third, one could go by the most direct route through Samaria. Usually the Jews would not take the short-cut through Samaria without compelling reasons. They would go by either of the two longer roads to Galilee from Judea in order to avoid contact with the Samaritans. The Jews had a saying that if one met a Samaritan walking along the road, one should walk into the ditch to avoid contact even between the two shadows! They believed that any contact with Samaritans would make them morally and religiously unclean.

Why does Jesus, a Jew, have compelling reasons to go through Samaria? He is eager to meet the woman at the well. He desires, in obedience to his Father, to make the gospel known in Jerusalem, Judea, Samaria, and beyond to Gentiles. John draws attention to the divine constraint that burns in Jesus' heart to be the Savior not only of the Jews but of the world. That is why he begins his account with the words, "And he had to pass through Samaria."

Who was this person whom Jesus feels constrained to meet? What do we know about the woman Jesus meets at the well?

THE PROBLEM OF HER RACE

First we need to think about her race. As a Samaritan she is a member of the wrong race—that is, from the perspective of the Jews. The Samaritans were a people of mixed race. Partially they were descended from the remnants of the northern tribes of Israel. After the reign of Solomon the nation of Israel had split, becoming two nations—the southern kingdom of Judah, made up of people from the tribes of Benjamin and Judah, with its capital in Jerusalem, and the northern kingdom of Israel, made up of people from the ten northern tribes, with its capital in Samaria. Many of the people from the kingdom of Samaria were taken captive after their defeat at the hands of the Assyrians and resettled in far eastern parts of the Assyrian Empire (in the region of Iraq and Iran today).

Long before Jesus' day these descendants of the ten northern tribes were no longer purely Israeli, for many of their ancestors had intermarried while they were living in exile (as Esther did, for example). Others who had returned to Samaria after their years of exile or who had remained in Samaria after the conquest had intermarried with the other peoples that the Assyrians had moved to Samaria in their policy of conquering and resettling (see 2 Kings 17:21–24).

In Jesus' time the Jews hated the Samaritans even more than they despised "pure" Gentiles, for they regarded them as polluting the blood of the patriarchs. For this reason the Jews often took one of the longer routes around Samaria rather than the direct and shorter road through the center of the country.

THE PROBLEM OF HER RELIGION

So the woman at the well, whom Jesus is so desirous of meeting, is a Samaritan, a person of mixed race. As a Samaritan her religion is also mixed. The Samaritans' religion was a blend of the worship of the true God with the pagan idolatry of the peoples from around Babylon who had been settled there in the northern part of Israel by the conquering Assyrians. The Samaritans accepted only the books of Moses as Scripture and had built their own temple on Mount Gerizim, for they claimed that Mount Gerizim was the proper place to worship the Lord. The Jews had fought against the Samaritans and burned down their temple in 128 B.C. because of the fierce religious hostility between these two peoples. The Jews despised Samaritans as heretics because of their confused theology and their improper worship. We need to ask ourselves if there are people whom we despise and from whom we separate ourselves because of what we consider to be their confused theology and their inappropriate worship.

THE PROBLEM OF HER GENDER

Jesus is eager to meet this woman despite her race and her theology. In addition to these two barriers that would have kept most Jews from talking with her, the woman at the well also has the problem of her gender. She is, of course, a woman. Why should this be considered a problem? Jewish rabbis or teachers at that time did not have women as disciples. Women were not allowed to be witnesses in court, for the rabbis considered women to be irrational and untrustworthy. In fact, there is said to have been a prayer of the Pharisees in which they thanked God that they were not Gentiles or slaves or women.

It is very striking that Paul reverses this prayer when he describes our unity in Christ: "in Christ Jesus you are all sons of God, through faith. For as many of you as were baptized into Christ have put on Christ. There is neither Jew nor Greek, there is neither slave nor free, there is no male and female, for you are all one in Christ Jesus. And if you are Christ's, then you are Abraham's offspring, heirs according to promise" (Galatians 3:26–29).

Paul clearly learned from Jesus' own example and teaching that the view of the Pharisees and the teachers of the Law was offensive to the Lord. Jesus, as God's Son, is the second person of the Trinity. It is he, the eternal Word, who is the Creator of both male and female in his image and likeness. Who better than Jesus to show by his example that women, designed and created by him, are the full equals of men, that every woman in this world is just as fully the representative and bearer of God's image as is every man. Jesus loves to honor women by asking them to bear witness to him, just as he called two women, Mary Magdalene and Mary the mother of James and Joseph, to be the first witnesses of his resurrection. Unlike his contemporaries Jesus trusts the witness of women. He is eager to meet this woman, for he gladly calls women to faith and discipleship.

THE PROBLEM OF HER SIN

Jesus feels constrained to overcome these barriers of race, religion, and gender. The woman at the well also has a fourth problem—her sin. Her sin is not the secret or "respectable" kind; rather, this woman is known by all to be a sinner, an immoral woman. She has been married five times and is now living with a man outside of any marriage contract.

Divorce at that time was fairly easy for men. If a man found another woman more to his liking or if he found fault with a woman for any reason (Matthew 19:3, 8), he could divorce her (this was the understanding of the more "liberal" wing of the Pharisees in the first century A.D.; and apparently there was a similar approach among the Samaritans). In such situations the woman was always viewed as the one at fault. Consequently, a woman divorced five times was a woman despised by everyone. A man did not need to marry her to have her, for she was a woman who could be passed from man to man. She would be scorned and hated by other women, for they would see her not only as a failure in her marriages but as a danger to their own marriages. Here was a woman in their small community who was known to be sexually available, and so in every way she would have low social status. Everyone would regard her as a "real sinner."

This badge of dishonor meant that the Samaritan woman was unacceptable not only to Jews but even to her own people. That is probably why she was at this particular well some distance from town, alone, at an unusual time of day. The women would usually go to draw water in the cool early morning or in the evening after the heat of the day had passed, and ordinarily they would go together, for this was a time for meeting friends and for social interaction with one's neighbors. But this woman is at the well by herself in the full heat of the day.

JESUS, FRIEND OF THE OUTCAST

Who is the one who goes out of his way to meet this mixed-race, heretical, sinful person? It is, of course, Jesus, who in this one passage is described as:

- The gift of God
- The one who gives living water
- A prophet
- One greater than the patriarch Jacob
- The Messiah
- The One who will explain everything to us
- "I . . . am he"
- The one who can tell us everything we ever did
- The Savior of the world

How does the Son of God, the Messiah, meet the woman at the well? How does the one who is both God and man, who in his Godhead and in his manhood is completely holy, who is separated from sinners, relate to this person who has so many barriers existing between himself and her?

SETTING ASIDE CUSTOM AND LAW

Jesus breaks his culture's customs and laws by asking the woman at the well for a drink of water (v. 7). In reflecting on this seemingly ordinary request we should note that Jews did not drink or eat from containers used by Samaritans. Rabbi Eliezer taught, "He who eats the bread of the Samaritans is like one who eats the flesh of swine" (and we know, of course, that the Jews were forbidden to eat pork). But Jesus breaks his people's social customs, and in fact the Jewish law of the time, when he asks the woman to use her container to draw water from the well for him and then give him a drink from this vessel that she has handled. No Jew had ever requested food or drink from her before. Jesus does not even have something to drink from of his own, something purified by Jewish law. He will have to drink from a container that she has handled. She is amazed because she is aware of the extraordinary nature of his request: "The Samaritan woman said to him, 'How is it that you, a Jew, ask for a drink from me, a woman of Samaria?'" (v. 9).

We should notice also how John draws attention to her amazement that Jesus is talking to a woman as well as to a Samaritan. No man had ever before addressed her as a social equal. His disciples, too, are surprised to find him talking with a woman when they return (v. 27). This surprise shows how little they yet knew him! All through the Gospel accounts we see Jesus treating women as equals, calling women to faith and to discipleship, teaching them the truth, and commissioning them for service in his kingdom.

Jesus sets aside the usual barriers that would have kept him apart from the woman at the well. He ignores social custom, even Jewish law, in order to reach out to her. In the eyes of the Pharisees and teachers of the Law and of all devout Jews at that time, Jesus would have been making himself ceremonially unclean—he would pollute himself by drinking water she had drawn for him, from a container she had touched.

Jesus acts as if the problem of race does not exist at all. And, of course, it does not. He is the Creator of every people group on the face of the earth; and as the Lord of Israel and the Lord of heaven and earth, he knew better than anyone how far from racially pure the people of Israel were. Indeed, he did not desire them to be racially pure, for he was the one who called Tamar, Rahab, and Ruth to come from outside Israel and to be incorporated into the line of his ancestry. In fact, of course, there can be no such state as racial purity, for all of us, from every race, every people, every tribe, and every language are descended from Eve and Adam.

From the moment he called Sarah and Abraham, God longed for the people of Israel to include those from all over the earth (see Psalm 87).[1] He was the Lord who had called individuals and groups from many nations to be a part of his holy nation. He was the one who had chosen women from outside Israel, women like Tamar, Rahab, and Ruth, to be his own ancestors. So Jesus has no regard for his fellow Jews' views about the importance of racial purity. For Jesus the fact that this Samaritan is a woman is not an issue to consider either. He treats her with respect as a social equal.

All of us have much to learn from Jesus' encounter with the Samaritan woman. Our social backgrounds and even our churches have many customs and regulations that keep us apart from people who are different from us. Jesus calls us to discard all such customs and regulations for the sake of the gospel and out of respect for the people from whom they separate us. He desires that we love our neighbor as ourselves, whoever those neighbors may be.

REVEALING HIS NEEDS

Jesus shows his vulnerability and need to the Samaritan woman— he is tired and thirsty. The Creator of the world, the One who is the source of every river, every spring, every ocean, every drop of rainfall, the One who is the fountain of living water, the One who needs nothing from anyone—this One asks the Samaritan woman for a drink. He dignifies her by acknowledging his need of something she can do for him. He shows his vulnerability to her. He is thirsty and tired, and she can help him. Again, this is such an ordinary request, but Jesus could not have done anything more dignifying.

Such a request would have scandalized his contemporaries, not only the Pharisees and rabbis with their rules and regulations for every detail of life, but even the ordinary people whose lives were burdened down with such teaching. Yet we find Jesus asking for help or receiving what sinners can give him on numerous occasions—for example, with Zacchaeus, the tax collector (Luke 19:1–9), when Jesus invites himself to Zacchaeus' home for a meal, and with the prostitute who anoints his feet with precious ointment after washing them with her tears and drying them with her hair (Luke 7:36–50).

In the same way, Jesus invites all of us to be his sisters and brothers, he refers to us as his friends, he calls us to ministry along with himself, and he declares that he is honored to know us (Hebrews 11:16). All of us can learn from the example of Jesus.

So often as Christians we think it inappropriate or even ungodly to have friends who are sinners, to have any personal and warm social interaction with unbelievers. We sometimes behave as if we have everything to give to the non-Christian and nothing to receive. We imagine that it would be demeaning for us to acknowledge any weakness or need. We think that letting unbelievers see that we don't have everything together and that we need or value what non-Christians have to give us or that we value unbelievers as persons might bring discredit on us and on the gospel.

This is folly, for the truth is that we are always morally flawed, our theology is never perfect, and like everyone else in this fallen world we are weak and needy. The gospel of Christ is not served by pretending otherwise. To acknowledge, as Jesus does, our need of the kindness, gifts, wisdom, or advice that an unbeliever may give us is encouraging and ennobling to those who may have been led to expect only scorn or condescension from us. I grew up in a home in which my parents were not at that time believers in the gospel of Christ. My father was a committed Communist. However, my parents had the best marriage I have ever seen, and they were wonderful parents. Every day of my life I am proud to say they are my inspiration as I think about how the Lord calls me to love my wife, my three sons, my daughters-in-law, and my, at present, six grandchildren.

RESPECTFUL DISCUSSION

Jesus treats the Samaritan woman as a rational and thoughtful person. He should know, of course, for he is the Creator of women as persons, persons who are just as much the image of God as any man he has made. As the Creator of women he is fully aware of her intellectual abilities and her capacity to learn and discuss theology. No teacher (and no man) has ever spoken to her in this way before. But Jesus enters into a theological discussion with her.

What subjects did they cover? John's account is brief, so one day we can ask her for a full recap of her conversation with Jesus. But even in John's few words we see them discussing the living water that only Jesus can give and that fills the soul to overflowing forever. They discuss the patriarch Jacob who had given that particular well to his descendants and who was honored by the Samaritans. They discuss the site of the proper place for worship—whether it should be Jerusalem as the Jews claimed or Mount Gerizim as the Samaritans insisted. Jesus identifies the nature of true worship that is soon no longer to be bound to a particular place but that the Father desires to be offered in spirit and in truth.

They also discuss the coming of the Messiah. The Samaritans expected the Messiah and called him the *Taheb*, the Restorer, on the basis of the promise of a great prophet like Moses who would teach all the truth, a promise recorded in Deuteronomy 18:17–19. The Samaritans had only the first five books of the Bible, but they expected the Messiah because of that promise of a great prophet in Deuteronomy.

They also discuss the fact that salvation will be from the Jews. The Samaritan woman would also have known this because of the prophecy in Genesis 49:9–10 that the Messiah would come as the lion from the tribe of Judah to rule all the nations. In discussing theology with her, Jesus is again demonstrating respect despite her race, her wrong theology, her gender, and her sin.

Are we prepared to follow Jesus' example and to take people and their theology seriously and respectfully? Are we willing to have thoughtful discussions with them, even if we consider their ideas to be confused, as with those Roman Catholics who offer prayers to Mary as their advocate with Christ, or if we think them to be heretical, as, for example, with the Jehovah's Witnesses or the Mormons or those who follow a New Age Jesus?

GENTLENESS AND GRACE

Jesus approaches the Samaritan woman graciously. He speaks to her with grace and gentleness even about her sin, which clearly weighs heavily upon her. She refers to this part of their conversation later by saying that he told me "all that I ever did" (v. 29). Her failures in the area of marriage and sexuality had become for her a definition of her whole life. Everyone else characterized her by her broken marriages, and so she had begun to think of herself in the same way. In her mind it is clearly this aspect of what Jesus says that causes her to draw the conclusion that he is a prophet (vv. 16–19). She knows that the Messiah will teach the whole truth of God, and so she realizes that Jesus must be the Messiah because of his deep and truthful knowledge of her life. Her response to Jesus' words leads in turn to Jesus' plain declaration that he is indeed the Messiah and to her putting her faith in him.

How sweetly and gently Jesus draws her to himself! In reflecting on Jesus' approach to her, we need to ask ourselves how we might behave in similar circumstances. How do we respond to the sin that is so often apparent in people's lives? Do we become guarded, reserved, and withdrawn? Do we communicate disapproval and personal rejection? Is scorn and contempt revealed in our tone of voice and our facial expression? Jesus shows none of these things.

As we reflect on this passage we need to remember that for the Son of God all of us should be outcasts. We should be outcasts socially from his presence, for he is the man who is God and who is therefore higher above us than the heavens are above the earth. We should be outcasts religiously and theologically, for we are all confused in our thinking (not one of us has all our doctrine correct) and have many errors in our lives, for we are all idolaters who worship many things in addition to the Lord. We should all be outcasts, above all, as those who have sinned, and so we are people with no right of entrance to meet with him who is the absolutely Holy One.

And yet Jesus comes to each of us with grace, gentleness, and respect. He meets each of us and leads us through confusion to the knowledge of the truth, just as he brings this Samaritan woman to that truth.

He shows us our sin without making us feel rejected and condemned in his holy presence. Instead he causes us to know that we are loved, forgiven, welcomed, and accepted, just as he accepts this lonely woman. He welcomes us to sit at his table and to eat with him, and he intends to serve us at the Marriage Supper of the Lamb. And who knows but there at his wedding feast we may find ourselves sitting next to the woman at the well, sharing stories of his merciful and amazing love!

Jesus, the Lord of heaven and earth, who needs nothing from us, asks for our friendship. He even declares himself proud to be our God, just as he is honored to be the God of the woman of Sychar.

Jesus entrusts us with responsible tasks in his service, just as he commissions this Samaritan woman to bear the good news to her husband and bring him back. She cannot do this, of course, for she has no husband, but she does bear the good news to her neighbors and brings them back to meet Jesus. She is the first witness to the Savior in her community, for Jesus gladly commissions women to be ambassadors of his reconciliation and to be witnesses to his divine nature, to his being the Christ, and to his amazing love.

This Samaritan woman is a very successful evangelist! Her words to her neighbors lead to Jesus' staying two more days in the village and to many of them meeting him and becoming believers. Like her, they come to know that this man is "the Savior of the world" (v. 42). Jesus delights to honor her witness and to do his work in that village. Jesus does the hard work, but he calls her to serve him in his great mission to call people to him, for he is indeed the One who desires to save people from every nation under heaven.

We are all in the position that Jesus describes in his words to his disciples (vv. 35–38). We sometimes get to reap a harvest as we see someone come to faith in Christ; but when we do enjoy this privilege, we are to remember that someone else has done the hard labor, and that someone else is Jesus.

SUGGESTED READINGS AND QUESTIONS

1. Do you think that too much was read into the words from John 4:4, "And he had to pass through Samaria"?

2. What to you are the most striking aspects of Jesus' encounter with the woman at the well?

3. What would it mean for you to "pass through Samaria"? What groups of people are equivalent to Samaritans, heretics, women, or sinners for you? Can you think of people for whom your committing yourself to follow Jesus' example would require you to begin to treat them differently?

4. Are there people you have had trouble respecting in your family, in your neighborhood, or in your workplace? What practical steps could you take to build a new relationship with people whom you might have treated without due respect in the past?

5. What other examples can you think of from the Gospels that so clearly demonstrate Jesus' respect for people?

6. What other examples from the Gospels can you think of that demonstrate Jesus' commitment to be the Savior of the world and not just the Savior of the Jewish people?

7. Are there individuals who are not believers whom it might be wise to ask to do something for you? Are there those for whom it might be important to reveal your vulnerability and need?

8. Who are the "Samaritans" for your church? What might it mean for your church, as a congregation, to be ready to "pass through Samaria"? What changes in attitude and practice might have to be made?

9. Read for our next chapter the account of Jesus at the home of Mary and Martha (Luke 10:38–42). Does this story trouble you, and if it does, why do you find it troubling?

19

MARTHA AND MARY:
SISTERS WHO LOVE JESUS

LUKE 10:38-42

In this past chapter we marveled at the way Jesus treated the Samaritan woman with such respect, gentleness, and grace. This woman had four problems from the perspective of a Jewish rabbi at that time—her race, her religion, her gender, and her sin. The racial, religious, cultural, and gender barriers that divided his society were set aside by Christ as if for him they did not exist at all. Jesus was able to see the human dignity of each person he encountered, even when that dignity was expressed in a different cultural form than his own and even when that dignity was deeply damaged by moral failure, as was true of the Samaritan woman.

Jesus' encounter with the Samaritan woman is a model and a challenge to every Christian believer today. Are we able to look beyond the outside of a person, past the surface matters of racial, religious, economic, cultural, gender, and educational difference? Can we see through such differences to each person's abiding glory as a bearer of God's image? Can we move beyond seeing gender, racial, and cultural diversity as problems and see them instead as part of the glory of our humanity? The God who made us all delights in variety, and so should we. Just as each snowflake is different from every other snowflake he has designed, so each person in this world is unique. We worship a God who loves diversity.

Even more challenging, can we see beyond the sin that disfigures a person to treat him or her with the respect that God's creation of that person in his likeness demands? Are we willing to value each individual we meet as Jesus did, and as he still does? He values each of us as having inestimable worth, the inestimable worth of his death for us.

Two films released in the 1990s make this point. *Dead Man Walking*, a true story of a man on death row for murder and rape, describes how he becomes a believer through a nun, his counselor as he awaits his execution. What is remarkable about this story is that the nun is able to look beyond the horrible crime the man has committed to see his human dignity. It is her recognition of his worth that leads to his conversion, making her a wonderful example of imitating Jesus' treatment of the Samaritan woman.

Another film that illustrates this principle is *Paradise Road*, a movie set in a Japanese prisoner of war camp during World War II. In this film the heroine of the story is a missionary. This missionary, along with several other women, is captured by the Japanese, spends several years in the POW camp, and endures severe mistreatment and suffering at the hands of the camp guards. Again, what is most powerful about the film is the way this believer in Jesus is able to see the dignity of each person in the camp, including the guards who abuse the women so terribly.

Turning back to the Gospels we see many occasions when Jesus shows respect, gentleness, and grace toward unbelievers and to those who have already come to faith in him. The Living Word is simply practicing for us in a perfect way what his written Word elsewhere commands us to do. For example, through the apostle Paul he says, "Let your speech always be gracious, seasoned with salt, so that you may know how you ought to answer each person" (Colossians 4:6).

Jesus is always full of grace to people, but his conversation is also seasoned with salt in every encounter. He desires to challenge each person he meets with the truth; he wants to stretch their understanding. He is eager to set right what is wrong in their thinking and their hearts. He has a longing to call them to faith in himself, and, he is ever working to bring them into a deeper life of discipleship. Think how greatly the life of the Samaritan woman changed after her discussion with Jesus!

This brings us to the subject of our present chapter—the account of Jesus visiting the home of Mary and Martha. This is a brief story that presents us with some challenging questions: What does Jesus ask of Mary and Martha (and of me)? What does he insist is most important in the life of those who follow him? What should be the attitude of our hearts when we offer acts of devotion to God? What are our motivations as Christians, as those who are disciples of Jesus?

These are wounding questions, but that is the way of the Spirit as he speaks to us with the sword of the Word.

THE SETTING

Jesus and his disciples are on their way to Jerusalem (see Luke 9:51), for the time would soon come for him to face his final test here in this world—his arrest, trial, conviction, and crucifixion. Jesus knows what is ahead, and even so he sets his face resolutely toward Jerusalem. On their way to Jerusalem, Jesus and his disciples stay for a while in Bethany. The home of Martha is in that city, and it is probable, though the text does not give us a sketch of her life, that Martha is a widow, as the home is referred to as belonging to her (Luke 10:38). In the society of that time a woman did not usually own property unless she was a widow.

Martha and Mary are sisters, and we learn on another occasion that they also have a brother named Lazarus. This, of course, is the same Lazarus whom Jesus raises from the dead. Martha and Mary call for Jesus to come and heal their brother when he becomes seriously ill. Jesus comes, but Lazarus dies before Jesus' arrival (John 11:1–12:10). Jesus enters into his tomb and calls him back to life, and Lazarus comes out of the grave, still wrapped in his graveclothes. After the resurrection of Lazarus we read how Mary anoints Jesus' feet with a pint of pure nard. Nard was an expensive ointment, a pint costing the equivalent of almost a year's wages for a laborer. So this is an enormously costly gift.

This family—Martha, Mary, and Lazarus—is obviously one that Jesus knows well, a family that Jesus counts as among his dear friends. On this particular occasion we find Jesus staying at the home of Martha. She and Mary, her sister, are already disciples of Jesus. Jesus and some of his disciples appear to be staying for the night in Martha's home, and so, of course, there are preparations for an evening meal.

THE STORY

The story is a simple one. Jesus, when he enters Martha's home, begins teaching those who are gathered there. Mary sits at his feet listening to him. Martha is, in contrast, very busy. She is, in fact, distracted by the preparations for the meal to come. She desires to serve Jesus the best meal that she is able to offer. We can all identify with Martha in this desire. Which of us would not want to give Jesus the best we have if he were a guest in our home!

Martha's anxiety to make sure the meal is just right for the Lord leads her to come and complain to him, "Lord, do you not care that my sister has left me to serve alone? Tell her then to help me." Jesus gently tells Martha that she has let herself become worried by all the preparations but that she has perhaps forgotten the most important thing. Mary, in contrast, has chosen the one thing that is most important, and it can never be taken away from her.

Here is a story to challenge us!

MISUNDERSTANDING JESUS' WORDS

Jesus' words to Martha are often misunderstood. Some have argued that Jesus is teaching that the contemplative life, the life of the monk or nun, closeted away from the world, away from the ordinary duties of life, is a spiritually superior life. Tens of thousands of people today would use just such a Scripture as this one to justify a life lived in complete contemplation, sometimes even with other people taking care of their physical needs. This, it is claimed, is how the spiritual athlete should live. This is Mary's "better" part. Such an understanding has been common in the Roman Catholic and Orthodox traditions.

In the evangelical tradition some have used these words of Jesus' to make a sharp separation between the secular and the sacred. Sacred duties are the ones truly pleasing to God—Bible study, prayer, evangelism, full-time ministry, any duties we do for the direct work of the church of God or for the advancement of the gospel. Secular duties are all our daily and ordinary jobs and work. Such a view would teach that only the sacred is truly pleasing to God. Everyone who is fully committed as a Christian (like Mary) should leave their secular work and become evangelists or be involved in some kind of full-time Christian ministry. This, it is said, is Mary's "better" part, and we all need to follow her example. Probably almost everyone reading this chapter is familiar with such an approach to this text.

This was the message that my wife, Vicki, heard several times a week from visiting pastors and missionaries in chapel services at the Christian college she attended. "If you are truly committed to Christ, you will become missionaries overseas; if you are not quite so committed, you will be involved in full-time Christian ministry here in the USA. However, if you are a third-class Christian [this was never stated that openly], you will get a secular job. But even if you do settle for the calling that is not the 'better' part, you can still support the more important work by tithing to support the 'better' work of the proclamation of the gospel."

This is the challenge repeatedly given to believers by some of the best-known evangelical leaders of our day as they address thousands of people involved in every kind of business and work imaginable: "You're involved in secular jobs. They are of little importance in the program of God. You all ought to leave your secular jobs and dedicate yourselves to the work of the kingdom. Let's get the job of world evangelization done in the next few years. We can complete this task if you all stop doing secular work!"

We have to recognize that while this teaching may sound wise or may appear practical as it calls many people to the proclamation of the gospel, it is in fact misguided. It is not biblical to make such a distinction between sacred and secular or to tell Christians that they ought to leave their jobs and become engaged in so-called "full-time Christian work."

Calvin wrote in response to such views, "On the contrary, we know that men were created for the express purpose of being employed in labor of various kinds, and that no sacrifice is more pleasing to God, than when every man applies diligently to his own calling, and endeavors to live in such a manner as to contribute to the general advantage."[1]

One of the beauties of faithful Reformed teaching, and we find this beauty in particular in the writings of Calvin, is that every calling is honored as a sacred calling. It is no more sacred for any believer to be involved in the ministry of the Word—as God calls some of his people to do—than it is for a believer to be involved, for example, in running a computer business or cutting people's hair or selling fruit or preparing meals or fulfilling any one of a thousand different callings. There is no place in the Bible where it is suggested that it is more pleasing to God, that it is more sacred, for someone to be committed to the teaching of the Word than to any other calling. James even says, "Not many of you should become teachers" (James 3:1).

God himself is quite capable of calling people to the teaching of the Word. God does not need us to tell people that the work they are doing is unimportant to the building of his kingdom. He does not desire teachers of his Word to be laying a burden of guilt on everyone else in the church about their daily work. Indeed, this is the very last thing people need to hear from pastors, teachers, and missionaries. Instead spiritual leaders are called to tell the people of God that what they are doing is pleasing to God, that God needs and calls faithful people to carry on serving him in all those places where they are already serving him. Notice Calvin's words: "No sacrifice is more pleasing to God, than when every man applies himself diligently to his own calling" from God. Making a sharp divide between the sacred and secular is *not* what Jesus means to communicate in his words to Martha.

WHAT DID JESUS MEAN?

First, we should take note that *Jesus delights to teach women as well as men.* This is evident also in the account of Jesus' conversation with the Samaritan woman. Most of Jesus' contemporaries did not regard women as having minds that were capable of being taught; so rabbis did not have women disciples. But Jesus does have women disciples, and he does regard women as capable of being taught and as being able to teach. Perhaps some of the best words ever written about this subject are the comments by Dorothy Sayers in her book and essay *Are Women Human?* In this work Dorothy Sayers reflects on the way Jesus treats women so differently from most of his contemporaries.[2]

Jesus treats women as fully the equals of men, and this is one thing that our story communicates. How many times have you heard a woman criticized because she wanted to stay with the men or listen to a lecture or discuss ideas or study theology rather than joining the other women doing meal preparation in the kitchen and keep to her proper place in the home? This is precisely what Martha is doing in her criticism of Mary and in her reflections on her own work for Jesus. But in contrast to such a view, Jesus teaches us that his word is for all of us to learn, that men have no particular prerogative or superior capacity to study theology or to learn Christian truth.

Mary is sitting at Jesus' feet, listening and learning, and Jesus commends her for this. Some of our male seminary students (not a majority—only a small minority, thank God!) need to learn this lesson. They can make some of our women students feel uncomfortable simply because they are women sitting in class, studying and making contributions to the learning that is taking place. Such men need to ask themselves whether they have the same thoughts about Mary sitting at Jesus' feet and drinking in his teaching! Jesus, in contrast to such despising of women, invites women to learn from him. He praises Mary for her desire to learn and to grow in her understanding.

We should also notice the position of Mary. *She is at Jesus' feet, a position of humility.* Mary knows that she needs to hear and understand the truth that Jesus is imparting; so she listens humbly and attentively. She clearly regards his teaching in their home as an amazing opportunity for learning and growth. Here in her sister's home is Jesus the Son of God sharing wisdom from his Father, and Mary decides to take full advantage of this precious time. One may gain the whole world, but if one loses one's soul through not understanding the truth of the gospel, the truth that Jesus teaches, then one has nothing at all. Mary understands this and grasps the absolute centrality of the gospel to human life. So she wants to listen and learn and humbly drink in all that Jesus has to say to her heart.

In contrast to Mary, *Martha becomes consumed by her service of Christ.* She makes the mistake of thinking that the best thing she can do for Jesus is to prepare for him as elaborate a meal as she possibly can. So she sets herself such an overwhelming task that she becomes distracted by "all the preparations" (v. 40, NIV). Martha is not setting a few cold cuts on the table so she can quickly complete the meal preparations and then come sit and learn at Jesus' feet. Her being so busy in her desire to serve leaves Martha no time or energy to listen to Jesus' teaching. Martha wants to do something for the Lord rather than to receive something from him. This appears to be the intention and motive of her heart. Her attitude comes out in the way that she criticizes her sister, Mary, and in the way that, implicitly, she criticizes Christ himself. "Do you not care?" she cries out to him.

All of us can become so busy about what we think we are doing for the Lord that we become consumed by our efforts to serve him. We begin to think that our hard labor is what truly matters in the kingdom rather than meekly sitting at Jesus' feet learning from his word and watching him work.

Francis Schaeffer used to say, perhaps more frequently than anything else (these words are written into the L'Abri Fellowship Consensus, the short document that describes the calling of those who work in that ministry), "We draw a distinction between Christian men and women building the kingdom of God, and men and women praying that God will build his kingdom and be pleased to use their efforts as he does." This may not sound like much of a difference, but there is, in truth, a great distance between these two mentalities.

If our thinking is like Martha's, we think of ourselves as doing important work for God, building his kingdom as we serve him. Then it seems to us that it is our acts of devotion—our love, our self-sacrifice, our service—that is of true significance. If we think this way, before long the work we are doing can easily become self-centered. At first we may be doing God's work in prayerful dependence on him, fully aware that unless the Lord builds, all our labor is in vain. But soon we find that we are building our own little works for God with an attitude of trust in our own gifts and in our own methods. And in the end we find that we are building a monument to ourselves.

Sadly, this is a mentality that we see in ministry all too frequently. Those working in ministry may begin well. But they can become so consumed by their own efforts to build the kingdom of God that they are simply building their own kingdoms instead. It is not Christ they are serving—rather it is their own ministries.

However, God is the one who builds his kingdom, and we are to pray that he might be pleased to use our weak and inadequate efforts as he does. The apostle Paul says in 1 Corinthians 3:6–7, "I planted, Apollos watered, but God gave the growth. So neither he who plants nor he who waters is anything, but only God who gives the growth." He then goes on to say that though each will be rewarded for his labor, we are to remember that this is "God's field, God's building" (1 Corinthians 3:9).

Consider an example. If ever you have the privilege of leading someone to Christ, let me suggest that you ask the new convert to tell you what God has been doing in his or her life before his or her coming to faith. Almost always the person will tell you (with a little prompting) of many different ways that God has been at work in his or her life. The immediate consequence of this is that we begin to realize that our part in helping the new convert come to faith was just one little piece of the work that God had been doing. We discover that in many cases God has been at work for many years and through a whole variety of means to call this individual to himself. We see in such an instance how it is indeed God who gives the increase, and that our part has merely been to sow or to water. What we have done is not insignificant, but what God has been doing is far more significant. We also see, just as Scripture teaches us, that without his work in the person's life he or she would never have come to faith, no matter what we have said or done.

All too easily we give ourselves far more credit than we deserve for any advance that takes place in the kingdom or for any growth there is in the church. God is indeed building his church, and he delights to use our efforts as he builds. The kingdom is most certainly advancing across the world, and the Lord is always ready to receive what we offer him in this progress of his rule. However, the Lord does not want us to become like Martha—so consumed with what we are doing for him that we forget how much we owe him, how much we need him, how much we still have to learn from him.

When we forget our true state of ongoing need, we become proud of our efforts for the Lord. And when we become proud of ourselves, we instantly become critical of others. Very soon we begin complaining to the Lord himself, and even against him: "Lord, why are you not noticing all this essential hard work that I am doing for you! Without my efforts the work would not get done. The kingdom would not grow. Don't you care about my tiring labor?"

In addition, we all need to learn the lesson that *"Man shall not live by bread alone, but by every word that comes from the mouth of God"* (Matthew 4:4). It is not that we don't need food, but there is something even more important—we need to know the truth. This is the lesson that the Lord wants to impress on Martha's mind. The Messiah is in her home. The meal she is so busy preparing is far less important than her need to learn at Jesus' feet. There will be time later to prepare a simple meal, one that will satisfy Jesus and everyone else who is present.

Jesus knows that food is necessary to live. He is a servant who delights in performing ordinary daily tasks; perhaps he might get up from his place and help Martha in the kitchen. That is the kind of man Jesus is. Not long after these events in Martha's home we will see him washing his disciples' feet, for Jesus is indeed a servant who gladly does the practical and even menial jobs that need to be done in a household.

Jesus is not like most males of his day who relegate women to domestic duties and consider that men should be waited on and served. He honors those who give themselves to service. Martha, however, is doing the right thing at the wrong time and with confused motives. Jesus does not rebuke her for preparing the meal; he rebukes her gently for the attitude of her heart.

Jesus' words to Martha also teach us about the nature of true devotion. What is the motive of my heart when I give some gift of service to the Lord? Sometimes the gifts we offer to the Lord are not so much gifts of true devotion to him but rather a busy effort of which we are proud and about which we are anxious, self-righteous, and critical of others—others who, we think, are less devoted to Christ than we are.

One of the saddest stories I've ever come across illustrates this problem. In the late seventies when I went to one of the Communist countries of central Europe and was teaching in that country, I was asked to preach at a small church with only about twenty people remaining in its membership. Before I arrived there for the service I heard the story of the former pastor. In the 1940s, 1950s, and early 1960s, he had been one of the greatest evangelists and teachers of God's Word in that area. He had been used by God to proclaim the gospel to many, many people. The church of which he was a pastor had grown to several hundred people, which was a huge number in a Communist country. It was the largest evangelical church in that part of the world.

However, this pastor began to think that only what he was doing was adequate. Consequently, he always criticized and found inadequate anyone else's ministry. He never encouraged anyone else to preach or to teach, believing that no one else could do quite as good a job. Over time, as he became older and less capable, the church began getting smaller and smaller.

By the time I arrived there, there were only twenty or so longtime members, people who had been converted and greatly helped by his ministry years earlier. But eventually even they had recognized the need for a new pastor. They had chosen one, and the man they had chosen was the one who invited me to come preach that Sunday. So he led the service, and I preached. It was one of the saddest occasions I have been part of because when I finished, the former pastor, now very elderly, got up and preached another full-length sermon because he felt that no other preaching was ever adequate. No matter who preached, he did this every Sunday. He had to have the final word. In his view, no one else's work or teaching could ever be truly commended or praised or used by God.

This story is a tragic illustration of the spirit of Martha taken to an extreme. We begin to be so proud, so self-righteous, and so anxious about what we are doing that nothing that anyone else does is sufficient in the service of God. Whatever our area of service in life, in our church, in the kingdom of God, we must not ever become a servant of God's people who cannot commend other people unreservedly. Do I feel the necessity to make qualifications every time I praise someone ("she's a good Bible teacher, but . . ." or "I sat in her wonderful Sunday school class, but . . ." or "she does a great job with the missions committee, but . . ." or "he's a good pastor, but . . .")? Such words tell anyone listening to me something troubling about my own heart—about my own arrogance and my own critical spirit—but very little about the other person at all.

These reflections underline for us the importance of our attempting to be honest about the motivations of our hearts: "Why do I do the things that I think I am doing for God?" This is the issue about which Jesus is challenging Martha. Am I truly serving the Lord out of love, or am I just displaying (to him, to others, to myself) my devotion in the Lord's service? This is Martha's problem. She is too acutely aware that she is the one running around being busy for the Lord, and this self-importance makes her critical of everyone else, even of the Lord himself.

Why do I do the things I do? Of course, I will never fully understand my own motivations, for my "heart is deceitful above all things, and desperately sick; who can understand it?" (Jeremiah 17:9). However, even though I may never, in this life, have a full knowledge of the inner workings of my heart, yet I must work toward purity and integrity of motivation. This is why David prays:

> *Who can discern his errors?*
> *Declare me innocent from hidden faults.*
> *Keep back your servant also from presumptuous sins;*
> *let them not have dominion over me!*
> *Then I shall be blameless,*
> *and innocent of great transgression.*
> *Let the words of my mouth and the meditation of my heart*
> *be acceptable in your sight,*
> *O LORD, my rock and my redeemer. (Psalm 19:12–14)*

Why do I do the things that I do for the Lord? Jesus' gentle rebuke of Martha is a challenge to me to examine the motivations for my service. It is a reminder to me to confess the lack of integrity and the double-mindedness in so much of what I do and say and to remember also that I need daily forgiveness.

Jesus' gentle rebuke also urges me to pray that the Holy Spirit will purify me from the inside out, so that through his working in my heart a day might come when I will no longer need to be ashamed of my impurity. I need to ask the Lord that one day my inmost thoughts might become truly pleasing to him. Just as Jesus' words to Martha rebuke me, so also his commendation of Mary— that she has chosen the better part—is a rebuke of much that I do. "Who will deliver me from this body of death? Thanks be to God through Jesus Christ our Lord!" (Romans 7:24–25).

SUGGESTED READINGS AND QUESTIONS

1. Do you still find yourself troubled by the story of Martha and Mary? If so, what is it about this story, or about teaching on it that you have heard, that causes you difficulty?

2. Have you been taught the view that some work is sacred while other work is only secular and that such secular work is less important to God? If someone were to suggest this to you in the future, how would you answer this view? What biblical passages would you appeal to in order to refute such teaching?

3. Have you heard the teaching that all Christians should be "full-time" servants of God? What Scriptures would you use to answer someone who told you that you ought to leave your present occupation to become a "full-time evangelist"?

4. How often are you, like Martha, distracted "by all the preparations" or whatever else you think is so important that it causes you to neglect what might be even more significant? What in particular tempts you to become distracted in such a way?

5. What "better" things do you often neglect as you think about your life?

6. Do you understand the distinction that Francis Schaeffer made between doing the work of the kingdom and praying that God will build his kingdom and be pleased to use your efforts as he does so? Where in your life do you struggle with this issue?

7. When you examine the motivation of your heart for the acts of devotion that you offer to God, what motivations do you see? How do you deal with the confusion and impurity of so much that is in your heart?

8. Read for our next chapter Acts 2:1–18; 21:7–9. What does it mean that women are to be given the gift of prophecy? What was the significance of the events on the Day of Pentecost?

20

YOUR DAUGHTERS WILL
PROPHESY

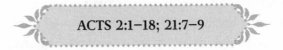

ACTS 2:1–18; 21:7–9

S hould women spend their whole lives as servants of others—
cleaning house, preparing food, and waiting on tables? Or are
women intended by God to be students of his Word? This may
seem like a stark and even absurd way to pose a question. However,
such questions may help us focus on some of the issues that confront us from the story of Jesus' words to Martha and Mary. Many
religious teachers in Jesus' day thought that a woman's place was
always in the home, that women did not have the rational capacity
to learn, the emotional stability to be faithful disciples of a rabbi, or
the trustworthiness to communicate accurately what they had seen
and heard. This was the prevailing view of the teachers of God's
Law at the time of Jesus' ministry.

Not only the men but also many women accepted this understanding of their abilities, just as in a fundamentalist Islamic
country today some women agree with imams and other religious
leaders who seek to prevent women from having access to education or from taking work outside the home. Consider the example
in Afghanistan where the Taliban turned back the clock of progress
for women and restricted their presence in the workplace, in public
education, and in open society. In addition strict dress codes were

imposed on women. The laws were so extreme in their prohibitions of women's place outside the home that widows had no means of making a living to support themselves and their children and were consequently reduced to terrible poverty. Punishment for ignoring these laws was so severe that at times even the death penalty was applied. In such a setting when views like this are taught with great power, even many of the women adopt the beliefs of those who subjugate them.

As we reflect on Jesus' life and ministry we see how very different is his teaching and his treatment of women. Over these past two chapters we have considered several examples of this. We watched Jesus having a theological discussion with the Samaritan woman at the well. She was surprised at his being willing to enter into such a dialogue with her (as were his disciples). In addition, we remembered how at the tomb Jesus called women to be the first witnesses of his resurrection to the apostles (Matthew 28:1–10). We saw how remarkable this was because Jesus lived in a society that would not accept women's testimony in a court of law. Yet Jesus chose women to testify to his resurrection. All through the Gospels we see Jesus treating women with respect and dignity, accepting their offerings and devotion, calling them to discipleship. His treatment of women was radically different from the prevailing cultural pattern.

In our last chapter we saw Mary learning at Jesus' feet, drinking in his teaching, knowing that he wanted her to be a disciple who knew and understood the message of the gospel. We also saw how Jesus gently rebuked Martha, not because there is no place for meal preparation and other daily tasks in the spiritual life or in the service of the Lord, but because there is a time to serve and a time to learn, a time to prepare food and a time to sit at the feet of the Lord and take in his word. There would be a time later to prepare a meal and eat it together. But at that time Mary chose the "better" thing (Luke 10:42, NIV) because she desired to take advantage of the opportunity to be instructed in the truth.

A question arises here that is germane to our reflections in the present chapter: what was the attitude toward women in the Old Testament? If the prevailing attitude of men in the society in which

Jesus lived meant such a low view of women, was this what the Old Testament had taught? We have been learning from our studies of individual women in Old Testament times that this low estimate of women is *not* taught in the Old Testament Scriptures. Rather, from creation onward we have seen the Lord treating women with the greatest possible dignity and honor.

Recognizing this high view of women in the Scriptures leads us to conclude that we need to differentiate between God's wisdom about women, taught to us by his Word, and the attitude of the average man in Israel or Judah. When we turn to think about God's attitude toward women, we see that God gives the gift of prophecy to women like Miriam, Hannah, Deborah, and Huldah. God calls both Deborah and Esther to positions of leadership and public honor among his people at difficult times in the history of the nation. We read of Abigail, a woman who has clearly been taught by God, instructing David, Israel's greatest king, to respond spiritually and righteously in a dangerous situation. We find God honoring the faith and courage of women such as Tamar (daughter-in-law of Judah), Ruth, and Rahab, and we remember that God gives them a place of distinction and prominence in the history of his kingdom.

Proverbs teaches us that a woman of faith and of noble character ought to be praised by the whole community. Proverbs 31 ends with this call to public praise: "Give her of the fruit of her hands, and let her works praise her in the gates."

Solomon, pronounced as the wisest king, recalls that when he was a child, he had been taught by his mother (Proverbs 1:8; 6:20–24; 31:26; cf. 31:1–9). He boasts that he had paid attention to her wise words. The central figure in the book of Proverbs is Wisdom, personified as a woman. The Old Testament does not teach the rational, emotional, and spiritual inferiority of women. Rather, it teaches the equality of women and men as persons made to reflect the likeness of God.

However, we know from the Gospels and from the teachings of the rabbis in the period around the time of Jesus that this teaching of the Old Testament and these examples of women's faith and faithfulness, of women's intellectual capacity and understanding of God's

Word, of women's ability to apply and to communicate the truth, had not become a part of the general spiritual wisdom of God's people.

Jesus, however, reinstates women as spiritual equals of men. It is clearly evident from the Gospels that Jesus' practice is radically different from the practice of the typical man in the time in which he lived and ministered.

This brief reflection on the radical message of Jesus brings us to the teaching of Acts 2 and the events of the Day of Pentecost. What is Pentecost all about? What is God doing on this great day? Clearly it is a day of great significance in the life of the early church and, further, in the whole history of God's kingdom. It marks a new beginning, a turning point in the history of God's work of salvation, and a great movement forward in the life of God's people in this world.

All Christians throughout history have looked back at the Day of Pentecost as one of the most significant events to celebrate in the calendar of the church and in the ongoing ministry of the Spirit among God's people. Jesus' death, Jesus' resurrection, Jesus' ascension to the right hand of the Father, and the subsequent pouring out of the Spirit on the Day of Pentecost together constitute a turning point. These events, which take place in a short period of time, mark the end of the Old Testament period with its focus on God's work in the nation of Israel and mark the beginning of the church age during which the gospel goes out to all nations. Pentecost, then, is a deeply significant moment in the history of the people of God.

After his resurrection Jesus tells his disciples to wait in Jerusalem until the coming of the Spirit in power (Acts 1:7–8). After the Spirit's descent they are to go out to Jerusalem, Judea, Samaria, and all the nations, to the very ends of the earth, making known the good news about Jesus and the kingdom of God. Their calling is to wait for the coming of the Spirit and then to go to every nation in the world.

THE FULFILLMENT OF JESUS' PROMISE

On the Day of Pentecost we find, in God's providence, people from "every nation under heaven" present in Jerusalem for the Feast of Pentecost (Acts 2:5). Pentecost was the feast of firstfruits; and as the gospel is proclaimed, we see Jews and God-fearing Gentiles from all these places hearing the good news and responding to it. Luke gives us the names of some of the countries represented by the people there in Jerusalem, a list that includes some from east, west, north, and south. People are gathered in Jerusalem from all points of the compass. It is the fulfillment of Jesus' words that those from every part of the world will take their place at the feast in the kingdom of God (Luke 13:29). What we observe on the Day of Pentecost is the firstfruits of God's harvest from all the nations.

As this ingathering of God's harvest takes place, with this great diversity of people present in Jerusalem, we also see the fulfillment of Jesus' word that the Holy Spirit would be poured out on the disciples with great power. The Spirit's presence is manifested in several ways.

• *Wind.* The wind that blows represents the life-giving power of God's Spirit. We see this wind at creation in Genesis 1, moving over the waters, bringing life. We find this wind in Ezekiel's vision of the valley of dry bones, raising the spiritually dead to new life (Ezekiel 37). Just so, the Spirit will give life to those who are dead in ignorance and sin wherever the gospel is proclaimed. The church can go out into the world with confidence that the Spirit will indeed give life in place of the death of unbelief, idolatry, and disobedience.

• *Fire.* The visible sign of fire represents the holiness of God and the cleansing power of God's Spirit. This fire is present at the burning bush, teaching Moses that he was standing on holy ground. Fire comes down and burns up the sacrifices on God's altar. We read of this fire coming to burn away the sin from God's people and to turn them to a life of righteousness. John the Baptist taught that Jesus would baptize with the Holy Spirit and with fire.

Just so, Christ comes into our lives by the Spirit to take away our sin, to burn it away like so much dead wood, and to give us a new life of righteousness. Even so, wherever people come to faith in Jesus there will be repentance and turning away from the old life of sin to a life of righteousness and holiness because the Spirit who comes to dwell in the believer is indeed the *Holy* Spirit, the one who hates sin and works to sanctify us, to make us holy.

• *Tongues.* This is the sign that is most often misunderstood. In the gift of tongues we hear the Tower of Babel reversed. In that story, God divided people from each other with the proliferation of languages so they could not understand one another, in order that sin might be restrained. On the Day of Pentecost the giving of tongues (where people of diverse languages are able to understand each other) represents the new humanity that God is creating—a new humanity to replace the old sinful, rebellious, power-seeking humanity of Babel; a new humanity made up of people from all nations; a new humanity in which God's people love and serve each other across all the divides that separate men and women from each other; a new humanity from all nations, tongues, races, and peoples.

There in Jerusalem, on this Day of Pentecost, we see the first-fruits of this new people of God in various ways. There are the firstfruits of the many tongues (languages) on earth as all these people hear the gospel proclaimed in their own language. There are the firstfruits geographically as people from the four points of the compass come to faith in Christ. And finally, there are the firstfruits racially as people from the descendants of Noah's three sons (Ham, Shem, and Japheth), represented by the peoples present, all come to faith. All are born again by the Spirit. Later it will be descendants of Ham, people from Cyrene in North Africa, who are some of the first to go and proclaim the gospel to the Gentiles, freely and gladly, in the church at Antioch (Acts 11:19–26).

• *The prophecy of Joel (Joel 2:28–32).* When Peter is asked what is taking place, he appeals to the prophecy of Joel. In this prophecy Joel describes the last days before the consummation of God's kingdom. There will be signs in heaven above and on the earth below. Jesus prophesied similar events before his coming again—the sun being darkened and the moon turned to blood. Joel is giving us signs of the end of the age, the signs in heaven and on earth, when the message of God's truth will be proclaimed to all the peoples on earth, and people from all the nations will be saved when they call on the name of the Lord. Joel states in his prophecy that young and old, men and women, will have God's Spirit poured out on them and will prophesy. Joel draws particular attention to this reality, emphasizing it by saying it twice, stating that the Spirit of God will be given to men and women equally, so that all will be able to make known God's truth.

Sometimes we are confused when we read about "the last days." What does this expression mean? What are the last days? The term *last days* is used to refer to the very end of this age. But the New Testament also describes the whole of this present age, the age between the first and second comings of Christ, as "the last days." We are living in the time of the consummation of the kingdom.

Now Christ has come; now Christ has died; now Christ has risen; now Christ has ascended and has poured out the Spirit. "The last days" or the time of "the end of the ages" is upon us. See, for example, Hebrews 1:2 ("in these last days he has spoken to us by his Son") or Hebrews 9:26 ("He [Christ] has appeared once for all at the end of the ages to put away sin by the sacrifice of himself") or 1 Corinthians 10:11 ("these things . . . were written down for our instruction, on whom the end of the ages has come"). For the past two thousand years and counting it has been the last days.

When Joel prophesies about the last days, he is speaking about this time in which we live. That is the point the apostle Peter makes in Acts 2:16. He answers the question of the people ("What does this mean?" [v. 12]) by saying, "this is what was uttered through the prophet Joel: 'And in the last days it shall be, God declares, that I will pour out my Spirit on all flesh. . . .'"

The predictions of Joel are the signs of this age, the marks of this present period of "the last days" (Acts 2:17) between the two comings of Christ. This present age in which we are living is the time that is intended to demonstrate the eternal reality of the kingdom to come. This is the age of the Spirit who reveals to us what the future kingdom of God will be like when Christ comes back; his work gives us a foretaste of the heavenly realm. The Spirit is described as the firstfruits of the age to come. In his work in us we see what the future holds. Joel tells us that the day is coming when the kingdom of God will be made up of people from "all flesh" (Acts 2:17)—from all the nations, from every race, tribe, and language. One day there will be no division of any kind between peoples. And this new age has already begun because the Spirit has come.

Most Christians gladly accept the equality and unity of Christians from every race and from every nation. Any church that has any passion for missionary outreach sees this unity and equality in the kingdom constantly demonstrated as the gospel goes out across the earth and as people from every nation are called to faith in Christ. Of course, we need to give ourselves to an ever greater realization of this unity and equality that the Lord gives us in the Spirit.

But there is another factor that we need to add in here. In addition to this racial and cultural equality in the new humanity, so openly demonstrated at the Day of Pentecost, there will also be spiritual equality between men and women. Let's look again at Joel's words: "this is what was uttered through the prophet Joel: 'And in the last days it shall be, God declares, that I will pour out my Spirit on all flesh, and *your sons and your daughters* shall prophesy.'"

However, many Christians have a hard time acknowledging the equality and unity between the sexes that Joel prophesies. In the kingdom to come this will be perfectly realized, but even now, especially now, because we are in the last days, because the Spirit has come, we should eagerly practice what Joel prophesies. Some may reply to my words, "But this is an obscure passage, and we need more scriptural input than this to acknowledge the spiritual equality of men and women."

First, we should note that nobody thinks of the end of Peter's quotation from Joel as being obscure: "And it shall come to pass that everyone who calls upon the name of the Lord shall be saved" (Acts 2:21).

Second, the words themselves are quite clear: "I will pour out my Spirit on all flesh, and *your sons and your daughters* shall prophesy . . . ; even on *my male servants and female servants* in those days I will pour out my Spirit, and they shall prophesy." Joel repeats his prediction for emphasis.

Third, the apostle Paul also speaks of this in a doctrinal passage that no one ought to regard as obscure. Paul teaches us that in Christ there is no Jew or Gentile, slave or free, male or female.

> [I]n Christ Jesus you are all sons of God, through faith. For as many of you as were baptized into Christ have put on Christ. There is neither Jew nor Greek, there is neither slave nor free, there is neither male nor female, for you are all one in Christ Jesus. And if

you are Christ's, then you are Abraham's offspring, heirs according to promise. . . . And because you are sons, God has sent the Spirit of his Son into our hearts, crying, "Abba! Father!" So you are no longer a slave, but a son, and if a son, then an heir through God. (Galatians 3:26–29; 4:6–7)

Without any question or qualification Paul is teaching us that we are equals in redemption. We all have the same status before God because of the work of Christ. We all receive full inheritance and the rights of the firstborn through Jesus. We all are given the Spirit of adoption, so that we can all cry out to God, "Daddy!" "Father!" (Romans 8:15).

Fourth, later on the apostle Peter refers to women and men as joint-heirs of the gracious gift of life (1 Peter 3:7). Joel prophesied that a time of spiritual equality would come. Peter declares that this prophecy of Joel is now fulfilled. What should this mean for us? All of us, across the gender barrier, are able to learn and to communicate God's Word. What we see in the ministry of Jesus Christ—his delight in treating women with dignity and honor, his eagerness to teach women, his glad recognition of women's witness—is to be the reality in all of our relationships and in all of our churches. Women and men are equally redeemed; women and men are equally given the Spirit; women and men are equally gifted to prophesy.

This assertion of equality of gifts raises another question: what is prophecy? The apostle Paul defines prophecy for us. It is speaking with the mind, after reflection on God's truth, for the strengthening, comfort, and encouragement of people. It includes declaring in an intelligible way the good news of the truth about Jesus Christ, so that the unbeliever is convicted of sin and comes to repentance and faith (1 Corinthians 14:1–25). Prophecy is also edifying God's church by clearly instructing his people with the truth. This gift of prophecy, of communicating God's truth, is a gift that all believers, all women and all men, are to seek and to be ready to exercise. That is Paul's command to us: "Pursue love, and earnestly desire the spiritual gifts, especially that you may prophesy" (1 Corinthians 14:1).

All of God's people, men and women, are to be prepared to listen to and to learn from one another. It is the height of spiritual arrogance and a denial of the nature of Christ's kingdom for a man to say that he cannot and will not listen to or learn from a woman. Will such a man remove the words of Deborah or Hannah or Mary from Scripture? Does such a man deny that he can learn anything from his mother, from his sister, from his wife, or from his daughter? If he does deny that he can learn from his sister, his mother, his wife, or his daughter, he cuts himself off from the wisdom of half of God's people. Peter declares that the prayers of such a man, a man who does not acknowledge that his wife is a joint-heir of the grace of life, are hindered.

All believers, male and female, read the words of godly, Spirit-filled women in the Scriptures. All believers, male and female, are called to recognize that God's gifts of instruction are given regardless of gender and are therefore to be glad to learn from one another. This is the way the kingdom of God will be for all eternity, with full spiritual equality between men and women, and this is the reality of how it should be now.[1]

SUGGESTED READINGS AND QUESTIONS

1. How had you understood the events of the Day of Pentecost before reading this last chapter? What had you understood about the gift of tongues?

2. Had you understood that the time we are living in is indeed the last days or have you thought of the last days as a brief time before the coming of Christ in glory? What are other characteristics of these last days in addition to those mentioned in this chapter?

3. We are taught that the gift of the Spirit to us is the down payment, the guarantee, the firstfruits, of the life to come. How do you relate this teaching to the events of the Day of Pentecost?

4. Why do you think so many Jewish men had failed to see and understand the scriptural teaching about the faith and spirituality of women and had failed to draw conclusions for their own life from the examples of godly women whose lives are described to us in the pages of the Old Testament?

5. Why do you think so many Christian men fail to see the clear example of the manner in which Jesus treated women with such honor and dignity?

6. Why do you think we hear so little about the words of the prophecy of Joel, words that Peter declared to be fulfilled on the Day of Pentecost?

7. Do you know Christian men (perhaps including yourself) who are reluctant to recognize the spiritual equality of women or who refuse to listen to or learn from women?

8. Have you earnestly sought the gift of prophecy, and how do you see Joel's prophecy being fulfilled in your life and ministry?

9. Read for our next chapter Ephesians 5:21–33 and Revelation 19:4–9; 21:1–5. What does it mean for you that the church is the bride of Christ?

21

THE BRIDE OF CHRIST

EPHESIANS 5:21–33; REVELATION 19:4–9; 21:1–5

I n the last chapter we saw how the redeeming work of Christ brought the pouring out of the Spirit on all believers—young and old, male and female. In previous chapters we had seen how Jesus, in his ministry, set an example for all his future disciples by the way he treated women. He never patronized women or looked down on them; he never regarded them as inferior or spoke slightingly of them; instead he showed respect, honor, and grace to women in all his dealings with them. This is true both when he encountered women who were already believers and also with those who had not yet come to faith in him. We might say that his life showed a promise of good things to come.

On the Day of Pentecost Christ fulfilled this promise that he had exemplified during his life by giving the Spirit he had received from his Father to all his followers. In his High-Priestly prayer to the Father on the night before he died, Jesus refers to the cluster of events around his death and resurrection as his being glorified (see John 17:1–5). In his being glorified we must include his death for us as our substitute to be our Savior, his resurrection from death to give us everlasting life, his ascension and his being seated at the Father's right hand to reign in glory on our behalf, and, finally, his glorification made complete with the coming of the Spirit as the ascended Jesus poured out the Holy Spirit "on all flesh" (Acts 2:17).

The Spirit's presence is the sign, the firstfruits, and the guarantee of the consummation of the kingdom at Jesus' return. By the Spirit's presence in our lives, we see just a glimpse of what life will be like when Christ comes back. Now, as just one of the signs of future glory, both sons and daughters are able to prophesy, to minister to one another, and to be a blessing to one another. In this we see one facet of the beauty of our redemption. In his work Christ came to set everything right that had been made wrong in the Fall. He is the Restorer; he is the Overcomer; he is the Deliverer who sets us free from every consequence of the Fall and who brings transformation and renewal to every aspect of our lives. In the last chapter we looked at one particular aspect of this multifaceted jewel of redemption—our spiritual equality as women and men.

The equality of creation is reaffirmed in redemption by the example of Christ and by the giving of the Spirit. As we saw, Paul teaches in Galatians 3:28 that in Christ there is no male and female; in Christ, the fundamental equality we have as human beings is renewed. Now all of us are heirs; we are all fully Isaacs, the firstborn sons of Abraham; we all inherit the fullness of the promise. We are all priests who have direct access to God through the one mediator, Jesus Christ. We all have the Spirit of Christ dwelling in our hearts—this is true of every disciple. We are all given the wisdom of the Spirit—both for our own lives and so that we may be a blessing to each other as we seek to serve one another day by day.

All of us, all believers, female and male, are called to instruct, to encourage, to comfort, and to edify one another, for we all are given the Spirit of prophecy. Christ lavishes his love on us all, for he is the bridegroom who cares for and cherishes his church. This thought brings us to the final subject of our reflections.

THE CHURCH AS THE BRIDE OF CHRIST

In our study of Proverbs we saw how God gives us a beautiful portrait of "The Woman of Noble Character." Proverbs, you will remember, uses the analogy of a woman to draw its picture of God's wisdom in chapters 8–9, and all who fear the Lord will attend to her voice. In several other passages in Proverbs, the compiler and author, King Solomon, speaks of having been instructed by particular women who embody in themselves this wisdom of God. For example, he writes, with deep gratitude, of the wisdom of his mother (see Proverbs 31:1–9).

This portrait of wisdom as a woman and Solomon's respect for the teaching of women should be an encouragement to all female believers. Women are to see themselves as worthy in God's eyes. Women should be encouraged to seek to become wise women of God and women of noble character. The prayer of every Christian woman should be that she might become one whose wisdom is listened to with respect by her husband, by her children, and by all the people of God. Every Christian man should recognize gladly these women of noble character and should praise them in the city gates, giving them honor before all of God's people.

In addition to choosing a woman as the portrait of true wisdom, in the Old Testament we also find that God further honors women by using marriage to portray his relationship with his people. We see this, for example, in the writings of the prophets Isaiah, Jeremiah, Ezekiel, and Hosea. God presents himself as a faithful husband, and his people are his bride, his wife, in whom he delights. The New Testament picks up this image and uses it both to teach us about marriage and also to teach us about our relationship with Christ. We will look at the three main passages where this is done.

In Ephesians 5 Paul instructs husbands by appealing to the love that Christ has for his church and his sacrifice of himself for his bride. He calls husbands to love their wives and to sacrifice themselves for them, just as Christ has done for us all. He instructs wives by appealing to the delight it is for the church to show respect, honor, and submission to Christ. Toward the end of this passage (v. 32), Paul teaches us that marriage is a picture of the love between Christ and his church. He says that marriage (in particular, the sexual union within a marriage) is a "profound . . . mystery." Marriage, he tells us, shows us a greater reality than itself. Marriage reveals to us the love that God has for his people in Christ. (Paul uses the word "mystery" to refer to the revelation of God's truth.) We have this glorious calling in our marriages that the union between a man and a woman should reveal the truth about Christ and the church to the watching world.

Obviously, this is a challenge, a high calling that ought to be on the hearts and minds of any believers who are married. We need to ask ourselves, what am I communicating to my children and to others around me by the way I love my wife or my husband? Am I revealing truth or falsehood about Christ and the church in our relationship day by day? What kind of a portrait of the union of Christ and his church am I showing to people?

These words of Paul in Ephesians 5 also suggest that the relationship between Christ and the church is more lasting than the relationship between a married couple: the lesser (the human relationship) reveals the greater, the more lasting (the divine relationship). If we turn to Jesus' teaching, we see that this suggestion is on the right track, for Jesus tells us explicitly that marriage is only temporary, that in the kingdom to come we will "neither marry nor be given in marriage"; rather, we will be "like angels in heaven" (Matthew 22:30).

Whatever this means precisely we will have to wait to discover, though we can be sure that it will be good and not disappointing. What it does imply, quite clearly, is that human marriage, as we know it, is for this age alone and that only the marriage between Christ and his bride is eternal. Our marriage to Christ is for all ages to come.

This is a comfort to those who are single, for all singles who know Christ are permanently wedded to him. That is why the Scriptures, for example, in Isaiah 54 and 62, encourage those who feel desolate and alone to rejoice. Nothing will ever take away the love that God has for them. Our relationship with him is a permanent and abiding union and love. Even those who have been violated and abused in this life, like Tamar (daughter of King David), will have their tears wiped away. One day they will know and enjoy eternal glory—glory that far outweighs the troubles of this life (cf. 2 Corinthians 4:17).

In Revelation 19 we see the marriage between Christ and his church con-

summated in the Marriage Supper of the Lamb. Jesus had used the image of a wedding banquet to teach about the nature of the kingdom of God (Luke 14:8–11, 15–24). In Revelation we read not of the image or of the picture but of the final reality. All believers will be invited to sit down at the Marriage Supper of Christ. All believers will have been made ready to be his bride. They will be clothed in fine linen, "righteous deeds" (Revelation 19:8).

These righteous acts include, first, the perfect obedience of Christ in our place that is reckoned to us by God, and, second, the daily obedience of our lives as Christ makes us righteous by his Word and by his Spirit. Our calling moment by moment is to offer ourselves to Christ and to seek to walk in his ways in dependence on the Spirit. We are to give ourselves to Christ that we might bear his fruit, just as a bride gives herself to her husband. This daily giving of ourselves to Christ will be consummated at the wedding feast where we are joined to him fully and when we celebrate his love for us, face-to-face with him. That will be the greatest day of rejoicing, far beyond any rejoicing we experience in this life. We will be glad, and with full and thankful hearts we will give God the glory for all his love for us.

In Revelation 21 we see that this wedding feast to which we are invited will prepare us for a permanent reality. We will be Christ's bride, exercising complete and perfect dominion on this earth. We will reign with Christ forever. Our redemption will be fully realized. We will dwell with God, and he will dwell with us, in perfect union.

All the sorrows and broken realities of this life will have passed away, never to return. Tears, mourning, separation, death—all of these will be gone forever. All things will be made new. The earth, our permanent home, will be renewed, so that there will be no more curse forever. Our bodies will be raised in glory, and every aspect of our selves will be made whole.

We ourselves will be people who will be able to offer to God the splendor of our lives. We will give to him our glory and honor, for we, his people, from all the nations, will be perfected by Christ. Whatever our greatest gifts, whatever the beauties of our personality and character, our labors and achievements, we will bring these to Christ to offer him praise and for his pleasure. We will bring our glory to him. This will be the permanent reality that we will enjoy. Year by year, forever, we will come from every nation and bring the gifts that Christ has showered on us, and we will return them to him as an expression of our love and adoration.

We will be transformed into the likeness of Christ, sharing his glory, made completely new. All the failures of this life, all the scars and brokenness of this life that we bear physically and emotionally, will be taken from us completely and forever. Each of us will be so glorious that, as in Scripture whenever an angel appeared people were tempted to worship him, so it will be with us. We can look forward with joyful expectation to the permanent reality of being the bride of Christ. Three passages from the prophets describe what our future will be:

> I will put my law within them, and I will write it on their hearts. And I will be their God, and they shall be my people. (Jeremiah 31:33)

> *Fear not, for you will not be ashamed;*
> > *be not confounded, for you will not be disgraced;*
> *for you will forget the shame of your youth,*
> > *and the reproach of your widowhood you will remember no more.*
> *For your Maker is your husband,*
> > *the LORD of hosts is his name;*
> *and the Holy One of Israel is your Redeemer. (Isaiah 54:4–5)*

> *[A]s the bridegroom rejoices over the bride,*
> > *so shall your God rejoice over you. (Isaiah 62:5)*

SUGGESTED READINGS AND QUESTIONS

1. How have you understood Jesus' words that we will be like the angels, that marriage as we know it will be no more? Do you find this disappointing, or is this an encouraging prospect?

2. In what ways have the promises of the prophets about God being the husband of his people been an encouragement to you? (See Isaiah 49:13–21; 54:1–12; 62:1–12; Jeremiah 31:31–34.)

3. As you reflect on the return of Christ, what do you look forward to most?

4. What particular tears do you long to have wiped away?

5. How do you visualize the Marriage Supper of the Lamb?

6. What splendor and glory do you hope to be able to offer to Christ in the kingdom to come (Revelation 21:24, 26)?

7. Does it surprise you to read in Revelation and elsewhere in Scripture that this earth is going to be our permanent home (Romans 8:18–21; 2 Peter 3:13; Revelation 21:1–5)?

EVE, THE FIRST WOMAN:

*A Wedding Sermon for Eve and Adam after the
Promise of Redemption*

L et us imagine ourselves at a wedding where the bride and groom have asked for a homily to be given on the subject of headship and submission. This was indeed the case for me at a recent wedding for which I preached, so I will reproduce the sermon here with only the names of the bride and groom altered to Eve and Adam.

HEADSHIP AND SUBMISSION IN MARRIAGE

Eve and Adam, thank you for giving me the privilege and responsibility of preaching at your wedding. It is a great joy to be able to help you celebrate this special day. You have asked me to speak on the subject of headship and submission in marriage. I am not usually told what to preach on. And when I am, I do not always feel constrained to obey, but today I will do as I am told!

Even when I am given a subject, I am certainly not usually asked to address *this* subject—it is one that most people want to shy away from rather than confront directly. Headship in marriage and submission are not the most popular ideas in this culture, for all around us the ideal is the fulfillment of the individual: *I must live for myself and nobody else—my life is to revolve around the pleasing of myself and the meeting of my own needs.* Such an approach to marriage or to any human relationship will, of course, destroy relationships and will set a married couple apart from day one.

So headship and submission it will be! The Scriptures you have chosen clearly teach us that God has indeed given us a structure for marriage. The apostle Paul in 1 Corinthians 11, commenting on Genesis 2, teaches us that the man is the head of the woman, for the woman was created from and for the man. And in Ephesians he declares, "The husband is the head of the wife even as Christ is the head of the church," and he adds, "Wives, submit to your own husbands, as to the Lord" (5:22–23). Paul could hardly express this more strongly! The apostle Peter repeats this call to submission (see 1 Peter 3:5–7).

As this is such a controversial and unpopular teaching—one influential Christian teacher has called an emphasis on a "theology of equals inimical to a doctrine of sexual hierarchy"[1]—we need to ask what is going on here. How are we to think about this? Why does God say such things? What are they to mean for you, Eve, and for you, Adam, in your marriage?

This pattern of headship comes from creation itself, or perhaps we should say from God himself. The Lord who made us, the Lord we worship, is a triune God. God is the three persons of the Father, Son, and Holy Spirit who have loved and delighted in each other from all eternity. Within the Trinity there is full equality—the Son and Spirit are just as fully God as is the Father. The Son and the Spirit have just as much authority, are just as powerful, just as holy, just as wise, just as good, just as loving, just as glorious as the Father. To deny this full equality of the persons of the Godhead is heresy, a serious departure from the truth. Yet, within the Trinity there is also a hierarchy— the Father is over the Son and the Spirit, and the western churches have taught that the Son is over the Spirit. The Son and the Spirit delight to submit themselves always to the Father's will; and the Spirit delights to submit to the Son and to do his will. However, in this sermon I want to focus our attention on the relationship of the Father and the Son.

This headship of the Father is not demeaning to the Son in any way. The Father is pleased to honor the Son always by giving him the most significant tasks imaginable: *creation*—it is by the Son's powerful Word that all things are made; *revelation*—every word that comes to us about God comes to us through the Son; *salvation*—it is by the Son's life of perfect righteousness and by his self-sacrificing death that our salvation is accomplished; *consummation*—by the Son's glorious coming the kingdoms of this world will finally become the kingdom of our Lord and of his Christ, and he shall reign forever.

The Son, for his part, is ever gladly submissive to the Father. He is always eager to do his Father's will, committed to obeying his Father's every word, ready to speak whatever the Father wants him to say, pleased to respect and honor his Father in everything he does, devoted to bringing glory to his Father. We look at this eternal relationship of headship and submission, and it is no vision of misery—rather it is an eternally shared glory! Think of Jesus praying, "Father, glorify me in your own presence with the glory that I had with you before the world existed" (John 17:5).

Adam and Eve, your relationship is to mirror the relationship between the Father and the Son, for the apostle Paul teaches us that your family, just like every other family on earth or in heaven, is named and patterned after the family of our heavenly Father, the family of the Trinity.

Adam, as the head of this new family being made today, you are to honor Eve by recognizing her equality with you as one, like you, who is made fully in the image of God. To deny her equality is a heresy, just as it is a heresy to deny the full deity of God the Son. You are to honor Eve by encouraging her to exercise her authority, to use her power and strength, her wisdom and goodness, her gifts of creativity, encouraging her to do in this world the gracious works of God that he has prepared for her. You are to be eager for her glory to be expressed in all she does.

Eve, you are called to honor Adam as your head, as your lord. It is to be your delight to submit to him, to do what pleases him, to consider daily how you may speak in ways that show how much you treasure his words and desires, to ponder in your heart how you can bring honor and glory to Adam in everything you say and do. This is not a vision of misery but the means of realizing a little bit of the shared glory that has been eternally expressed between the Father and the Son.

Paul appeals to our creation in the likeness of God when he writes of headship and submission, and he also appeals to our redemption by Christ. Paul is not falling prey to the chauvinism of first-century Jewish or Greco-Roman culture when he calls men and women to this pattern of marriage. No, for he writes that "The husband is the head of the wife even as Christ is the head of the church" (Ephesians 5:23). It is as we look at the grace of God in saving us by the love of Jesus that we see the clearest and most beautiful picture of what headship in marriage means.

Husbands are to love their wives as Christ loved the church and gave himself up to death for us all. Christ is the head of us all, but serving him is a great joy because he gave himself completely for us. He spent eternity thinking and planning and preparing for how he would save us. He spent his life here on earth devoting himself to serving us, even to the point of washing our feet. Then, at the very end and climax of expressing his love for us, he submitted himself to the evil rulers of his day by being put to death on the cross for our salvation. He spends all his time now drawing us to himself by his love, treasuring us, praying for us, considering how we may serve him, and finding fulfilling work for us to do— work that will honor his Father and that will build his kingdom here in this world. Even when we see Christ face-to-face in all his glory he will still serve us at his table at the Marriage Supper of the Lamb. What a joy it is for us to submit ourselves to him and to do what he desires!

Adam, this is the kind of head you are to be to Eve. You are to imitate Christ, spending your time thinking about how you may serve Eve, how you may bring good into her life, not harm; you are to delight in finding ways to help her flourish and blossom, to use her gifts in the service of our heavenly Father; you are to give yourself fully for her, glad to wash her feet or to do anything else that will demonstrate your love for her. You are to cherish and treasure her, just as Christ cherishes and treasures you and is proud to know you. You are never to lord it over her, never to order her around, never to take advantage of your greater strength, never to demean her, never to be rude to her, never to make unreasonable demands of her but rather always to love her as Christ has loved you and as Christ continues to love you every moment of your life. It is to be your delight to sit her down at your table and to wait on her as Christ will one day wait on you at his wedding feast.

Eve, you are to honor Adam as your lord. Every day you are to ask, "What can I do that will please him?" You are to show him unceasing respect and love. A man who is not respected by his wife is like a whipped cur, unable to hold up his head. Adam is to be able to go out into the world knowing he has a wife who loves and adores him, who respects and honors him, who delights to serve him and please him. Such respect and honor will give him a strong sense of dignity and self-worth, and this sense of being loved and honored will enable him to do great things in the kingdom of God.

This is a remarkable calling that you are both given today. What an honor and glory God sets before you! Eve and Adam, you are to show to the world the beauty of the eternal love between the Son and the Father. You are to display to everyone who enters your home and who shares your life the wonder of the gracious love of Christ for his people and of their devotion to him.

Is all this possible, is it all realizable, or is what I have been saying just an impractical ideal that, given our sinful nature, we can just go away from this service and forget? Without the Lord it is impossible, but with his grace and power, with his indwelling love, with his forbearance and his forgiveness at work in you both and through you both, then you can indeed begin to live this way. That is the Lord's promise, and as a song says, "He can do anything but fail!" He comforts us with the words, "I will never leave you nor forsake you" (Hebrews 13:5).[2] His promise is that as you look to him today and every day, your path will shine brighter and brighter, for "The path of the righteous is like the light of dawn, which shines brighter and brighter until full day" (Proverbs 4:18).

Adam, love Eve today and every day of your life to come. Commit yourself to delight in her and to becoming one flesh with her, enjoying the great gift of each other's body and so imitating the joyful union of Christ with his church.

Eve, honor and respect Adam, give yourself unreservedly to him, delight in him, become one with him.

> The LORD bless you and keep you;
> the LORD make his face to shine upon you and be gracious to you.
>   (Numbers 6:24–25)

Amen!

SUGGESTED READINGS AND QUESTIONS

1. For many people today the whole issue of acknowledging hierarchy in any form is problematic. How have you thought about this issue? Would you agree with the view that to speak of hierarchy at all is to bring into our lives a vision of misery?

2. All of us have encountered poor examples of the exercise of headship or leadership in marriage, in family, in churches, in the workplace. As you reflect on the poor examples you have seen, what was at the heart of the problems?

3. Have you seen good examples of headship or leadership in marriage, in family, in churches, in the workplace? As you reflect on these, what was at the heart of such good examples?

4. Have you considered before reading this chapter the reality of equality and headship that exists within the Trinity? As you think about this, how would you express the beauty of the relationship between the Father and the Son as it is described for us in the Scriptures?

5. Do you think it is appropriate or do you consider it to be illegitimate to appeal to the relationship of the Father and the Son as a model for equality and headship within marriage?

6. What do you see to be the primary biblical requirements for anyone who is called on to exercise headship or leadership in any setting—home, church, workplace, etc.?

7. All of us, both men and women, are called on to be in positions of headship in various settings in our lives. As you reflect on your own exercise of headship or leadership in the family or at work or in the church, how would you grade yourself on the manner in which you have fulfilled this calling?

NOTES

CHAPTER 1

1. The simple fact that all races can intermarry indicates that we are genetically one species. The differences between the races are very superficial matters of height, skin color, and texture and color of hair.

2. This is only a portion of the whole. This folk song appears to come from northern England, probably Yorkshire, but its exact origins are uncertain. It can be found in many books of English songs and ballads.

3. In most animal species, including the apes, coming together sexually is a matter of procreation, and its frequency is regulated by the female coming into oestrus. In a human relationship of love between a woman and a man, sex is usually far more frequent and in God's kindness appears to give much greater pleasure.

4. Phillip E. Johnson, *Darwin on Trial* (Downers Grove, IL: InterVarsity Press, 1993); John C. Collins, *Science and Faith: Friends or Foes?* (Wheaton, IL: Crossway Books, 2003). Both of these books have helpful suggestions for further reading.

CHAPTER 2

1. God commands us to communicate the gospel of Christ to unbelievers with respect, gentleness, and grace. See Peter's command in 1 Peter 3:15 and the words of Paul in Colossians 4:6. See my book *The Heart of Evangelism* (Wheaton, IL: Crossway Books, 2001) for a careful study of these passages and of our calling to treat those around us with the same kindness and honor that the Lord has shown to us.

2. In C. S. Lewis's book *Perelandra* (most recent edition Scribner, 2003), the second in his science fiction trilogy, there is a marvelous account of the temptation of the first woman, the Eve of Venus, an account in which Lewis explores the ways in which Satan might have tempted Eve. It is evident that Lewis has used the Genesis summary of the temptation as the basis for his fictional account on Venus.

3. See Francis A. Schaeffer, *Genesis in Space and Time* (Ventura, CA: Regal Books, 1972).

4. "As for you, you were dead in your transgressions and sins, in which you used to live when you followed the ways of this world and of the ruler of the kingdom of the air, the spirit who is now at work in those who are disobedient. All of us also lived among them at one time, gratifying the cravings of our sinful nature and following its desires and thoughts. Like the rest, we were by nature objects of wrath" (Ephesians 2:1–3, NIV); see also Isaiah 59:1–2; Romans 3:4–8, 19.

5. C. S. Lewis, *Surprised by Joy: The Shape of My Early Life* (London: Harvest Books, 1955), 228–229.

6. Some commentators think that Paul is just describing himself when he was a young believer or that he is describing someone else who is a "carnal" Christian—that is, a Christian who is not dedicated to serving God. Others even conclude that Paul is describing himself as an unbeliever, before his conversion. But why is there such reluctance to admit that Paul is simply recounting his experience as a mature Christian? What happens in all of us is that as we grow as believers in Christ, we become more aware of the ugliness of our sin. It is not that we actually become more sinful, but that we have a deeper and more acute sense of the beauty of righteousness and the cost of Christ's dying for us, and it is this growing sense of the seriousness of the truth about God and about ourselves that causes the passion of Paul's cry: "Wretched man that I am!"

7. See Francis Schaeffer, *Pollution and the Death of Man* (Wheaton, IL: Crossway Books, 1992), for a helpful discussion of this problem.

CHAPTER 3

1. Friedrich Nietzsche, *The Gay Science, with a Prelude in Rhymes and an Appendix of Songs*, Book III, Section 125, in Walter Kaufmann, *Existentialism from Dostoevsky to Sartre* (Cleveland: Meridian Books, 1957).

2. The following quotations are taken from Joseph Campbell's defense of Hindu thinking in his interviews with Bill Moyers: Joseph Campbell and Bill Moyers, *The Power of Myth* (New York: Anchor Books, 1991). The following quotes make clear the notion that in Hinduism there is an ultimate denial of the distinction between good and evil and that, therefore, there is no alternative but to affirm and accept the evil that appears to damage our world:

   Heraclitus said that for God all things are good and right and just, but for man some things are right and others are not. When you are a man, you are in the field of time and decisions. One of the problems of life is to live with the realization of both terms, to say, "I know the center, and I know that good and evil are simply temporal aberrations and that, in God's view, there is no difference."

   Since in Hindu thinking everything in the universe is a manifestation of divinity itself, how should we say no to anything in the world? How should we say no to brutality, to stupidity, to vulgarity, to thoughtlessness? . . . For you and for me—the way is to say yes.

3. As a university student in Manchester in northern England, I came to the conclusion that there is no foundation for the distinction between good and evil and no way to account for the broken reality of our existence in this world. I came to the conclusion that life is utterly absurd and went out one day to throw myself over a cliff. On the edge of that cliff I was overwhelmed by the beauty of nature, even in the middle of winter, and felt compelled to keep searching for meaning. A few days later I met the first true Christian who took my struggles and questions with utmost seriousness and began to answer my questions and show me the wonderful answers that are found in the Bible. For a full account of this time in my life, see *The Heart of Evangelism* (Wheaton, IL: Crossway Books, 2001), 117–123.

4. Below are a set of readings for Advent that I prepared using many of the more familiar messianic prophecies and finishing with their fulfillment in the birth of Jesus.

December 1	Genesis 3:1–20	Seed of Eve
December 2	Genesis 22:1–18	Only beloved son and sacrifice
December 3	Genesis 48:15–16; 49:8–10	Lion of Judah
December 4	Numbers 23:18–24; 24:3–9, 15–19	Star of Jacob
December 5	Deuteronomy 18:14–22	Prophet like Moses
December 6	2 Samuel 7:1–17	Son of David
December 7	Psalm 2	Messiah: Son of God and King
December 8	Psalm 16 and Job 19:23–27	Holy One and Resurrected Redeemer
December 9	Psalm 22	The One forsaken by God
December 10	Psalm 72	Royal Son, deliverer of the afflicted
December 11	Psalm 110	Priest and Lord at God's right hand
December 12	Isaiah 7:14; 9:1–7	Immanuel, Mighty God, Prince of Peace
December 13	Isaiah 11:1–10	Branch from Jesse's roots
December 14	Isaiah 42:1–10	Covenant and Light of the Nations
December 15	Isaiah 49:1–7; 50:4–11	Servant of Kings, sustainer of the weary
December 16	Isaiah 52:13–53:12	Suffering Servant and Lamb of God
December 17	Jeremiah 23:1–6; 33:14–18	Righteous Branch
December 18	Ezekiel 34:1–31	The Good Shepherd
December 19	Daniel 7:9–14 and Micah 5:2–5a	The Son of Man and Ruler from Bethlehem
December 20	Zechariah 9:9–10; 12:10–13:1	King on a donkey and pierced firstborn
December 21	Malachi 3:1–4; 4:1–6	Covenant Messenger and sun of righteousness
December 22	Luke 1:5–38	Son of the Most High
December 23	Luke 1:39–80	The tender mercy of God
December 24	Matthew 1:18–25; John 1:1–14	Savior from sin and Word made flesh
December 25	Luke 2:1–20; Matthew 2:1–12	The birth of Jesus

5. Jesus promises to give each of us a new name, a name that will express our new identity as each of us is made whole and perfect through his work in us. See Revelation 2:17 and also the new name of Peter ("rock") that Jesus gave to Simon, though at the time he was anything but a rock!

6. In Ephesians 2:14–18 and 3:1–13 Paul exults in the mystery of the gospel that unites Jews and Gentiles (and people from all other kinds of race, economic backgrounds, and cultures that bring hostility between them); see also Galatians 3:28; Colossians 3:10–11. In Ephesians 3:10 Paul intimates that the heavenly authorities (presumably archangels and cherubim) will see this amazing revelation of the power of the gospel to unite divided peoples.

7. "Oh, no single piece of our mental world is to be hermetically sealed off from the rest, and there is not a square inch in the whole domain of our human existence over which Christ, who is Sovereign over all, does not cry: 'Mine!'" So stated Dutch reformer Abraham Kuyper in the inaugural address of the opening of the Free University of Amsterdam.

8. See Paul's words in 1 Corinthians 6:13.

9. Think of Eric Liddell saying, "When I run, I feel God's pleasure" (portrayed in the film *Chariots of Fire*).

10. Michael Green used this phrase, "arrows of glory from heaven," to describe those remarkable occasions when we see God answering our prayers to heal someone who is desperately sick.

11. See George MacDonald's wonderful story "The Gifts of the Child Christ."

12. This poem was written to celebrate the promise of Genesis 3:15.

CHAPTER 4

1. Gordon J. Wenham, *Word Biblical Commentary*, Vol. 1 (Nashville: Thomas Nelson, 1987), 273.

2. Ibid.

3. Francis Schaeffer preached a fine sermon on this subject of the Christian's calling to do the Lord's work in the Lord's way. See Francis Schaeffer, *No Little People* (Wheaton, IL: Crossway Books, 2003).

4. Allen P. Ross, *Creation and Blessing* (Grand Rapids, MI: Baker Book House, 1988), 319.

CHAPTER 5

1. Jesus denounces the addition of human rules to God's commandments with great passion. See his words in Matthew 15:1–20, and also Paul's in Colossians 2:20–23. In my forthcoming book *Learning Evangelism from Jesus* (Wheaton, IL: Crossway Books, 2009), one chapter will look at Jesus' critique of legalism.

2. The Scripture makes it clear that God will step in and bring severe discipline to his people—sometimes in the form of sickness, sometimes even of death (see the account of Ananias and Sapphira in Acts 5:1–11 and also Paul's words to the Corinthians in 1 Corinthians 11:27–30).

3. In India, the practice of suttee, burning a wife on her dead husband's funeral pyre, was made illegal in the early decades of the 1800s, largely as a result of the efforts of William Carey and William Wilberforce. However, even to this day suttee sometimes takes place. When I lectured in India in 1988, a widow had recently burned herself on her husband's funeral pyre, and vast numbers of people went to the site to honor her act.

CHAPTER 6

1. I remember Francis Schaeffer preaching this sermon. The text can be found in *Joshua and the Flow of Biblical History* (Wheaton, IL: Crossway Books, 2004), 79–90.

2. Numbers 25 recounts the incident of the Israelites' involvement in Baal worship at Shittim. King Balak had hired the false prophet Balaam to curse Israel, but God prevented this plan by giving Balaam visions of his future blessing of Israel. Balaam then tried a different approach to subvert Israel—the enticement of the false religion of the god Baal and the ritual prostitution that was a part of the worship of Baal.

3. See, for example, Exodus 9:13–16.

4. Exodus gives an account of Jethro, Moses' father-in-law, coming to faith and making an offering to the Lord after he hears about the acts of God on behalf of his people Israel (Exodus 18:1, 5–12).

5. See 1 Samuel 18–20, especially chapter 20. Jonathan's commitment to protect David and to warn David of his father's plans to kill him brings out Saul's anger against his own son for his loyalty to David.

6. My colleague and teacher of ethics, David Jones, writes as follows:

   Veracity (i.e., habitual truthfulness) is a desirable character trait that should be cultivated, especially among God's people for whom the truth is supremely important. That should be the governing principle in all ordinary discourse. Yet there are extreme or emergency situations when truth-telling would be manifestly against the purpose for which God has given us speech: to build up and not destroy. How to act in those circumstances is a matter of discernment, but the biblical narrative does not exclude lying (to lie = "to make an untrue statement with intent to deceive").

   Looking at the conduct of Rahab and the Hebrew midwives we observe (1) their motives were pure—Rahab explicitly acted out of faith; (2) their intentions were good—to spare the lives of the Hebrew boys, to prevent the Hebrew spies from being discovered; and (3) their speech-acts were just inasmuch as Pharaoh and the authorities in Jericho had no right to information that would enable them to carry out their murderous plans for the Hebrews. Thus, in both cases Rahab and the midwives acted righteously, not only from the perspective of motive and intent, but also of means. Even if the deception had not been successful, their conduct was morally praiseworthy because of its intrinsic integrity, not consequences.

   For an extended discussion see David Jones, *Biblical Christian Ethics* (Grand Rapids, MI: Baker, 1994), Chapter 7, "The Resolution of Moral Conflicts," especially the excursus on truthfulness, 144–151.

7. All human authority is strictly limited, for only God has absolute authority over us all. Whenever there is a conflict between our submission to God and the demands of any human over us, clearly it is appropriate to obey God rather than a subordinate authority (see, for example, Acts 5:29).

CHAPTER 7

1. There is a wonderful account of the Battle of Agincourt and of Henry V's remarkable victory in William Shakespeare's play *Henry V*.

2. Hal Lindsey, *There's a New World Coming: An In-depth Analysis of the Book of Revelation* (Eugene, OR: Harvest House, 1984), 94.

3. Ray C. Stedman, *God's Final Word—Understanding Revelation* (Grand Rapids, MI: Discovery House, 1991). If one does a Google search on the Web for "sixth seal nuclear winter," one will find many examples of this particular interpretation of the sixth seal of Revelation 6.

CHAPTER 8

1. When God first calls Abraham, he gives the charge to him and to all his descendants that they are to be a blessing to the nations (Genesis 12:1–3). We can justly refer to this passage as the Old Testament's Great Commission. This theme of the calling of Israel to bear witness to the nations is one of the central themes of the book of Psalms.

2. We should probably assume that the Magi knew of the Balaam prophecy as it speaks clearly of the birth of a king in Israel in the context of the appearance of a star. The carol "We Three Kings of Orient Are" reflects on the Magi's awareness of this prophecy from the book of Numbers and also sees the gifts of the Magi as reflecting their knowledge of the Books of Moses. When the northern tribes of Israel with their kingdom centered on Samaria were taken captive by the Assyrians, they took the Books of Moses with them to the East. We will be able to ask the Magi one day about the extent of their acquaintance with the Pentateuch, but we are probably right to assume some knowledge.

3. See the article on Tom Wolfe by Bonnie Angelo ("Master of the Universe") in *Time*, February 13, 1990, 90.

4. When my father died, it was just a matter of a few days before unscrupulous men started calling or turning up and offering to do unnecessary work for my mother at exorbitant prices. I have also come across several recent examples of pastors preying on widows in order to try to gain either sexual favors or money.

5. God commands all his people to care for widows. He also insists that it is a primary obligation of rulers to intervene on their behalf (Psalm 146:9; Isaiah 1:17; Acts 6:1–4; 1 Timothy 5:3–10; James 1:27).

6. One of the most difficult assignments I have ever had was to preach at the funeral of a pastor who had been my closest friend during our years at seminary. He had committed suicide, and so the occasion was extraordinarily painful for the congregation he had served and who loved him dearly. I found the honest words of Jeremiah in Lamentations 3 to be the most helpful on that occasion. That chapter expresses bitterness of soul and deep disappointment and also contains some of the most comforting words in all of Scripture: "This I call to mind, and therefore I have hope: The steadfast love of the LORD never ceases; his mercies never come to an end; they are new every morning; great is your faithfulness" (vv. 21–23).

7. I have personally met those who have converted from Islam to Christian faith and who have had to flee for their lives.

CHAPTER 9

1. See the excellent reflections on the Law in Gordon Wenham, "The Gap Between Law and Ethics," *Journal of Jewish Studies* 48 (1997): 17–29; Christopher J. H. Wright, *Old Testament Ethics for the People of God* (Downers Grove, IL: InterVarsity Press, 2004), 253–326.

CHAPTER 10

1. We often find Jesus eating with sinners and being welcomed by them into their homes. His participation in intimate fellowship with "sinners" scandalized Jesus'

contemporaries. They believed that moral purity requires personal separation from sinners. Jesus rejects such a view with great passion. See, for example, Matthew 9:10–13; Luke 15:1–2; 19:1–10.

2. In Judaism the song of Hannah is regarded as the prime role model for how to pray and is read on the first day of Rosh Hashanah as the *haftarah*. Recent examples of renditions with music include Mary Lou O'Hern, "Hannah's Song" and Brad Eberly, "Hannah's Song."

CHAPTER 11

1. "You shall not oppress your neighbor or rob him. The wages of a hired servant shall not remain with you all night until the morning" (Leviticus 19:13). See also Deuteronomy 24:15; 25:4; Matthew 10:10; 1 Corinthians 9:9; 1 Timothy 5:18.

2. God commands the people of Israel to open their hearts to the needy at all times, and especially at the festivals that celebrate his acts on their behalf (Deuteronomy 15:7; Leviticus 19:9; Isaiah 58:7).

CHAPTER 12

1. Writing about Abraham and others like him, the writer of Hebrews refers to them as "strangers and exiles on the earth" who were "seeking a homeland." He then declares of them that they were not seeking a homeland here on this earth; rather, "they desire a better country, that is, a heavenly one. Therefore God is not ashamed to be called their God, for he has prepared for them a city" (Hebrews 11:13–16).

CHAPTER 13

1. Examples of Bible passages that seek to confront the problem of suffering and the acts of those who do evil are Psalms 10; 22; 53; 73; 94; Jeremiah 5.

2. The following information about the widespread problems of abuse and rape are from the National Sexual Assault Hotline (1-800-656-HOPE):

Every two and a half minutes, somewhere in America, someone is sexually assaulted.

One in six American women is a victim of sexual assault, and one in thirty-three men.

In 2004–2005, there were an average annual *200,780 victims* of rape, attempted rape, or sexual assault.

About 44 percent of rape victims are under age eighteen, and 80 percent are under age thirty.

Contrary to the belief that rapists are hiding in the bushes or in the shadows of the parking garage, almost two-thirds of all rapes were committed by someone who is known to the victim. Most (73 percent) of sexual assaults were perpetrated by a non-stranger—38 percent of perpetrators were a friend or acquaintance of the victim, 28 percent were an intimate, and 7 percent were other relatives (National Crime Victimization Survey, 2005).

CHAPTER 14

1. "As they went out, they found a man from Cyrene, Simon by name. They compelled this man to carry his cross" (Matthew 27:32; see also Acts 2:10; 13:1. The church that was earliest committed to taking the gospel to the Gentiles was in Antioch and had members from Cyrene.

2. "Do not let your adorning be external—the braiding of hair and the putting on of gold jewelry, or the clothing you wear—but let your adorning be the hidden person of the heart with the imperishable beauty of a gentle and quiet spirit, which in God's sight is very precious" (1 Peter 3:3–4). "Charm is deceitful, and beauty is vain, but a woman who fears the LORD is to be praised" (Proverbs 31:30).

3. From the film *Chariots of Fire*, 1981.

4. "Let every person be subject to the governing authorities. For there is no authority except from God, and those that exist have been instituted by God. Therefore whoever resists the authorities resists what God has appointed, and those who resist will incur judgment" (Romans 13:1–2; see also 2 Peter 2:4–10).

5. Old Testament laws required Israel to include the poor, widows, orphans, and aliens in the feast times (Exodus 22:21; 23:9; Deuteronomy 14:28–29; 16:9–12, 13–15).

CHAPTER 15

1. The Jews faced the temptation to withdraw from the world when they were in exile, but Jeremiah wrote a letter to them urging them to serve God in Babylon (see Jeremiah 29). Christians face the temptation to create a haven from the world and to retreat from relationships with unbelievers. However, Jesus requires us not to succumb to this temptation but to follow him into the world (see John 17:15).

CHAPTER 16

1. I remember being asked to give an evangelistic lecture at a college in England. When the student committee chose the subject of "Sex," I simply set out the contrast between the common practice of promiscuity in our culture and God's calling to chastity and then fidelity. Many of the non-Christians present were relieved and encouraged to hear someone praising chastity and fidelity as virtues and expressed the unhappiness and lack of fulfillment in being treated as sexual objects and in treating others that way.

2. Examples of the *Magnificat* set to music include Claudio Monteverdi's *Vespers for the Blessed Virgin*, 1610 or the extended setting by Johann Sebastian Bach, *BWV* 243. There is also a beautiful contemporary setting by the Estonian composer Arvo Part.

3. The Counter-Reformation was a reaction to the Protestant Reformation and sought to define Roman Catholic doctrine and practice in opposition to the Protestant positions. This led to what some Roman Catholics today would acknowledge as exaggerated emphases and a certain rigidity of doctrine.

CHAPTER 17

1. In his encyclical *Redemptoris Mater* John Paul II spells out his developed theology of Mary. He repeatedly refers to Mary's cooperation in her Son's work of redemption, to her unceasing intercession for believers and for the world, to her work of protection of God's people and of nations, to her absolute purity and sinlessness, to her bodily assumption into heaven and her present reign as Queen of the Universe. A few passages from the encyclical give the flavor of the whole: "Mary's motherhood continues unceasingly in the Church as the mediation which intercedes, and the Church expresses her faith in this truth by invoking Mary 'under the titles of Advocate, Auxiliatrix, Adjutrix and Mediator'" (39). "The Church draws abundantly from this cooperation, that is to say from the maternal mediation which is characteristic of Mary, insofar as already on earth she cooperated in the rebirth and development of the Church's sons and daughters" (44). "We believe [here he is quoting Paul VI from 1968] that the Most Holy Mother of God, the new Eve, the Mother of the Church, carries on in heaven her maternal role with regard to the members of Christ, cooperating in the birth and development of divine life in the souls of the redeemed" (47). "Mary, present in the Church as the Mother of the Redeemer, takes part, as a mother, in that 'monumental struggle against the powers of darkness' which continues throughout human history. And by her ecclesial identification as the 'woman clothed with the sun' (Rev. 12:1) it can be said that 'in the Most Holy Virgin the Church has already reached that perfection whereby she exists without spot or wrinkle. Hence, as Christians raise their eyes with faith to Mary in the course of their earthly pilgrimage, they 'strive to increase in holiness.' Mary, the exalted daughter of Sion, helps all her children, wherever they may be and whatever their condition, to find in Christ the path to the Father's house" (47). "She is also the one who, precisely as the 'handmaid of the Lord,' cooperates unceasingly with the work of salvation accomplished by Christ, her Son" (49). "Mary, though conceived and born without the taint of sin, participated in a marvelous way in the sufferings of her divine Son, in order to be Coredemptrix of humanity" (Mark I. Miravalle, *The Dogma and the Triumph* (Santa Barbara, CA: Queenship Publishing Company, 1998), 122).

2. Several texts make it clear that even Mary and her other sons and daughters experienced some confusion concerning Jesus' ministry (Luke 2:48; Mark 3:31–34; John 2:4).

3. Mystery is part of much of our knowing, particularly of matters that are deeply significant to us—not only our knowledge of God, but also our knowledge of each other as human persons who are always impenetrable to us in the sense that another person cannot be fully known by us. There is also mystery in our knowledge of the physical universe—the more we know about both the vastness of the universe and of the nature of matter itself, the more we are faced with the limitations of our knowledge.

4. I am indebted to Francis Schaeffer for these baptism questions. I was very struck by them the first time I heard him ask them at an infant baptism. Every time I have asked them of parents, first privately as we discuss the baptism of their child and then publicly at the baptism itself, the parents have had to wrestle with these questions, for they put the issues starkly.

CHAPTER 18

1. In Psalm 87 we see the Lord's desire to call people from every nation and to declare that even the historic enemies of his people Israel are spiritually "born" in Zion and have their names written in his book of life.

> *Among those who know me I mention Rahab and Babylon;*
>   *behold, Philistia and Tyre, with Cush—*
>   *"This one was born there," they say.*
> *And of Zion it shall be said,*
>   *"This one and that one were born in her";*
>   *for the Most High himself will establish her.*
> *The* LORD *records as he registers the peoples,*
>   *"This one was born there." (vv. 4–6)*

CHAPTER 19

1. John Calvin, *A Commentary on the Harmony of the Evangelists*, vol. 2, trans. William Pringle (Grand Rapids, MI: Eerdmans, 1949), 144.

2. Read this wonderful essay on the way Jesus related to women in Dorothy Sayers, *Are Women Human?* (Grand Rapids, MI: Eerdmans, 2005).

CHAPTER 20

1. It should be evident from the first chapter of this book that I believe both in the equality of men and women in marriage and in the structure of headship that God has given in marriage. The wedding sermon in the Appendix makes this very clear. In addition, because the church is the family and household of God, and therefore is given by God a similar structure to marriage and the family, I believe that the New Testament clearly teaches that God has called men to be elders in the church with the teaching and ruling authority. However, this structure does not invalidate or set aside in any way our equality from creation, our equality in redemption, and our equality of spirituality. Nor does this structure set aside the calling of all of us, both men and women, to be humble, submissive to each other, and ready to learn from each other—husbands from their wives, as well as wives from their husbands; men who are elders in the church being humble, submissive, and ready to learn from other men and women in the church, as well as men who are not elders and women in the church being humble, submissive, and ready to learn from the elders of the church. For a fuller exposition of my views on this matter see my lectures on "Gender and Faith in Church and Society," available on Covenant Seminary's website (www.covenantseminary.edu). See also the lecture "Women: Equality and Authority in the Church."

APPENDIX

1. Paul Jewett, *Man as Male and Female* (Grand Rapids, MI: Eerdmans, 1975), 85, insists that it is impossible to defend Paul's teaching in Ephesians 5 about headship in marriage. He argues that Paul betrays the insight of equality in Christ that he sets out in Galatians 3:28 ("there is no male or female . . . in Christ Jesus"). He suggests that Paul is so influenced by his rabbinic training that he cannot escape from it and so is unable to implement fully his vision of equality. This argument

of Jewett has had widespread influence in the church. However, I believe it is clear that Paul roots his understanding of headship in marriage in the doctrine of the Trinity. There we affirm both equality and headship without any difficulty or without imagining that the headship of the Father is demeaning to the Son.

2. In its entirety this verse reads, "Keep your life free from love of money, and be content with what you have, for he has said, 'I will never leave you nor forsake you'" (Hebrews 13:5).

SCRIPTURE INDEX

343

GENERAL INDEX

Abel, 34

Abigail, 187–188, 305; and David, 178–179; historical setting of her story, 174; marriage of to David, 183–184, 188; marriage of to Nabal, 174–176. See also *Abigail, characteristics of her wisdom*

Abigail, characteristics of her wisdom: appeal of to God's providence, 180–181; appeal of to God's vengeance rather than David's, 180; faithfulness of, 182; generosity of, 181; honesty of, 179–180; humility of, 181; knowledge that a soft answer turns away wrath, 179; seeing God's hand at work in history, 181–182; thoughtful advice, 182

Abimelech, 58, 68, 69

Abraham, 57–58, 122, 123, 128, 134, 135, 247, 250, 336n1; in Egypt, 62–64; as an exile, 337n1 (of chapter 12); as father of the faithful, 249, 251; in Gerar, 68–69; God's promises to, 60–61, 67; and Hagar, 65–67; lack of faith of, 63–64; similarity of to Hannah, 170; tests of faith of, 62, 68–69, 83–84

Absalom, 191; ambition of, 197; murder of Amnon by, 197

Adam, 13; alienation of from creation, 36; creation of, 14–22, 27, 231; Eve's alienation from, 34–36; God's curse on, 34–35; as the image-bearer of God, 18; leadership role of in relationship with Eve, 22; loneliness of, 19–20. See also *Fall, the*

Addiction, 34

Africa, 210–211

Agincourt, Battle of, 111

Ahab, 215

Ahasuerus (Xerxes), 214, 220, 222, 223; kingdom of (Medo-Persia), 210–212

Ahinoam, 191, 192

Amnon, 193–195; consequences of the rape of Tamar, 196–199; hatred of Tamar after he rapes her, 195–196; his rape of Tamar, 192–195

Are Women Human? (Sayers), 295

Arrogance, 32

Asher, 110

Assyrians, 278

Austen, Jane, 129

Authority, obedience to, 178

Autonomy, personal, 127

Baal, 124

Baalam, 90, 123–124, 334n2, 336n2

Babylonians, 213

Balak, 334n2

Baptism, 265, 339n4

Barak, 109, 111, 117, 121

Bathsheba, 190

Beauty, inner, 216, 338n2 (of chapter 14)

Benjamin, 110, 278

bin Laden, Osama, 96

Boaz, 125, 128, 134, 135, 142, 155; generosity of, 143–144; and God's laws, 149; kindness and self-sacrificing love of, 146–48

Bosnia, 129

Burial of the Count of Orgaz, The (El Greco), 251, 252, 253, 258

Cain, 34, 54

Caleb, 175

Calvin, John, 294

Campbell, Joseph, 332n2

Chemosh, 124, 138

Child-bearing, and salvation, 53–54

Children: lack of as a stigma in ancient times, 60, 165; as a reflection of God's glory, 53; as a reflection of ourselves in sin, 53

Chilion, 128, 129

Christianity/Christians, 33, 43, 44, 121–122, 178, 190, 204, 215, 229, 284; and building the kingdom of God, 296–298; call of to love unbelievers, 227, 338n1 (chapter 15); and communicating the gospel message to others, 26, 331n1; in Iran, 224; need of to address moral problems in the church, 161–162; response of to Mary, 250; and sexuality, 243. See also *secular versus sacred duties debate*

Christmas, 221

Church, the, as the Bride of Christ, 316–320

Claudius, 218

General Index

Naphtali, 106, 110
Nathan, 191, 196, 197
Nazirites, 164
Nebuchadnezzar, 213, 215
Nero, 218
New Jerusalem, 198
Nietzsche, Friedrich, 41–42
Nunc Dimittis, 267

Obadiah, 215
Obedience, 217–218, 338n4
Onan, 75, 77, 79
Orpah, 129, 131
Othniel, 105–106

Palestine, 210
Paradise (1997), 290
Passover, Feast of, 266–267, 268–269
Paul, 42, 107, 206, 218, 279, 340–341n1;
  on the equality of all in redemption
  through Christ, 310–311; on himself as
  a sinner, 33, 332n6; instructions of to
  husbands, 317–318, 326; on men and
  women as joint-heirs of grace, 250–251;
  on the submission of women, 324
Peninnah, 159–160
Pentecost, 306, 315; as the fulfillment of
  Jesus' promise, 306–312, 315; mani-
  festation of the Holy Spirit in through
  wind, fire, and the giving of tongues,
  307–308; and the prophecy of Joel,
  308–309; and spiritual equality between
  men and women, 310–312
Perelandra (Lewis), 331n2
Perez, 83
Peter, 218, 308, 310, 311, 333n5
Pharaoh, 63, 64
Pharisees, 279, 280, 283
Phinehas, 156–158
Poetry: of Hannah's song, 166–167; Hebrew,
  167; of the Psalms, 167
Polygamy, 191–192
Pride, 32
Pride and Prejudice (Austen), 129
Prophecy, gift of, 107–108; to both men and
  women, 305, 310
"Prosperity gospel," 169
Prostitution, 162; ritual, 124; shrine, 80–81,
  157. See also *Rahab*
Purim, Feast of, 221, 222

Rabbi Eliezer, 281
Race, genetics of, 331n1
Rachel, 160

Rahab, 87–88, 103–104, 209, 335n6; and
  the destruction of Jerusalem, 98–99;
  faith of, 95; historical setting of her
  story, 88–91; lies of, 92, 95–96; response
  of to the king's men searching for spies,
  92–93; understanding Rahab's behavior
  in saving the spies, 93–98
Redemption. See *God, redemptive work of*;
  Jesus, roles of as the Seed of Eve
Redemptoris Mater (Pope John Paul II), 339n1
Reformation, the, 247–258
Reuben, 110
Revelation, book of, interpretation of,
  115–116
Righteousness, 83, 162
Roman Catholics, 275–276, 293; beliefs of
  concerning Mary, 251–254, 258, 339n1
Ruth, 74, 76, 77, 129, 131, 209; blessings
  of God on, 134–135, 137; decision of
  to stay with Naomi, 131–133; gleaning
  of in Boaz's fields, 139–144; and God's
  providence, 138–139; historical setting
  of her story, 123–128; immediate setting
  of her story, 128–129; kinship/redeemer
  (*goel*) motif of, 128, 144–146; marriage
  of to Boaz, 146–149; and the missionary purpose of God, 122–123; parallels
  between her time and ours, 126–127;
  return of to Bethlehem, 133, 137–138; as
  a story of faithfulness, 155–156

Samaria, 278
Samaritans, 278, 280, 281, 285; religion of,
  278–279
Samson, 164
Samuel, 164, 165, 169, 173–174
Sarah, 122, 123, 128, 134, 135, 160, 251; bar-
  renness of, 60–61; descendants of, 62;
  in Egypt, 62–64; fulfillment of God's
  promises to, 69–79; in Gerar, 68–69;
  God's promises to, 60–61, 67; lack of
  faith of, 64–67, 68; laughter of, 67–68;
  odd cultural practices concerning her
  and Abraham, 57–58; tests of faith of,
  62, 83–84
Satan, 45, 46, 53, 223. See also *Fall, the*
Saul, 123, 174, 178
Sayers, Dorothy, 295
Schaeffer, Francis, 15, 31, 52, 296, 334n3,
  339n4
Schindler, Oscar, 96
Secular versus sacred duties debate,
  293–294
"Seed of Eve," 54–55
Self-loathing, 33–34

351